D1250032

FAST
According to the Quran & Sunnah

© Maktaba Dar-us-Salam, 2011
King Fahd National Library Cataloging-in-Publication Data

Zulfiqar, Muhammad
 Fast according to the Quran & Sunnah. / Muhammad
Zulfiqar - Riyadh, 2011

  252 p; 14x21cm

ISBN: 978-603-500-161-8

  1- Fasting (Islam)   1-Title

252.3 dc   1432/9062

L.D.no. 1432/9062
ISBN: 978-603-500-161-8

First Edition: December 2011
Supervised by: ABDUL MALIK MUJAHID
P.O. Box: 22743, Riyadh 11416 K.S.A. Tel: 00966-01-4033962/4043432 Fax: 4021659
E-mail: Riyadh@dar-us-salam.com. Website: www.darussalamksa.com, info@darussalamksa.com

K.S.A. Darussalam Showrooms:
  Riyadh
Olaya branch: Tel 00966-1-4614483 Fax: 4644945
Malaz branch: Tel 00966-1-4735220 Fax: 4735221
Suwaydi branch: Tel 00966-1-4286641
Suwailam branch: Tel & Fax: 00966-1-2860422
● **Jeddah**
  Tel: 00966-2-6879254 Fax: 6336270
● **Madinah**
  Tel: 00966-4-8234446 Fax: 00966-4-8151121
  Al-Khobar
● Tel: 00966-3-8692900 Fax: 8691551
  Khamis Mushayt
● Tel & Fax: 00966-7-2207055 / 0500710328
  Yanbu Al-Bahr
● Tel: 00966-4-3908027 Mob.: 0500887341
  Al-Buraida
● Tel: 00966-6-3696124 Mob.: 0503417156
  Fax: 00966-6-3268965
U.A.E
● **Darussalam, Sharjah U.A.E**
  Tel: 00971-6-5632623 Fax: 5632624
  darsalam@emirates.net.ae
PAKISTAN
● **Darussalam, 36 B Lower Mall, Lahore**
  Tel: 0092-42-37240024 Fax: 37354072
● **Rahman Market, Ghazni Street**
  Urdu Bazar, Lahore
  Tel: 0092-42-37120054 Fax: 37320703
● **Karachi**, Tel: 0092-21-34393936 Fax:34393937
● **Islamabad,**Tel & Fax :0092-51-2500237,51-2281513
U.S.A
● **Darussalam, New York** 486 Atlantic Ave, Brooklyn
  New York-11217, Tel: 001-718-625 5925
  Fax: 718-625 1511
  E-mail: darussalamny@hotmail.com.
● **Darussalam, Houston**
  P.O Box: 79194 Tx 77279
  Tel: 001-713-722 0419 Fax: 001-713-722 0431
  E-mail: houston@dar-us-salam.com
  www.dar-us-salam.com
CANADA
● **Nasiruddin Al-Khattab**
  2-3415 Dixie Rd.Unit # 505
  Mississauga, Ontario L4Y 4J6, Canada
  Tel: 001-416-4186619
FRANCE
● **Distribution: Sana**
  116 Rue Jean Pierre Timbaud,75011, Paris, France
  Tel: 0033 01 480 52928 Fax: 0033 01 480 52997

U.K
● **Darussalam, International Publications Ltd.**
  Leyton Business Centre
  Unit-17, Etloe Road, Leyton, London, E10 7BT
  Tel:0044 20 8539 4885Fax:0044020 8539 4889
  Website:www.darussalam.com
  Email:info@darussalam.com
● **Darussalam, International Publications Limited**
  Regents Park Mosque 146 Park Road,
  London NW8 7RG Tel: 0044- 207 725 2246
  Fax: 0044 20 8539 4889
● **Dar Makkah International**
  23-25 Parliament Street, Off Jenkins st. Off Coventry rd.
  Small Heah - Birmingham B10-OQJ
  Tel: 0044 0121-7739309-07815806517-07533177345
  Fax: 0044 121-7723600
AUSTRALIA
● **Darussalam:** 153, Haldon St. Lakemba (Sydney)
  NSW 2195, Australia
  Tel: 0061-2-97407188 Fax: 0061-2-97407199
  Mobile: 0061-414580813 Res: 0091-297580190
  Email: abumuaaz@hotmail.com
● **The Islamic Bookstore**
  Ground Floor-165 Haldon Street
  Lakemba, NSW 2195, Australia
  Tel: 0061-2-97584040 Fax: 0061-2-97584030
  Email: info@islamicbookstore.com.au
  Web site:www.islmicbookstore.com.au
SRI LANKA
● **Darul Kitab** 6, Nimal Road, Colombo-4
  Tel: 0094 115 358712 Fax: 115-358713
  E-mail:info@darulkitaonline.com
INDIA
● **Darussalam, India**
  58 & 59, Mir Bakshi Ali Street, Riyapettah,
  Chennai - 600014, Tamil Nadu, India
  Tel: 0091 44 45566249 Mob.: 0091 9884112041
● **Islamic Books International**
  54, Tandel Street (North)
  Dongri, Mumbai 4000 09, India
  Tel: 0091-22-2373 4180
  E-mail:ibi@irf.net
● **Huda Book Distributors**
  # 455, Purani Haveli, Hyderabad- 500002
  Tel: 0091 40 2451 4892
  Mob.: 0091 98493 30850
● **M/S Buraqh Enterprises**
  # 176 Peter's Road
  Indira Garden, Royalpettah,
  Chennai - 600014 India
  Tel.: 0091 44 42157847
  Mob.: 0091 98841 77831
  E-mail: buraqhenterprises@gmail.com

FAST

According to the Quran & Sunnah

Professor Muhammad Zulfiqar

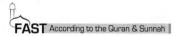

Contents

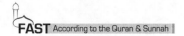

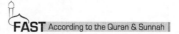

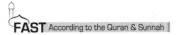

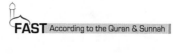

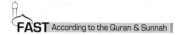

Saum – Fast

The linguistic meaning of *Saūm*

The word *siyām* (sing. *saūm*) is derived from sama, which means to restrain from eating, drinking, talking, etc. If an individual refrains from these things, he is a sāim. The Noble Qur'ān uses the word in the general sense when it revealed the conversation between the angel and Mary, the mother of Jesus. The angel instructed her:

فَكُلِى وَٱشْرَبِى وَقَرِّى عَيْنًا ۖ فَإِمَّا تَرَيِنَّ مِنَ ٱلْبَشَرِ أَحَدًا فَقُولِىٓ إِنِّى نَذَرْتُ لِلرَّحْمَٰنِ صَوْمًا فَلَنْ أُكَلِّمَ ٱلْيَوْمَ إِنسِيًّا ﴿٢٦﴾

"So eat and drink and be glad. And if you see any human being say: Verily, I have vowed a fast unto the most Gracious (Allah) so I shall not speak to any human being this day". (Maryam 19:26)

The phrase, "I shall not speak" is the interpretation of the Arabic word *saūm*. The reason for this interpretation is that *saūm* cannot mean fast, i.e., to restraint from food, because Mary had just been told to eat from the fruits of the palm tree. This general meaning is common to the Arabic language.

The juristic meaning of *Saūm*

In the terminology of the *Shari'ah*, the word *saūm* means to abstain from food, drink and sexual activity from dawn to sunset, with the intention

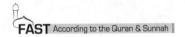
of doing so sincerely and solely for Allah, the Exalted. This is because fasting purifies the soul and cleanses it from the evil that might cause it to become a miser and their ill behavior.[1]

The linguistic and juristic meaning of Ramadān

The word Ramadān is called as such to indicate the heating sensation (of the stomach as a result of thirst). Others have said that it is called as such because Ramadān scorches out the sins with good deeds, as the sun burns the ground; others have said that it is called as such because the hearts and souls are more readily receptive to the admonition and remembrance of Allah during Ramadān, as the sand and stones are receptive to the sun's heat. The framers of this beautiful language may have been inspired in naming this month Ramadān. Otherwise, the relation between the heat and its properties is miraculously similar to that of Ramadān. While the heat represents the matter that helps shape, form, and mold virtually every matter – from metal and plastics, to plants and living cells – Ramadān undoubtedly helps a serious believer remold, reshape, reform, and renew his physical and spiritual disposition and behavior.[2]

Legal status of Ramadān

According to Qur'ān it is an obligatory action. Allah says:

$$\text{يَٰٓأَيُّهَا ٱلَّذِينَ ءَامَنُواْ كُتِبَ عَلَيۡكُمُ ٱلصِّيَامُ كَمَا كُتِبَ عَلَى ٱلَّذِينَ مِن قَبۡلِكُمۡ لَعَلَّكُمۡ تَتَّقُونَ ﴿١٨٣﴾}$$

"O you who believe! Observing *As-Saūm* (the fasting) is prescribed for you as it was prescribed for those before you, that you may become *Al-Muttaqūn* (the pious)." (Al-Baqarah 2:183)

Shortly afterwards, Allah also says:

---

1. *Tafsir* Ibn Kathir: 1/496,497
2. Essentials of Ramadān the Fasting Month, P: 16

شَهْرُ رَمَضَانَ ٱلَّذِىٓ أُنزِلَ فِيهِ ٱلۡقُرۡءَانُ هُدٗى لِّلنَّاسِ وَبَيِّنَٰتٖ
مِّنَ ٱلۡهُدَىٰ وَٱلۡفُرۡقَانِۚ فَمَن شَهِدَ مِنكُمُ ٱلشَّهۡرَ فَلۡيَصُمۡهُۖ

"The month of Ramadān in which was revealed the Qur'ān, a guidance for mankind and clear proofs for the guidance and the criterion (between right and wrong). So whoever of you is resident during the month must observe fast..." (Al-Baqarah 2:185)

The entire Muslim Nation has agreed that it is obligatory to fast during the month of Ramadān, and it being one of the pillars of Islam. It is something that is known about the religion. The one who rejects it as a practice is a disbelieving apostate who has left the fold of Islam.[3]

The Divine wisdom behind the decree of fasting is that it involves purification of the human soul from immoralities and vices; for fasting blocks the evil ways of Satan, as Satan circulates in the body of a person just like the circulation of blood. Whenever a person eats or drinks, his soul becomes vulnerable to his desires, his will weakens, and he becomes reluctant toward worship. This is contrary to the case of a person who is fasting. Moreover, fasting induces the renunciation of wordly pleasure and personal desires and draws a Muslim's attention to the Hereafter. Fasting also makes one sympathize with the poor and needy by gaining a sense of their sufferings from the hardships of hunger and thirst.

The reference to the earlier *Ummahs* in the verse shows the importance on the one hand, and gives an encouragement to the Muslims on the other. It indicates that although there may be inconvenience in fasting but the same inconvenience was also faced by the earlier communities. This brings a psychological comfort to the Muslims, because if an inconvenience in faced by a large number of people, it becomes easier to bear.[4]

The verse simply says that fasting has been enjoined on Muslims as it was enjoined on past communities. From this it does not necessarily follow that the fasts which was enjoined upon the earlier communities is identical in all respects with the fasts enjoined upon this *ummah*. There

3. Fiqh As-*Sunnah*: 1/366
4. Ruhul-Ma'ani: 1/453

may have been difference in the number and the timings of the fasts, etc. Actually there is a big difference between the fasts as later generations completely altered it.

Fasting was only for special classes of people in the previous religions. In the Hindu religion, fasting is mandatory only for the high priests in the Brahmin class. In the some Latin religions, it is only women who must fast without exception. In Judaism, the faster eats only after the break and there is no more food. The Arabs, before Islam, would not eat after sleeping.

The subject of fasting in Christianity is very difficult to discuss, simply because Christianity as a whole is very short on religious laws. Besides, there is fundamental disagreement among the scholars to whether Jesus commanded fasting. Fasting in Christianity seems to have evolved with time and is effected by social, political, and economic factors.

Jesus fasted 40 days before starting his mission. It is possible that he fasted on the Day of Atonement, which was an established tradition in Judaism. By the 4th century, there was no sign of 40 days fasting in Christianity. There are traditions which Christians live. The fast in Rome was different from the fast in Alexandria. Some abstain from meat, while others from fish and birds. Some will not eat fruits and eggs; some just fast on white bread. Some will abstain from all the above. Certain days had been made for fasting in later centuries to commemorate some events, such as the life of Jesus. There was a fast for three days in English law. During the time of Edward VI, James I and the Elizabeth, meat was prohibited during the fast, and James justified that saying: "The fishing industry and maritime commerce must become encouraged and it must be profitable."[5]

Obligation of Ramadān from the sayings of Allah's Messenger (ﷺ)

Ibn Umar (ﷺ) narrated, Allah's Messenger (ﷺ) said:

---

5. Arkane Arba'ah by Abul Hasan Nadwi

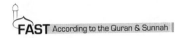
بُنِيَ الْإِسْلَامُ عَلَى خَمْسٍ شَهَادَةِ أَنْ لَا إِلَهَ إِلَّا اللهُ وَأَنَّ مُحَمَّدًا رَسُولُ
اللهِ وَإِقَامِ الصَّلَاةِ وَإِيتَاءِ الزَّكَاةِ وَالْحَجِّ وَصَوْمِ رَمَضَانَ

Islam is based on (the following) five principles:

1- To testify that *La illaha illallah wa anna Muhammad-ur-Rasul Al-lah* (none has the right to be worshiped but Allah and that Muhammad is the Messenger of Allah)

2- Iqamat-as-*Salāt* (to perform the compulsory congregational) prayers.

3- To pay *Zakah*

4- To perform Hajj (i.e. pilgrimage to Makkah)

5- To observe *Saūm* (fasts) during the month of Ramadān.[6]

Talhah bin 'Ubaid-Ullah (☉) narrated that a Bedouin with unkempt hair came to Allah's Messenger (☉) and said, "O Allah's Messenger! Inform me what Allah has made compulsory for me as regards to the prayer." He replied: "You have to perform the five compulsory *salāt* in a day and night (24 hours), unless you want to offer *nawafil*." The Bedouin further asked, "Inform me what Allah has made compulsory for me as regard fasting." He replied, "You have to observe *Saūm* (fast) during the whole month of Ramadān, unless you want to fast more as *nawafil*" The bedouin further asked, "Tell me how much *zakah* Allah has enjoined on me." Thus, Allah's Messenger informed him about all the laws (i.e, fundamentals) of Islam. The Bedouin then said, "By Him who has honored you, I will neither perform any *nawafil* nor will I decrease what Allah has enjoined on me." Allah's Messenger (☉) said:

أَفْلَحَ إِنْ صَدَقَ أَوْ دَخَلَ الْجَنَّةَ إِنْ صَدَقَ

"If he is saying the truth he will succeed or said he will be granted paradise"[7]

'Āishah (☉) narrated that the Quraish used to observe fast on the day of

6. Bukhari: 8
7. Bukhari: 1891

Āshūra during the pre-Islamic period, and then Allah's Messenger (ﷺ) ordered (Muslims) to observe the fast on it until fasting during the month of Ramadān was obligated. The Prophet (ﷺ) said:

مَنْ شَاءَ فَلْيَصُمْ وَمَنْ شَاءَ أَفْطَرَ

"He who wants to fast (on Āshūra) may fast and he who does not want to observe fast [during it] does not have to fast."[8]

Ad-Dhahabi says: "According to the believers anyone who leaves the fast of Ramadān without being sick is worse than a fornicator or an alcoholic. They doubt his Islam and they suspect he might be a *zindeeq* (disbeliever) and one of those who destroy Islam."[9]

Shaykhul Islam Ibn Taymiyyah said: "If a person does not fast in Ramadān knowing that it is *harām* [to leave it] but makes it *halal* (permissible) for himself to abandon it, he must be executed; if he does it because he is immoral [but believes it is *harām* (impermissible)], then he must be punished for not fasting."[10]

The obligation of fasting is directed to both the resident and the traveler, the healthy and sick, ritually pure or impure (such as menstruating women and women is postnatal bleeding period), and those in a state of unconsciousness; all of them are accountable for the obligation of fasting. They are commanded to observe it so as to be aware that it is obligatory upon them and that it has to be observed whether at its due time or later in the case of legal excuse. It is obligatory upon some of them to perform it at its prescribed time, namely the healthy and the resident people, excluding menstruating women and women in a state of postnatal bleeding. Others are only obliged to make up for it later, namely the menstruating women and women in a state of postnatal bleeding, and those who are too ill to observe it at its due time and can observe it later. However, there are some who may choose either, whether to observe it at its prescribed time or later, such as the travellers and ill people who can observe fasting

---

8. Bukhari: 1893
9. Fiqh As-*Sunnah*: 1/545
10. Majmo al-Fatawa: 25/265

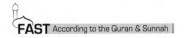

with difficulty but without causing them harm.

As for one who breaks his fast during Ramadān due to legal excuse and then the excuse ends – such as a traveller returning from his travel, a menstruating woman or woman in a state of postnatal bleeding who becomes ritually pure, a disbeliever who converts to Islam, an insane person who regains sanity, and a child who reaches puberty – they are to observe the fasts for the rest of the day (if the excuse is over in the day time) and to make up for that day afterwards. Similarly, if people are informed in the daytime (or after daybreak) that the month of Ramadān has already begun, they are to observe fasting for the rest of the day and then to make up for that day later after Ramadān.[11]

We will discuss all these points in detail.

---

11. Al-Mulkhasul – Fiqhi: 1/375-377

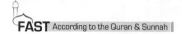

Merits and
Virtues of Saum

Forgiveness and great reward for the men and women who observe *Saūm*

Allah says:

إِنَّ ٱلْمُسْلِمِينَ وَٱلْمُسْلِمَٰتِ وَٱلْمُؤْمِنِينَ وَٱلْمُؤْمِنَٰتِ وَٱلْقَٰنِتِينَ وَٱلْقَٰنِتَٰتِ وَٱلصَّٰدِقِينَ وَٱلصَّٰدِقَٰتِ وَٱلصَّٰبِرِينَ وَٱلصَّٰبِرَٰتِ وَٱلْخَٰشِعِينَ وَٱلْخَٰشِعَٰتِ وَٱلْمُتَصَدِّقِينَ وَٱلْمُتَصَدِّقَٰتِ وَٱلصَّٰٓئِمِينَ وَٱلصَّٰٓئِمَٰتِ وَٱلْحَٰفِظِينَ فُرُوجَهُمْ وَٱلْحَٰفِظَٰتِ وَٱلذَّٰكِرِينَ ٱللَّهَ كَثِيرًا وَٱلذَّٰكِرَٰتِ أَعَدَّ ٱللَّهُ لَهُم مَّغْفِرَةً وَأَجْرًا عَظِيمًا ﴿٣٥﴾

Verily the Muslims men and women, the believers men and women, the men and the women who are obedient (to Allah), the men and women who are truthful, the men and women who are humble, the men and women who give *sadaqat* (i.e. *zakah* and alms etc) the men and women who observe *saūm*, the men and women who guard their chastity (from illegal sexual acts) and men and women who remember Allah much (with their hearts and tongues) Allah has prepared for them forgiveness and a great reward (i.e.

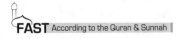

Paradise). (Al-Ahzab 33:35)

Ar-Raiyan is one of the gates of Paradise

Shal (ﷺ) narrated that the Prophet (ﷺ) said:

$$\text{إِنَّ فِي الْجَنَّةِ بَابًا يُقَالُ لَهُ الرَّيَّانُ يَدْخُلُ مِنْهُ الصَّائِمُونَ يَوْمَ الْقِيَامَةِ}$$
$$\text{لَا يَدْخُلُ مِنْهُ أَحَدٌ غَيْرُهُمْ}$$

"There is a gate in Paradise called *ar-Raiyan*, and those who observe the fast will enter through it on the Day of Resurrection and none except them will enter through it. It will be said, 'Where are those who used to observe fast?' They will get up, and none except them will enter through it. After this entry the gate will be closed and no body will enter through it.

Abu Hurairah (ﷺ) narrated that Allah's Messenger (ﷺ) said, "Whoever gives two kinds (of things or property), in charity for Allah's cause, will be called from the gates of Paradise and will be addressed, 'O slaves of Allah! Here is prosperity, so, whoever was amongst the people who used to offer their prayers will be called from the gates of the *salat*; and whoever was amongst the people who used to participate in jihad will be called from the gate of jihad; and whoever was amongst those who used to observe the fast will be called from the gate of *ar-Raiyān*; whoever was amongst those who used to give charity, will be called from the gate of *as-Sadaqah*.'" Abu Bakr (ﷺ) said, "Let my parents be sacrificed for you, O Allah's Messenger! No distress or need will befall him who will be called from those gates. Will there be anyone who will be called from all these gates?" The Prophet (ﷺ) replied:

$$\text{نَعَمْ وَأَرْجُو أَنْ تَكُونَ مِنْهُمْ}$$

"Yes, and I hope you will be one of them."[1]

---

1. Bukhari: 1896,1897.

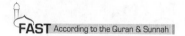

All Previous Sins will be forgiven

Abu Hurairah (رضى الله عنه) narrated that the Prophet (ﷺ) said, "whoever established prayer on the night of Qadr with sincere faith and hoping for a reward from Allah, then all his previous sins will be forgiven." (He added:)

مَنْ صَامَ رَمَضَانَ إِيمَـانًا وَاحْتِسَابًا غُفِرَ لَهُ مَا تَقَدَّمَ مِنْ ذَنْبِهِ

"Whoever observes fasts in the month of Ramadān with sincere faith and hoping for a reward from Allāh, then all his previous sins will be forgiven."[2]

In another narration:

إِنَّ فِى الْجَنَّةِ لَبَابًا يُدْعَى الرَّيَّانَ يُدْعَى لَهُ الصَّائِمُونَ فَمَنْ كَانَ مِنَ الصَّائِمِينَ دَخَلَهُ وَمَنْ دَخَلَهُ لَمْ يَظْمَأْ أَبَدًا

"There is a gate in Paradise called ar-Raiyyān, and those who fast shall be invited into it; whoever was among those who fasted, then he will enter it, and whoever enters it, he will never thirst again."[3]

Explanation

Rayyan is a door of Paradise which means "Full with water.' A fasting person bears the pang of hunger and thirst, and bearing thirst is harder than hunger, therefore, the door appointed for the fasting people is called" the door full with water, or the well-watered door.

Gates of Paradise are Opened

Abu Hurairah (رضى الله عنه) narrated that the Messenger of Allah (ﷺ) said:

إِذَا جَاءَ رَمَضَانُ فُتِّحَتْ أَبْوَابُ الْجَنَّةِ وَغُلِّقَتْ أَبْوَابُ النَّارِ

2. Bukhari: 1901
3. Tirmidhi: 765

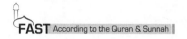

$$وَصُفِّدَتِ الشَّيَاطِينُ$$

"When Ramadān comes, the gates of Paradise are opened and the gates of fire are closed, and the Devils are fettered." [4]

Explanation

The doors of paradise are opened and the doors of Hell are closed means their literal opening and closing. Another possible meaning is that the month of Ramadān is given special importance in Muslim society, and the good deeds become more attractive so that the Muslims are inspired to perform a variety of good deeds. They make a determined struggle to avoid sins; therefore these good deeds are doors to Paradise and the sins are doors to Hell.

Saūm is for Me and I shall Reward for it

Abu Hurairah (ﷺ) narrated: "I heard Allah's Messenger (ﷺ) say:

$$قَالَ اللهُ عَزَّ وَجَلَّ كُلُّ عَمَلِ ابْنِ آدَمَ لَهُ إِلاَّ الصِّيَامَ هُوَ لِي وَأَنَا$$
$$أَجْزِي بِهِ فَوَالَّذِي نَفْسُ مُحَمَّدٍ بِيَدِهِ لَخِلْفَةُ فَمِ الصَّائِمِ أَطْيَبُ عِنْدَ$$
$$اللهِ مِنْ رِيحِ الْـمِسْكِ$$

'Every deed of the son of Adam is for him, except fasting. It is for Me and I shall reward for it. By the one in whose Hand is the soul of Muhammad, the smell of the mouth of the fasting person is better to Allah than the fragrance of musk.'"[5]

The change in the ordor of the mouth is a vived physical testimony of this discipline. As much as we hate bad breath in fasting, it is a good thing, for it is caused by the coating which appears on the upper surface of the tongue soon after the commencement of the fast. After desiring food,

---

4. Muslim: 1079
5. Muslim: 1151(160)

the body begins to digest such waste material and deposits of fat as are available in it. This coating on the tongue is an outward proof that inner elimination is in progress. As soon as the digestive organs have been purified, the mouth returns to normal.[6]

The Fasting Person has two Moments of Joy

Abu Hurairah (ﷺ) said that the Messenger of Allah (ﷺ) said: "Allah the Most High, said:

كُلُّ عَمَلِ ابْنِ آدَمَ لَهُ إِلاَّ الصِّيَامَ فَإِنَّهُ لِي وَأَنَا أَجْزِي بِهِ وَالصِّيَامُ جُنَّةٌ فَإِذَا كَانَ يَوْمُ صَوْمِ أَحَدِكُمْ فَلاَ يَرْفُثْ يَوْمَئِذٍ وَلاَ يَسْخَبْ فَإِنْ سَابَّهُ أَحَدٌ أَوْ قَاتَلَهُ فَلْيَقُلْ إِنِّي امْرُؤٌ صَائِمٌ. وَالَّذِي نَفْسُ مُحَمَّدٍ بِيَدِهِ لَخُلُوفُ فَمِ الصَّائِمِ أَطْيَبُ عِنْدَ اللهِ يَوْمَ الْقِيَامَةِ مِنْ رِيحِ الْمِسْكِ وَلِلصَّائِمِ فَرْحَتَانِ يَفْرَحُهُمَا إِذَا أَفْطَرَ فَرِحَ بِفِطْرِهِ وَإِذَا لَقِيَ رَبَّهُ فَرِحَ بِصَوْمِهِ

'Every deed of the son of Adam is for him, except fasting. It is for Me, and I shall reward for it.' Fasting is a shield, so if it is a day when one of you is fasting, let him not utter any abscene speech that day nor raise his voice. If anyone reviles him, or argues with him, let him say: 'I am a man who is fasting.' By the one in whose hand is the soul of Mohammad! The smell of the mouth of the fasting person will be better to Allah on the day of resurrection than the fragrance of musk. The fasting person has two moments of joy that he rejoices in: When he breaks his fast he rejoices at breaking his fast, and when he meets his Lord he will rejoice in his fasting."[7]

6. Essentials of Ramadān the Fasting Month, P:12
7. Muslim: 1151 (163)

Explanation

"Fasting is for Me and I shall reward for it." Allah has specially mentioned fasting and His bestowing the reward for it Himself. This is in spite of the fact that all acts of worship are for Him and the reward for them is from Him, is because all acts of worship through which the slaves seek to draw nearer to Allāh, the Al-Mighty, the All-powerful – such as prayer, Hajj, charity, asceticism, i'tikaf, supplication, slaughtering sacrificial animals and other acts of worship have all been performed by the pagans as acts of worship to their gods and things that they set up as partners with Allah. But no one has heard that any group from among these ancient pagans worshiped their idols through fasting, nor they attempted to draw nearer to them through it, or offered thanks to them through it. Fasting is not known as an act of worship except in the Divinely revealed Laws. This is why Allah, the Almighty, the All-powerful said: 'Fasting in for Me.' That is, no one shares in it with Me, and none beside Me has been worshiped through it, so I will give the reward for it, because it was performed for Me alone. And I will be responsible for giving the rewords for, I will not appoint another to do it, whether it be one of the angels who is allowed to come near (to Me) or anyone else."[8]

Allah will Remove his Face Seventy Autumns from the Fire

In another narration Allah's Messenger ﷺ said:

$$مَنْ صَامَ يَوْماً فِي سَبِيلِ اللهِ عَزَّ وَجَلَّ بَاعَدَ اللهُ مِنْهُ جَهَنَّمَ مَسِيرَةَ$$
$$مِائَةِ عَامٍ$$

"Whoever fasts one day in the cause of Allāh, the Mighty and Sublime, Allāh will separate him the distance of one hundred years from the Fire."[9]

Abu Sa'eed Al-Khudri (ﷺ) narrated that the Messenger of Allah (ﷺ) said:

---

8. Jami' Al-Usool 9/454
9. Nasa'i: 2256

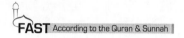

مَا مِنْ عَبْدٍ يَصُومُ يَوْمًا فِي سَبِيلِ اللهِ إِلاَّ بَاعَدَ اللهُ بِذَلِكَ الْيَوْمِ وَجْهَهُ عَنِ النَّارِ سَبْعِينَ خَرِيفًا

"There is no one who fasts one day in the cause of Allah, but Allah will remove his face (the distance of) seventy autumns from the fire in return for that day." [10]

O Seekers of the Good Come Near

Abu Hurairah (رضي الله عنه) narrated that the Messenger of Allah (ﷺ) said:

إِذَا كَانَ أَوَّلُ لَيْلَةٍ مِنْ شَهْرِ رَمَضَانَ صُفِّدَتِ الشَّيَاطِينُ وَمَرَدَةُ الْجِنِّ وَغُلِّقَتْ أَبْوَابُ النَّارِ فَلَمْ يُفْتَحْ مِنْهَا بَابٌ وَفُتِّحَتْ أَبْوَابُ الْجَنَّةِ فَلَمْ يُغْلَقْ مِنْهَا بَابٌ وَيُنَادِى مُنَادٍ يَا بَاغِيَ الْخَيْرِ أَقْبِلْ وَيَا بَاغِيَ الشَّرِّ أَقْصِرْ وَلِلَّهِ عُتَقَاءُ مِنَ النَّارِ وَذَلِكَ كُلَّ لَيْلَةٍ

"On the first night of the month of Ramadān, the *shayatīn* are shackled, the jinns are restrained, the gates of the fires are shut such that no gate among them would be opened. The gates of Paradise are opened such that no gate among them would be closed, and a caller calls: 'O seeker of the good, come near!' and 'O seeker of evil, stop!' There are those whom Allah frees from the Fire. And that is every night." [11]

A Shield against the Fire

Uthman bin Abul-'Ās Ath-Thaqafi narrated that Allah's Messenger (ﷺ) said:

الصِّيَامُ جُنَّةٌ مِنَ النَّارِ كَجُنَّةِ أَحَدِكُمْ مِنَ الْقِتَالِ

---

10. Muslim: 1153
11. Tirmidhi: 682

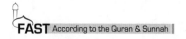

"Fasting is a shield against the fire just like the shield of anyone of you while fighting."[12]

In another narration:

الصَّوْمُ جُنَّةٌ مَا لَمْ يَخْرِقْهَا

"Fasting is a shield, as long as he does not pierce it."[13]

Abu Hurairah (ﷺ) narrated that the Prophet (ﷺ) said:

الصِّيَامُ جُنَّتُهُ وَ حِصْنٌ حَصِينٌ مِنَ النَّارِ

"Fasting is a protection and a strong fortress that keeps [a person] safe from the Fire."[14]

Fasting and the Qur'ān's Intercession

'Abdullāh bin Amr bin 'Āl-As (ﷺ) narrated that the Messenger of Allah (ﷺ) said:

الصِّيَامُ وَالْقُرْآنُ يَشْفَعَانِ لِلْعَبْدِ يَوْمَ الْقِيَامَةِ، يَقُولُ الصِّيَامُ: أَيْ رَبِّ مَنَعْتُهُ الطَّعَامَ وَالشَّهَوَاتِ بِالنَّهَارِ فَشَفِّعْنِي فِيهِ، وَيَقُولُ الْقُرْآنُ، مَنَعْتُهُ النَّوْمَ بِاللَّيْلِ فَشَفِّعْنِي فِيهِ، قَالَ: فَيُشْفَعَانِ

"Fasting and the Qur'ān intercede (with Allah) for the slave on the day of Resurrection, saying: 'O Lord! I prevented him from (eating) food and from (giving into his) desires during the day, so make me intercessor for him.' The Qur'ān will say: 'I prevented him sleeping at night, so make me an intercessor for him.'" He (ﷺ) added: "Then Allah will grant them intercession."[15]

12. Ibn Majah: 1639
13. Nasai: 2233
14. Al-Jami' as-Sagheer: 1/232
15. Sahih at-Targheeb: 980

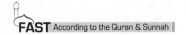

A Trench between him and the Fire

Abu Umamah Al-Bahili (ﷺ) narrated that the Prophet (ﷺ) said:

مَنْ صَامَ يَوْماً فِي سَبِيلِ اللهِ جَعَلَ اللهُ بَيْنَهُ وَبَيْنَ النَّارِ خَنْدَقاً كَمَا
بَيْنَ السَّمَاءِ وَالأَرْضِ

"Whoever fasted for a day in Allah's Cause, Allah will place a trench between him and the Fire as wide as the distance between the heaven and the earth."[16]

In another narration Allah's Messenger (ﷺ) said:

وَمَنْ صَامَ يَوْمًا ابْتِغَاءَ وَجْهِ اللهِ خُتِمَ لَهُ بِهِ دَخَلَ الْـجَنَّةَ

"Whoever fasts one day seeking the pleasure of Allah, if that is the last day of his life, he will enter Paradise."[17]

Away with one who Attains Ramadān but is not Forgiven

Ka'b bin Ujrah (ﷺ) narrated that the Messenger of Allah (ﷺ) approached the Minbar. So we approached and he mounted one step (of the Minbar) and said: "Ameen" then when he had mounted the second step, he said (again): "Ameen" And when he had mounted third step, he said: "Ameen." When he had descended, we said: "O Messenger of Allah! We have heard something from you today that we had not previously heard." He replied:

إِنَّ جِبْرِيلَ عَلَيْهِ الصَّلَاةُ وَالسَّلَامُ عَرَضَ لِي فَقَالَ: بُعْدًا لِـمَنْ
أَدْرَكَ رَمَضَانَ فَلَمْ يُغْفَرْلَهُ قُلْتُ: آمِينَ، فَلَمَّا رَقِيتُ الثَّانِيَةَ قَالَ:
بُعْدًا لِـمَنْ ذُكِرْتَ عِنْدَهُ فَلَمْ يُصَلِّ عَلَيْكَ، قُلْتُ آمِينَ، فَلَمَّا
رَقِيتُ الثَّالِثَةَ قَالَ بُعْدًا لِـمَنْ أَدْرَكَ أَبَوَاهُ الْكَبِيرَ عِنْدَهُ أَوْ أَحَدَهُمَا،

---

16. Tirmidhi: 1624
17. Saheeh at-Targheeb: 985

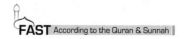

$$\text{فَلَمْ يُدْخِلَاهُ الْـجَنَّةَ قُلْتُ آمِين}$$

"Verily Gabriel ﷺ appeared to me and he said: 'Away with one who attains Ramadān but is not Forgiven,' upon which I said: 'Āmeen' then when I mounted the second (step), he said: 'Away with one in whose presence I am mentioned and he does not invoke prayers on me,' upon which I said: 'Āmeen.' Then when I had mounted the third (step), he said: 'Away with him whose parents – or one of his parents – are overtaken by old age and they do not admit him to the paradise,' upon which I said: 'Āmeen.'" [18]

As-Saūm is Expiation

Abu Hurairah (ﷺ) narrated that the Prophet (ﷺ) said:

$$\text{الصَّلَوَاتُ الْخَمْسُ وَالْجُمْعَةُ إِلَى الْجُمْعَةِ وَرَمَضَانُ إِلَى رَمَضَانَ}$$
$$\text{مُكَفِّرَاتٌ لِمَا بَيْنَهُنَّ اذا اجْتُنِبَتِ الْكَبَائِرُ.}$$

"The five prayers, from one Friday prayer to the next, and from one Ramadān to the next all expiate the sins that are committed between them, as long as one avoids the major sins."[19]

Hudhaifah (ﷺ) narrated that 'Umar (ﷺ) asked the people: "Who remembers the narration of the Prophet (ﷺ) about the fitnah (trail or affliction)?" Hudhaifah (ﷺ) said: "I heard the Prophet (ﷺ) saying:

$$\text{فِتْنَةُ الرَّجُلِ فِي أَهْلِهِ وَمَالِهِ وَجَارِهِ تُكَفِّرُهَا الصَّلَاةُ وَالصِّيَامُ}$$
$$\text{وَالصَّدَقَةُ}$$

'The Fitnah of a person in his property, family and neighbors is expiated by his prayer, fasting and giv-

18. Al-Hakim: 4/153,154, Ibn Khuzaimah: 1888
19. Ahmad: 2/400

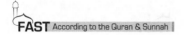

ing in charity.'" Umar said: "I do not ask about that, but I ask about the fitnah which will spread like the waves of the sea." Hudhaifah replied: "There is a close gate in front of it." 'Umar asked: "Will that gate be opened or broken?"

He replied: "It will be broken." Umar said: "Then the gate will be not be closed again until the day of Resurrection." We said to *Masruq*: "Would you ask Hudhaifah whether 'Umar knew what that gate symbolized?" He asked him and he replied: "He (Umar) knew it as one knows that there will be night before tomarrow morning."[20]

Explanation

In the above mentioned *hadith* Allah's Messenger (ﷺ) said: "as long as one avoids the major sins."

The Qur'ān also describes this point. Allah says:

$$إِن تَجْتَنِبُواْ كَبَآئِرَ مَا تُنْهَوْنَ عَنْهُ نُكَفِّرْ عَنكُمْ سَيِّئَاتِكُمْ وَنُدْخِلْكُم مُّدْخَلًا كَرِيمًا ﴿٣١﴾$$

"If you avoid the great sins which you are forbidden to do, we shall expiate from you your (small) sins, and admit you to a Noble entrance (i.e. Paradise)." (An-Nisā' 4: 31)

Minor sins are pardoned with the performance of the five prescribed prayers, Jumuah and with observing fasts while major sins like associating someone with Allah in worship, disobedience of Parents, false oath, false evidence, encroachment on an orphan's property, calumny against chaste women etc., are not forgiven without repentance.

Scholars have said: If the sin involves the right of Allah and not of a person, then there are three conditions to be met in order for that repentance to be accepted by Allah:

---

20. Bukhari: 1895

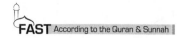

1-   To desist from committing it

2-   To feel sorry for committing it.

3-   To decide not to recommit it.

But if the sin involves a person's right, it requires a forth condition, i.e to absolve oneself from such right. If it is a property, he should return it to its rightful owner. If it is slandering or backbiting, one should ask the pardon of the offended person.[21]

Seeking Allah's Face

Hudaifah (&) narrated: "I placed the head of the Messenger of Allah (&) to rest on my chest and he & said:

مَنْ قَالَ لَا إِلَهَ إِلَّا الله - إِبْتِغَاءَ وَجْهِ الله - خُتِمَ لَهُ بِهَا دَخَلَ الْـجَنَّةَ،
وَمَنْ صَامَ يَوْمًا إِبْتِغَاءَ وَجْهِ الله خُتِمَ لَهُ بِهَا دَخَلَ الْـجَنَّةَ، وَمَنْ
تَصَدَّقَ بِصَدَقَةٍ إِبْتِغَاءَ وَجْهِ الله خُتِمَ لَهُ بِهَا دَخَلَ الْـجَنَّةَ

'Whoever said that none has the right to be worshipped except Allah, seeking by it Allah's Face, it will be ordained for him thereby that he will enter Paradise. And whoever observes fast, seeking by it Allah's Face, it will be ordained for him thereby that he will enter Paradise. And whoever gives something in charity, seeking by it Allah's Face, it will be ordained for him thereby that he will enter Paradise."[22]

Nothing like *Saūm*

Abu Umamah (&) said: "Tell me something that I may learn from you. He said:

عَلَيْكَ بِالصَّوْمِ فَإِنَّهُ لَا مِثْلَ لَهُ

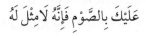

---

21. Riyad-us-Saliheen: 17
22. At-Targeeb wat-Tarheeb: 2/85; Ahmad: 5/391

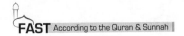
'Take to fasting, for there is nothing like it.'"

In an other narration, I said: "O Messenger of Allah, tell me of something by which Allah will benefit me. He said:

عَلَيْكَ بِالصِّيَامِ فَإِنَّهُ لَا مِثْلَ لَهُ

'Take to fasting, for there is nothing like it.'"

In another narration, I asked the messenger of Allah (ﷺ): "Which deed is best?" He said:

عَلَيْكَ بِالصَّوْمِ فَإِنَّهُ لَا عِدْلَ لَهُ

'Take to fasting, for there is nothing equal to it.'"[23]

Explanation

"There is nothing like it," means either from the dimension of reward and recompense or from the aspect of shielding oneself against sins. And perhaps it refers to both.

Among the Truthful ones and Martyrs

Amr bin Murrah Al-Juhani ؓ narrated: A man come to the Prophet (ﷺ) and said: "O Messenger of Allah! What do you think, if I bear witness that none is worthy of worship except Allah and that you are the Messenger of Allah, perform the five prayers, pay *zakah*, fast the month of Ramadān and stand in prayer during its nights, among which group I will be?" He said:

مِنَ الصِّدِّيقِينَ وَالشُّهَدَآءِ

"Among the truthful ones and the martyrs"[24]

Observing *Saūm* is Recommended for Young People

'Abdullāh bin Mas'ud (ؓ) narrated that Allah's Messenger (ﷺ) said:

23. Nasai: 2222, 2223, 2224
24. Al-Mawarid, p,36 no:19, Majma' Az-Zawaid: 1/46

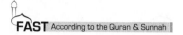

مَعْشَرَ الشَّبَابِ مَنِ اسْتَطَاعَ مِنْكُمُ الْبَاءَةَ فَلْيَتَزَوَّجْ وَمَنْ لَـمْ يَسْتَطِعْ فَعَلَيْهِ بِالصَّوْمِ فَإِنَّهُ لَهُ وِجَاءٌ

"O young people! Whoever among you is able to marry, should marry, and whoever is not able to marry, is recommended to observe *saūm* as fasting will diminish his sexual power."[25]

The Supplication of the Fasting Person is not Turned Back

Abu Hurairah narrated that the Messenger of Allah (ﷺ) said:

ثَلاَثَةٌ لاَ تُرَدُّ دَعْوَتُهُمْ الإِمَامُ الْعَادِلُ وَالصَّائِمُ حَتَّى يُفْطِرَ وَدَعْوَةُ الْـمَظْلُومِ يَرْفَعُهَا اللهُ دُونَ الْغَمَامِ يَوْمَ الْقِيَامَةِ وَتُفْتَحُ لَهَا أَبْوَابُ السَّمَاءِ وَيَقُولُ بِعِزَّتِى لأَنْصُرَنَّكِ وَلَوْ بَعْدَ حِينٍ

There are three whose supplications are not turned back: A just ruler, a fasting person until he breaks his fast, and the supplication of one who has been wronged, which is raised by Allah up to the clouds on the Day of Resurrection. The gates of Heaven are opened for it, and Allah says: 'By my might I will help you (against the wrongdoer) even it is after a while.'"[26]

Allah Tells Proudly to the Angels

Allah's Messenger (ﷺ) said:

أَتَاكُمْ رَمَضَانُ شَهْرُ بَرَكَةٍ وَيُغْنِيكُمُ اللهُ فِيهِ فَيُنَزِّلُ الرَّحْمَةَ وَيَحُطُّ الْـخَطَايَا، وَيَسْتَجِيبُ فِي الدُّعَاءِ، يَنْظُرُ اللهُ إِلَى تَنَافُسِكُمْ وَيُبَاهِي بِكُمْ مَلاَئِكَتَهُ، فَأَرُوا اللهَ مِنْ أَنْفُسِكُمْ خَيْرًا فَإِنَّ الشَّقِى مَنْ حُرِمَ

25. Bukhari: 5065
26. Ibn Majah: 1752

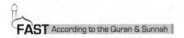
فِيهِ رَحْمَةَ اللهِ

"The month of Ramadān has come to you all. It is a month of blessing. Allah covers you all during it. He sends down the Mercy, removes the sins and insures the supplication. Allah looks at you competing for good works during it and He tells proudly to the angles about you all. Therefore, show Allah goodness from yourselves. For verily the wretched person is the one who is deprived of Allah's Mercy during it (Ramadān)."[27]

---

27. Majma'uz-Zawa'id: 3/142

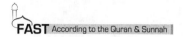

Ascertaining the Crescent

Do not Observe Fasting Unless you See the Crescent of the Moon

'Abdullāh bin Umar (رضي الله عنه) narrated that Allah's Messenger (ﷺ) mentioned Ramadān and said:

لَا تَصُومُوا حَتَّى تَرَوْا الْهِلَالَ وَلَا تُفْطِرُوا حَتَّى تَرَوْهُ فَإِنْ غُمَّ عَلَيْكُمْ فَاقْدُرُوا لَهُ

"Do not observe fasting unless you see the crescent, the moon (of Ramadān), and do not give up fasting until you see the crescent, the moon of (Shawwāl), but if the sky is overcast and you can not see the moon, then act on estimation."[1]

In another narration:

الشَّهْرُ تِسْعٌ وَعِشْرُونَ لَيْلَةً فَلَا تَصُومُوا حَتَّى تَرَوْهُ فَإِنْ غُمَّ عَلَيْكُمْ فَأَكْمِلُوا الْعِدَّةَ ثَلَاثِينَ

"The month (can be) 29 nights (i.e. days); do not fast until you see the crescent, the moon, and if the sky is

---

1. Bukhari: 1906

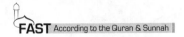

overcast, then complete Sha'bān as thirty days."[2]

In another narration Allah's Messenger (ﷺ) mentioned Sha'bān:

صُومُوا لِرُؤْيَتِهِ وَأَفْطِرُوا لِرُؤْيَتِهِ فَإِنْ غُبِّيَ عَلَيْكُمْ فَأَكْمِلُوا عِدَّةَ شَعْبَانَ ثَلَاثِينَ

"Start observing *saūm* (fasts) on seeing the crescent, the moon (of Ramadān), and give up observing *saūm* (fast) on seeing the crescent, the moon (of Shawwāl); if the sky is overcast (and you cannot see it), then complete thirty days of Sha'bān."[3]

Explanation

In case the moon of Ramadān is not sighted on the 29th of Sha'bān due to the sky being blurred by dust or clouds, one should complete 30 days of Sha'bān and then observe fasting. The observance of fast merely on the basis of suspicion or assumption that the moon of Ramadān might possible have been sighted on the 29th of Sha'abn itself, is forbidden.

The Month may be only Twenty-Nine Days

Umm Salamah (﵂) narrated that the Prophet (ﷺ) swore that he would not enter upon some of his wives for a month. When twenty-nine days had passed, he came to them in the morning – or in the evening – and it was said to him: "You swore, O Prophet of Allah, that you would not enter upon us for a month." He said:

إِنَّ الشَّهْرَ يَكُونُ تِسْعًا وَعِشْرِينَ يَوْمًا

"The month may be only twenty-nine days."[4]

---

2. Bukhari: 1907
3. Bukhari: 1909
4. Muslim: 1085

We Fasted with Allah's Messenger (ﷺ) for Thirty Days

Ibn Mas'ūd ؓ said:

لَـمَا صُمْنَا مَعَ النَّبِيِّ (ﷺ) تِسْعًا وَعِشْرِينَ أَكْثَرُ مِـمَّا صُمْنَا مَعَهُ ثَلاَثِينَ

"We fasted with the Prophet (ﷺ) for twenty nine days, more often than we fasted with him for thirty days."[5]

Ibn Abbas (ﷺ) narrated that the Prophet (ﷺ) said:

أَتَانِي جِبْرِيلُ ﷺ فَقَالَ: الشَّهَرُ تِسْعٌ وَعِشْرُوْنَ يَوْماً

"Jibril came to me and said: 'The month is twenty nine days.'"[6]

More Tentativeness in Ascertaining the Days of Sha'bān

'Abdullāh bin Abi Qais said: "I heard 'Āishah (ﷺ) say that the Messenger of Allah (ﷺ) used to be more tentative in ascertaining the days of Sha'ban then any other month. Then he would fast upon the sighting (of the crescent) of Ramadān. If it was obscured from him, he would complete thirty days (of Sha'bān) and then fast."[7]

Collective Decision in Sighting the Crescent

Abu Hurairah ؓ narrated that Allah's Messenger (ﷺ) said:

وَفِطْرُكُمْ يَوْمَ تُفْطِرُونَ وَأَضْحَاكُمْ يَوْمَ تُضَحُّونَ وَكُلُّ عَرَفَةَ مَوْقِفٌ وَكُلُّ مِنًى مَنْحَرٌ وَكُلُّ فِجَاجِ مَكَّةَ مَنْحَرٌ وَكُلُّ جَمْعٍ مَوْقِفٌ

"Your breaking of the fast ('Eīd Al-Fitr) is the day

---

5. Abu Dawud: 2322
6. Nasai: 2135
7. Abu Dawud: 2325

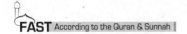

that (all of) you break your fast, and your sacrificing ('Eīd Al-Adhā), is on the day that (all of) you
sacrifice, and all of 'Arafat is a place of standing, and
all of Mina is a place for slaughtering, and all of the
mountain paths of Makkah are a place for slaughtering, and all of the mountain paths of Makkah are a
place of slaughtering, and all of Jam' (Muzdalifah) is
a place of halting."[8]

If a person sees the new moon by himself, he does not fast until the people fast nor does he break his fast until the people break their fast.

Connecting Sha'bān with Ramadān

Abu Hurairah ◈ narrated that the Prophet (ﷺ) said:

$$ لَا يَتَقَدَّمَنَّ أَحَدُكُمْ رَمَضَانَ بِصَوْمِ يَوْمٍ أَوْ يَوْمَيْنِ إِلَّا أَنْ يَكُونَ $$

$$ رَجُلٌ كَانَ يَصُومُ صَوْمَهُ فَلْيَصُمْ ذَلِكَ الْيَوْمَ $$

"None of you should observe saūm (fast) for a day
or two ahead of Ramadān unless he has the habit of
observing saūm (Nawafil) (and if his fasting coincides with that day) then he can observe saūm on that
day."[9]

Explanation

"If a person is in the habit of observing saūm on a particular day," means
that if it is his routine to observe saūm on these days, then he can do so,
one or two days before the advent of Ramadān. The reason being that in
that case his saūm will not be for the reception of Ramadān but a matter
of routine.

Fasting on a day in which there is Doubt

Silah bin Zufar said: "We were with 'Ammar bin Yasir when a roasted

8. Abu Dawud: 2324
9. Bukhari: 1914

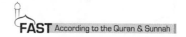

sheep was brought and he said: "Eat," but someone among the people said: "I am fasting." Ammar said:

مَنْ صَامَ الْيَوْمَ الَّذِى يَشُكُّ فِيهِ النَّاسُ فَقَدْ عَصَى أَبَا الْقَاسِمِ (ﷺ)

"Whoever fasts on a day in which there is doubt, he has disobeyed Abul-Qasim."[10]

Each Land has its Own Sighting of the Crescent

Kuraib narrated that Umm Al-Fadl bin Al-Harith sent him to Muawiyah in Ash-Sham. He said: I arrived in Ash-Sham and I finished her errand, and the crescent of Ramadān appeared while I was in Ash-Sham, where I saw the crescent moon on the night of Friday. Then I came to Al-Madinah at the end of the month, and I asked 'Abdullāh bin Abbas (ﷺ), who mentioned the crescent and said: "When did you see the crescent?" I said: "We saw it on the night of Friday." He said "Did you see it?" I said: "Yes and the people saw it, and they fasted, and Muawiyah fasted." He said: "But we saw it on the night of Saturday. And we will keep fasting until we complete thirty days, or we see it." I said: "Is the sighting and fasting of Muawiyah not sufficient for you?" He said: "No this is what the Messenger of Allah (ﷺ) enjoined upon us."

Abu Bakhtari said: "We went out for Umrah, and when we stopped in Batn Nakhlah, we looked for the crescent and we saw it. Some of the people said: It is the three nights old, and some of them said: It is two nights old.

Then we met Ibn Abbas and we said: 'We spotted the crescent, some of the people said that it was three nights old, and some of the people said it was two nights old.' He said: 'On what night did you see it?' We said: 'On such – and – such a night.' He said: 'The Messenger of Allah (ﷺ) said:

إِنَّ اللهَ مَدَّهُ لِلرُّؤْيَةِ فَهُوَ لِلَيْلَةِ رَأَيْتُمُوهُ

---

10. Tirmidhi: 686

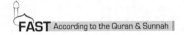

"Indeed Allah courses it to appear for long enough that it can be seen, so on the night that you saw it, that was when it appeared.""""[11]

Explanation

The sighting of the moon at one place being sufficient for another place is controversial. The group which states that the sighting of the moon at one place is valid for another holds that the *hadith*:

صُوْمُوْا لِرُؤْيَتِهِ وَأَفْطِرُوْا لِرُؤْيَتِهِ

"Observe *saūm* on sighting the crescent and termi-
nate it on sighting it (the new moon),"

is addressed to all the Muslims, and for this reason the sighting at one place holds good for another place. The group which holds that the sight-ing of the moon at one place is not enough for the Muslims of other localities contended that the words are addressed to the people who have actually sighted the moon. The Muslims of the localities of the other areas who have not sighted the moon are not addressed by these words. They say that the sighting of the moon goes with each area according to which they will decide about starting the *saūm* and celebrating 'Eīd, as mentioned in the above narrations.

There is a third group also, which is of the opinion that for such areas which are in close proximity and do not have much difference in the tim-ings of sunrise and sunset, the sighting of the moon at one place holds good for the other. In any case, it is a moderate view, which can be im-plemented without fear of it being wrong. According to this view, at least in one country the sighting of the moon at one place holds good for all other areas.

The two months of 'Eīd, do not decrease

Abu Bakra ☙ narrated, the Prophet (ﷺ) said:

---

11. Muslim: 1087,1088

شَهْرَانِ لَا يَنْقُصَانِ شَهْرَا عِيدٍ رَمَضَانُ وَذُو الْحَجَّةِ

"The two months of 'Eīd, do not decrease, Ramadān and Dhul-Hijjah."[12]

Explanation

Abu 'Eisa said: "Ahmad commented on the meaning of this *hadith*, Ramadān and Dhul-Hijja will not both be decreased in the same year, if one of them is decreased, then the other will be complete." Ishaq said: "If it is twenty nine days, it will still be complete, not deficient." So according to the view of Ishaq it is possible that the two months would be decreased in the same year.[13]

The most common interpretation of this *hadith* is: The good deeds done in these two months are rewarded fully whether these months are of 29 or 30 days. There is no harm if Muslims unknowingly start observing *saūm* on a wrong day, or stay at 'Arafat during Hajj on a day other than the prescribed one, on condition that the crescent should be watched carefully. For example, if two persons witness that they have seen the crescent and the people observe *saūm* or stay at 'Arafat accordingly, and later the two witness turn to be liars, the acts of worshipping performed by the Muslims will not be rejected by Allah.[14]

Testimony of a Single Trustworthy Muslim for the Crescent of Ramadān.

Ibn Umar (رضي الله عنهما) narrated: "The people gathered to see the crescent. I informed the Messenger of Allah (ﷺ) that I had seen it. He fasted and ordered the people to Fast."[15]

Testimony of Two Men about Sighting the Crescent of Shawwāl

Husain bin Al-Harith al-Jadali narrated that a governor of Makkah deliv-

12. Bukhari: 1912
13. Tirmidhi: 702
14. Fathul Bari: 4/161, 162
15. Abu Dawud: 2342

ered a speech and said: "The Messenger of Allah (ﷺ) took an oath from us, that we perform our rites after sighting the crescent. If we do not sight it, and two just persons testify to (seeing) it, we should perform the rites on the basis of their testimony." (Abu Malik said): "I asked Al-Husain bin Al-Harith: 'Who is this governor of Makkah?'" He said: "I don't know." Sometime later he met me and said: "He is Al-Harith bin Hatib, the brother of Muhammad bin Hatib." The governor then said: "Among you is a person who is more knowledgeable about Allah and his Messenger than me. He testified to this, from the Messenger of Allah (ﷺ) and then pointed with his hand towards a man."

Al-Hussein said: "I said to an older man beside me: 'Who is he that the governor pointed to?'"

He said: "This is 'Abdullāh bin Umar and he spoke the truth." He ('Abdullāh bin Umar) was more knowledgeable about Allah then him. He ('Abdullāh bin Umar) said: "Allah's Messenger (ﷺ) ordered us with that."[16]

Ribi bin Hirash narrated from a man among the companions of the prophet (ﷺ) who said: "The people differed (about sighting the crescent of Shawwāl) on the last day of Ramadān. Then two Bedouins arrived and testified before the Prophet (ﷺ) that they had seen the crescent the previous evening. The Messenger of Allah (ﷺ) ordered the people to break their fast." In his narration, Khalaf (one of the narrators) added: "And that they go to *musalla* the (following) morning."[17]

'Abdur-Rahmān bin Zaid bin Khattāb said, while delivering a speech on a day concerning which there was doubt (as to whether Ramadān had come to an end or not): "Verily, I sat with the Companions of the Messenger of Allah (ﷺ) who said: 'Fast due to its sighting, break your fast due to its sighting and performed the pilgrimage rites by it. If it is cloudy, then complete thirty days. If two Muslims bear testimony to it, fast and break the fast.'" In the *hadith* of Abdur-Rahmān bin Zaid and in the *hadith* of Al-Harith, they indicate by implication, that it is not allowed to start the fast or break the fast due to the witness of only one person. How-

---

16. Abu Dawud: 2338
17. Abu Dawud: 2339

ever, since starting the fast has been exempted based on evidence (quoted above), it leaves only the issue of breaking the fast, for which there is no evidence that it may be done on the basis of one witness only. This is the abridgement of the argument as found in *Tuhfah al-Ahwadhi*.[18]

Offering 'Eīd Prayer the Following Morning

Umair bin Anas bin Malik narrated: My paternal uncles among the Ansar who were among the companions of the Messenger of Allah (ﷺ) told me: "The new crescent of Shawwāl was covered with clouds, so we fasted the next day. Then some riders came at the end of the day and testified to the prophet (ﷺ) that they had seen the new crescent the night before. The Messenger of Allah (ﷺ) commanded them to break their fast and to go out to offer the 'Eīd prayer the following morning."[19]

Explanation

1. If the news of the appearance of a new crescent is received in the afternoon, then the 'Eīd prayer will be offered the next day, but the fast of the day will immediately end upon receiving the news.

2. Sighting the new crescent by the nearest city is accepted. The caravan reached Al-Madinah after concerning a whole days journey; the people of Al-Madinah finished their fast on the basis of the moon being sighted from such a distance.

Supplication at the Sight of the Crescent

Talhah bin 'Ubaidullah ؓ narrated: At the sight of the new moon (of the luner month), the Prophet (ﷺ) used to supplicate:

اللَّهُمَّ أَهِلَّهُ عَلَيْنَا بِالأَمْنِ وَالإِيمَانِ وَالسَّلَامَةِ وَالإِسْلَامِ، رَبِّي وَرَبُّكَ اللهُ.

"Allahumma ahillahu 'alaina bil amni wal iman, was

18. *Tuhfah al-Ahwadhi* 3/373, 374
19. Ibn Majah: 1653

salamati wal-Islam, Rabbi wa Rabbuk Allah (Allah,
let this moon appear on us with security and Imān;
with safety and Islam. (O moon!) Your Rub and mine
is Allah."[20]

Muslims near the North or South Pole

Muslims who live in the land of Scandinavia and the area north of it have
to deal with the problem of the night and day being very long and very
short. Sometimes the day will continue for 22 hours and the night will
be 2 hours. While during other season, the situation may be reversed.
In some of the areas night lasts for 6 months and day will last a similar
amount of time. The problem in these lands is not particularly related to
fasting. Rather, it also includes the prayer. However, if the country has
a day and a night, then it is obligatory to act according to the dictates of
that, regardless of whether the day is extremely long or short. However,
if the land does not have a night and day, like the areas close to the north
or south poles where the day will last 6 months or the night will last 6
month, then these people estimate their fasting and prayer. But the question is: what do they base their estimation upon? Some of the people
of knowledge say that they estimate based upon the times of Makkah,
because Makkah is the mother of cities. Thus, all of the cities refer to it
because the mother is the thing which is followed, like the *Imam* for example. Other have said that in that land they should consider based upon
the middle course. Thus, they should consider the night as 12 hours and
the day as 12 hours, because this is the balanced time regarding the day
and night. Some of the people of knowledge have said that they consider
the closest land to them that has a regular day and night. This view is the
most correct, because the closest land to them has the most right to be
followed and it is the closest to their climate geographically; therefore,
based upon this, they should look at the night and day of the closest land
to them, and they should restrict themselves to following it, whether it is
for the fasting or the prayer.[21]

---

20. Tirmidhi: 3451; Saheeh Al-Jami'as-'Sagheer: 3811
21. Fatawa Islamiah 3/258, 259

Intention

The real basis of all actions is the *niyyah* (intention) and every one will be rewarded or punished according to his *niyyah*. It is true that the *niyyah* is found in one's heart or that one has first to make up his mind for what he subsequently proceeds to do but it is not necessary to express it verbally. In fact, the latter course is a *bid'ah* (innovation in the religion) because no proof of it is found in the *Sunnah*.

Ikhlas (sincerity) is a must for every action. In every righteous deed one should have in view only the pleasure of Allah. If some extraneous purpose is combined with Ikhlas as then it will not be accepted by Allah.

Allah says:

وَمَا أُمِرُوا إِلَّا لِيَعْبُدُوا اللَّهَ مُخْلِصِينَ لَهُ الدِّينَ

"And they were commanded not, but that they should worship Allah, keeping religion pure for him."[1]

Umar bin Khattab ؓ said: "I heard Allah's Messenger (ﷺ) saying:

إِنَّمَا الْأَعْمَالُ بِالنِّيَّاتِ وَإِنَّمَا لِكُلِّ امْرِئٍ مَا نَوَى فَمَنْ كَانَتْ هِجْرَتُهُ إِلَى دُنْيَا يُصِيبُهَا أَوْ إِلَى امْرَأَةٍ يَنْكِحُهَا فَهِجْرَتُهُ إِلَى مَا هَاجَرَ إِلَيْهِ.

"The reward of deeds depends upon the intentions and every person will get the reward according to what he

---

1. Al-Baiyinah 98:5

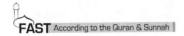

has intended. So whoever emigrates for worldly benefits or for a woman to marry, his migration will be for what he emigrated for."[2]

Sulaiman bin Yasar said: The people dispersed from around Abu Hurairah, and Nātil, who was from the people of Ash-Sham, and said: "O Shaikh! Tell me a *hadith* that you heard from the Messenger of Allah (صلى الله عليه وسلم)." He said: "Yes. I heard the Messenger of Allah (صلى الله عليه وسلم) say: 'The first of the people concerning whom judgement will be passed on the Day of Resurrection will be a man who was martyred. He will be brought and (Allah) will remind him of His blessings, and he will acknowledge them. He will say: "What did you do with them?" He will say: "I fought for Your sake until I was martyred." He will say: "You are lying, rather you fought so that it would be said he is brave, and it was said." Then he will be ordered to be dragged on his face and thrown into the Fire.

Then a man who acquired knowledge and taught it, and read Qur'ān will be brought and Allah will remind him of His blessings, and he will acknowledge them. He will say: "What did you do with them?" He will say: "I acquired knowledge and taught it, and I read Qur'ān for Your sake." He will say: "You are lying. You acquired knowledge and taught it so that it would be said, he is a scholar, and you read Qur'ān so that it would be said, he is a reciter, and it was said." Then he will be ordered to be dragged on his face and thrown into the Fire. And a man whom Allah made rich, and to whom He granted all kinds of wealth will be brought, and Allah will remind him of His blessings and he will acknowledge them. He will say: "What did you do with them?" He will say: "I did not leave any way in which You love wealth to be spent but I spent it for Your sake." He will say: "You are lying, rather you did that so that it would be said, he is generous, and it was said." Then he will be ordered to be dragged on his face and thrown into the Fire.'"[3]

---

2. Bukhari: 1
3. Sahih Muslim: 1905

The Intention for Fasting

Niyyah (intention) is a required condition of the obligatory fast of Ramadān as well as other obligatory fasts, such as making up missed fasts or fasts of expiation. *Niyyah* is the difference between whether the actions are religious or irreligious. For instance, fast for political reasons, as a weapon of passive resistance, hunger strikes, striving for dietary reasons, weight control, or even medical advice – all of these are not proper Islamic fasting, because they lack one main component: the *niyyah*. This is why *niyyah* for fasting is to worship Allah by abstaining from that which will break the fast from the break of dawn to sunset.

Hafsah, the wife of the Prophet (ﷺ) narrated that the Prophet (ﷺ) said:

مَنْ لَمْ يُجْمِعِ الصِّيَامَ قَبْلَ الْفَجْرِ فَلاَ صِيَامَ لَهُ

"Whoever did not intent to fast before *Fajr*, then there is no fast for him."[4]

Explanation

According to some of the people of knowledge, this only means that there is no fast for the one who does not decide to do so before *Fajr* begins during Ramadān, or when making up for Ramadān, or when fasting to expiate a vow; when he did not intend it during the night, then it will not be accepted from him. As for voluntary fasting, then it is permissible for him to intend to do it after the morning begins. This is the view of Ash-Shafi'i, Ahmad and Ishaq.[5]

Whoever did not know that the month of Ramadān had begun until after the time of *Fajr* had entered, then he must refrain from those things that break the fast for the rest of his day, because it is a day of Ramadān. It is not permissible for the person who is a resident of a place and healthy to partake of any of the things that would break the fast during Ramadān. He must also make up for the day of fasting because he did not pass the night with the intention to fast before the time of *Fajr*. It has been con-

4. Abu Dawud: 2454
5. Tirmidhi: 730

firmed from the Prophet (ﷺ) that he said: "Whoever did not intent to fast before *Fajr*, then there is no fast for him."

If a person intends to break his fast during the day but does not do so, then according to the most correct opinion, his fast is not adversely affected; he is like a person who wants to speak during the prayer but does not speak. Some of the scholars think that he is not fasting as soon as he stops intending to fast, so as a precaution, he should make up that fast later. Apostasy, however, invalidates the intention; there is not dispute on this matter. The person who is fasting Ramadān; it is sufficient to have the intention at the beginning of the month. If the intention is interrupted by breaking the fast due to travel or sickness, for example, he has to renew the intention to fast when the reason for breaking the fast is no longer present.[6]

The Intention for Voluntary Fasting

Umm Ad-Dardā' said: Abū Ad-Dardā' used to ask: "Do you have food?" If we answered in the negative, he would say, "Then I am observing *saūm* (fast) today."

Abu Talha, Abu Hurairah, Ibn Abbas and Hudhaifa ﷺ would do the same.

Salamah bin Al-Akwa ﷺ narrated: Once the Prophet (ﷺ) ordered a person on the day of Āshūra (the tenth of Muharram) to announce: "Whoever has eaten, should not eat any more, but observe *saūm* (fast), and who has not eaten should not eat, but complete his *saūm* (fast) (till the end of the day)."[7]

'Āishah, the Mother of the believers (ﷺ) said: The Messenger of Allah (ﷺ) said to me one day: "O Āishah! Do you have anything (to eat)?" I said: "O Messenger (ﷺ) of Allah, we do not have anything." He said: "Then I am fasting." Then the Messenger of Allah (ﷺ) went out, then a gift was brought to us. When the Messenger of Allah (ﷺ) came back, I said: "O Messenger of Allah, a gift was brought to us, and I kept some-

---

6. Rulings pertaining to Ramadān, p. 40, 41
7. Bukhari: 1924

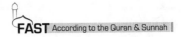

thing for you." He said: "What is it?" I said: "Hais" He said: "Bring it."
So I brought it to him and he ate, then he said: "I woke up this morning
fasting."

(One of the narrators) Talhah said: "I narrated this *hadith* to Mujahid and
he said: 'That is like a man who allocates charity from his wealth; if he
wishes, he may give it, and if he wishes, he may keep it.'"[8]

---

8. Muslim: 1154

Sahur

(Just Before Dawn Meal)

Islam is a natural religion based on moderation, middle course, and away from excessiveness. Therefore it urges to eat and drink as a predawn meal and also that the predawn meal is to be taken a little before the dawn appears; and the breaking of the fast should be soon after the sun has set, so that the time for remaining hungry and thirsty does not become prolonged needlessly, and the Prophet (ﷺ) stated it is a source of blessing.

Sahūr is Blessing

Anas ؆ narrated that the Messenger of Allah (ﷺ) said:

تَسَحَّرُوا فَإِنَّ فِي السُّحُورِ بَرَكَةً

"Take *sahur*, for there is a blessing in it." [1]

Explanation

This *hadith* tells us that *sahur* is musnun (*Sunnah* of the Prophet ﷺ), even if one takes a small quantity of food. This meal is blessed and maintains one's energy and vitality during the fast. Against this, if a person goes to sleep after taking his dinner to save himself from the inconvenience of getting up before dawn or takes *sahur* early, he will be, on one side, disobeying the Messenger of Allah (ﷺ), while on the other hand, he will

---

1. Muslim: 1905

be feeling hunger and thirst very early as he himself has increased the period of fasting by not taking the *sahur*. *Subhan Allah*! How the weaknesses of a man have been taken into account in the teachings of Islam while suitable provision has been provided to over come them.

Blessed Breakfast

Al-Irbad bin Sariyah ☀ narrated that the Messenger of Allah (☀) invited me to *sahur* during Ramadān and said:

$$هَلُمَّ إِلَى الْغَدَاءِ الْـمُبَارَكِ$$

"Come to the blessed breakfast."[2]

Explanation

The Prophet (☀) does not speak of his own desire, but only speaks what has been revealed to him. It is, therefore, necessary that even if a person feels no desire for food so early in the morning, he should at least have a date or a morsel or two, or even a few sips of water, in order to be a recipient of the blessings promised by the Prophet (☀).

You should Take *Sahūr*

Al-Miqdām bin Madikarib ☀ narrated that the Prophet (☀) said:

$$عَلَيْكُمْ بِغَدَاءِ السُّحُورِ فَإِنَّهُ هُوَ الْغَدَاءُ الْـمُبَارَكُ$$

"You should take *sahur* for it is the blessed breakfast (*ghada*)."[3]

Explanation

The term *ghada* means meal or breakfast, which is eaten in the beginning of the day. Since the predawn meal for the one fasting is synonymous to the daytime meal. In the blessed *hadith*, it is called the breakfast or the

---

2. Abu Dawud: 2344
3. Nasā'i: 2166

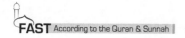

ghada. We could term the *sahur*, in our common usage as breakfast.

Do Not Neglect *Sahūr*

'Abdullāh bin Al-Harith narrated that a man from among the companions of the Prophet (ﷺ) said:

"I entered upon the Prophet (ﷺ) when he was having *Sahūr* and He said:

إِنَّهَا بَرَكَةٌ أَعْطَاكُمُ اللهُ إِيَّاهَا فَلاَ تَدَعُوهُ

'It is a blessing that Allah has given to you, so do not neglect it.'"[4]

Difference between our Fasting and the Fasting of the People of the Book

Amr bin Al-'Ās (ﷺ) narrated that the messenger of Allah (ﷺ) said:

إِنَّ فَضْلَ مَا بَيْنَ صِيَامِنَا وَصِيَامِ أَهْلِ الْكِتَابِ أَكْلَةُ السَّحَرِ

"The difference between our fasting and the fasting of the people of the book is eating *Sahūr*."[5]

Eating Too Much

Allah says:

وَكُلُواْ وَٱشْرَبُواْ وَلَا تُسْرِفُوٓاْ إِنَّهُۥ لَا يُحِبُّ ٱلْمُسْرِفِينَ

"And eat and drink but waste not by extravagance, certainly He (Allah) likes not Al-Musrifun (those who was to by extravagance)." (Al-Arāf 7:31)

Abu Hurairah (ﷺ) narrated that the Messenger of Allah (ﷺ) hosted a guest who was a disbeliever. The Messenger of Allah (ﷺ) ordered that

---

4. Nasā'i: 2164
5. Muslim: 1096

a sheep be milked for him and he drank it, then another and he drank it, then another, and he drank it, until he had drunk the milk of seven sheep. Then the next morning he became Muslim, and the Messenger of Allah (ﷺ) ordered that a sheep be milked for him and he drank it, then he ordered that another be milked but he did not finish it. The Messenger of Allah (ﷺ) said:

$$ اَلْـمُؤْمِنُ يَشْرَبُ فِي مِعًى وَاحِدٍ وَالْكَافِرُ يَشْرَبُ فِي سَبْعَةِ أَمْعَاءٍ $$

"The believer eats in one intestine and the disbeliever eats in seven."[6]

Nāfi' said: "Ibn 'Umar saw a poor man and he put some food in front of him, and put more, and he started to eat a great deal. He said: 'Do not let this man enter upon me, for I heard the Messenger of Allah (ﷺ) say: 'The disbeliever eats in seven intestines.'"[7]

Miqdām bin Madikarib said: "I heard the Messenger of Allah (ﷺ) say:

$$ مَا مَلَأَ آدَمِيٌّ وِعَاءً شَرًّا مِنْ بَطْنٍ حَسْبُ الآدَمِيِّ لُقَيْمَاتٌ يُقِمْنَ صُلْبُهُ فَإِنْ غَلَبَتِ الآدَمِيَّ نَفْسُهُ فَثُلُثٌ لِلطَّعَامِ وَثُلُثٌ لِلشَّرَابِ وَثُلُثٌ لِلنَّفَسِ $$

'A human being fills no worse vessel than his stomach. It is sufficient for a human being to eat a few mouthfuls to keep his spine straight; but if he must (fill it), then one third for food, one third for drink and one third for air.'"[8]

i) Overeating results in food not doing digested and leaves the body without any benefit. So, one should eat only the amount that can be digested easily and benefit the body.

ii) The purpose of eating is only to stay alive. Hence, instead of wasting time in preparing formal and delicious dishes, one should

---

6. Muslim: 2063
7. Muslim 2060 (183)
8. Ibn Majah: 3349

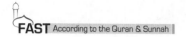

spend his time is good and useful deeds.

'Atiyyah bin 'Āmir Al-Juhani said: "I heard Salmān, when he was forced to eat food, say: 'It is sufficient for me that I heard the Messenger of Allah (ﷺ) say:

إِنَّ أَكْثَرَ النَّاسِ شِبَعاً فِى الدُّنْيَا أَطْوَلُهُمْ جُوعاً يَوْمَ الْقِيَامَةِ

"The people who most eat their fill in this world will
be the most hungry on the Day of Resurrection."'"[9]

i)   Whosever consumption is little, can easily bear hunger. Enduring hunger for such a person on the Day of Judgment also becomes relatively easy.

ii)   Those who have big appetites and are eager to eat much, do not think about the lawfulness or unlawfulness of the food. Consequently, they will deserve punishment on the Day of Judgment.

iii) Belching is a sign of eating a stomach full, which is not desirable.

The wise peron eats to live and does not live to eat. The best type of food is that which is there to be used, not that which is there to be served. People indulge in making all kinds of food (during Ramadān) and treating food preparation as a virtual art form; thus housewives and servants spend all their time in preparing the food. This keeps them away from worship, and people spend more on food during Ramadān than they ordinarily do at other times. Thus the month becomes the month of indigestion, obesity and gastic illness in which people eat like gluttons and drink like thirsty camels. When they stand to pray *tarawīh* they do so reluctantly, and some of them leave after the first two *rak'ahs*.[10]

---

9. Ibn Majah: 3351
10. Rulings Pertaining to Ramadān, p. 22

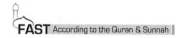

Time of *Sahūr*

White Thread Appears Distinct from the Black

Adiyy bin Hatim ﷺ narrated that when the verse:

$$\text{حَتَّى يَتَبَيَّنَ لَكُمُ الْخَيْطُ الْأَبْيَضُ مِنَ الْخَيْطِ الْأَسْوَدِ مِنَ الْفَجْرِ}$$

"Until the white thread appears to you distinct from the black thread of dawn" was revealed Adiyy (bin Hatim) said: "O Messenger of Allah, I put two strings under my pillow, a white string and a black string, so that I can tell night from day." The Messenger of Allah (ﷺ) said:

$$\text{إِنَّ وِسَادَتَكَ لَعَرِيضٌ إِنَّمَا هُوَ سَوَادُ اللَّيْلِ وَبَيَاضُ النَّهَارِ}$$

"Your pillow must be very big, for that refers to the blackness of the night and the whiteness of the day.[11]"

Ascending White Light Should not Prevent You

Qais bin Talaq narrated from his father who said that the Messenger of Allah (ﷺ) said:

$$\text{كُلُوا وَاشْرَبُوا وَلاَ يَهِيدَنَّكُمُ السَّاطِعُ الْـمُصْعِدُ فَكُلُوا وَاشْرَبُوا}$$
$$\text{حَتَّى يَعْتَرِضَ لَكُمُ الأَحْمَرُ}$$

"Eat and drink, and the ascending white light should not prevent you from it, so continue to eat and drink until the redness appears horizontally."[12]

Sahl bin Sa'd narrated: When the following verse was revealed: "Eat and drink until the white thread appears to you, distinct form the black

---

11. Muslim: 1090
12. Abu Dawud: 2348

thread," but "of dawn" was not revealed, some people who intended to observe *Saūm* (fast), tied black and white threads to their legs and went on eating until they differentiated between the two. Allah then revealed the words, of 'dawn' and it became clear that, that it meant night and day.[13]

Regarding the verse: "O you who believe! Fasting is prescribed for you, as it was prescribed for those before you," Ibn Abbas said: "During the lifetime of the prophet (ﷺ), when the people prayed *Al-Atamah* (*Salāt Al-'Ishā'*) it became unlawful for them to eat and drink and have intercourse with women. They would fast till the next sunset. A man deceived himself by having intercourse with his wife after he had prayed *Ishā* and did not break his fast. So Allah, the Mighty and Sublime, intended to make that easier for those remained, and grant them permission and benefit. Allah, the Glorious, said: 'Allah knows that you used to deceive yourselves,' and by this Allah benefited the people, and grant for them ease."[14]

Al-Bara ؓ narrated: It was the custom among the companions of Muhammad (ﷺ) that if any of them was observing *saūm* and food was presented (for *iftar*) but he slept before eating, he would not eat that night and the following day until sunset.

Qais bin Sirma al-Ansari was observing *saūm* and came to his wife at the time of *iftar* and asked her whether she had anything to eat. She replied: "No, but I would go and bring something for you" he used to do hard work during the day, so he was overwhelmed by sleep and slept. When his wife came and saw him, she said: "Disappointment for you." When it was midday on the following day, he fainted and the Prophet (ﷺ) was informed about the whole matter, upon which the following verses were revealed: "It is made lawful for you to have sexual relations with your wives on the night of *saūm* (the fasts)..."

So they were rejoiced greatly by it. Allah also revealed: "And eat and drink until the white thread (light) of dawn appears to you distinct from

---

13. Bukhari: 1917
14. Abu Dawud: 2313

the black thread (darkness of the night)."[15]

Explanation

The last *hadith* seems to be in conflict with the one before it; however it shows that prior to that the rule of eating and drinking until dawn, if a person had fasted during the day and had taken a nap after *iftar* (regardless of whether he had performed his *'Ishā'* prayer or not), the door of having food, drink and sexual relations was legally closed for him. Scholars of *hadith*, however, see no conflict between the two and suggest that either of the two actions (sleep or *'Ishā'* prayer) was enough to bar a person from indulging in those acts until the next *iftar* time. Therefore, Allah granted the permission to perform those acts from after sunset until dawn, which was a great relief for them.

Interval between the Sahur and Salātul Fajr

Zaid bin Thabit ﷺ narrated: "We took the *Sahūr* with the Prophet (ﷺ), and then he stood for *salāt*." I asked: "What was the interval between the *Sahūr* and the *Adhan*?" He replied: "The interval was sufficient to recite fifty verses of the Qur'ān."[16]

Sahl bin Sa'd ﷺ narrated: "I used to take my *sahur* meal with my family and then hurry to present myself for the *Fajr* prayer with Allah's Messenger (ﷺ)."[17]

Zirr bin Hubaish said: "I had *Sahur* with Hudhaidfah, then we went out to pray. When we came to the Masjid we prayed two *rak'ahs* and then the iqamah for the prayer was said, and there was only a short time between them."[18]

Delaying *Sahūr*

Abū 'Atiyyah said: "I said to 'Āishah (ﷺ) that among us are two com-

---

15. Bukhari: 1915
16. Bukhari: 1921
17. Bukhari: 1920
18. Nasai: 2155

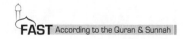

panions of the Prophet (ﷺ), one who hastens *iftar* and delays *Sahūr*, while the other delays iftār and hastens *Sahūr*." She said: "Which of them is the one who hastens *iftar* and delays *sahur*?" I said: "Abdullāh bin Masud." She said: "That is what the Messenger of Allah (ﷺ) used to do."[19]

The *Adhan* of Bilal should not Stop from Taking *Sahūr*

'Āishah (ﷺ) narrated that Bilal used to pronounce the *Adhan* at night, so Allah's Messenger (ﷺ) said:

$$كُلُوا وَاشْرَبُوا حَتَّى يُؤَذِّنَ ابْنُ أُمِّ مَكْتُومٍ فَإِنَّهُ لَا يُؤَذِّنُ حَتَّى يَطْلُعَ$$
$$الْفَجْرُ$$

"Carry on taking your meals (eat and drink) until Ibn Umm Maktūm pronounces the Adhān, for he does not pronounce it until dawn."[20]

Ibn Umar (ﷺ) narrated: "The Messenger of Allah (ﷺ) had two mu'adhdins, Bilal and Ibn Umm Maktum, the blind man. The Messenger of Allah (ﷺ) said: "Bilal calls the *Adhan* at night, so eat and drink until Ibn Umm Maktumm calls the *Adhan*." And there was no more [of a time difference] between them than the time it took for one to climb down and the other to climb up.[21]

Samurah bin Jundab ﷺ narrated that the Messenger of Allah (ﷺ) said:

$$لَا يَغُرَّنَّكُمْ مِنْ سَحُورِكُمْ أَذَانُ بِلَالٍ وَلَا بَيَاضُ الأُفُقِ الْـمُسْتَطِيلُ$$
$$هَكَذَا حَتَّى يَسْتَطِيرَ هَكَذَا$$

"Do not let the *Adhan* of Bilal nor the vertical whiteness on the horizon like this distract you from your *Sahūr*, until (the whiteness) is like this."

---

19. Nasai: 2160
20. Bukhari: 1918, 1919
21. Muslim: 1092 (38)

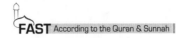

Hammad described it with his hands and said: "Meaning when it is horizontal."[22]

Explanation

We learn from this *hadith* that in the days of the prophet (ﷺ) there used to be two *Mu'adhadhins* and two *Adhan* in the morning. The First *Adhan* was meant to warn the people who were taking the *Sahur* that it was about to finish and they should make preparation for *Fajr* prayer. Soon after that there was a second *Adhan* by another mu'adhadhin which signified that the time for food was finished and people should attend to *salāt*. As far as the question of time between the two *Adhan* is concerned, the scholars have stated that after announcing the *Adhan*, Bilal would engage in prayer, etc, and would wait for the daybreak. When the time for the daybreak drew near, he would then come down and inform Ibn Umm Maktum who would then make *wudū*; and then proceed to call the *Adhan* at the beginning of the day break.[23]

A Man who Hears the Call while a Vessel is in his Hand

Abu Hurairah ؓ narrated that the Messenger of Allah (ﷺ) said:

إِذَا سَمِعَ أَحَدُكُمُ النِّدَاءَ وَالإِنَاءُ عَلَى يَدِهِ فَلاَ يَضَعْهُ حَتَّى يَقْضِيَ
حَاجَتَهُ مِنْهُ

"If one of you hears the call for prayer and the vessel is in his hand, he should not put it down until he fulfills his need from it."[24]

Explanation

If the time for the end of *Sahūr* has approached and the call to the morning prayer has begun, it is still allowed for the fasting person to finish what he has in his hand.

---

22. Muslim: 43 (1090)
23. Ibn Allan: 7/44, 45
24. Abu Dawud: 2350

Observing *Saūm* in the State of Janabah

Abu Bakr said: "I heard Abu Hurairah ﷺ speaking and one of the things that he said was: "If dawn comes when a person is *junub*, he should not fast." I mentioned that to Abdur Rahman bin Al-Harith to his father and he denied that. Abdur-Rahman set off with him, and we entered upon 'Āishah and Umm Salamah (ﷺ). Abdur Rahman asked them about that and they both said: "The Prophet (ﷺ) would be *junub* in the morning, not as the result of a wet dream, then he would fast." We went and entered upon Marwan, and Abdur Rahman mentioned that to him. Marwan said: "I urge you to go to Abu Hurairah and prove to him that he was wrong." We went to Abu Hurairah, and Abu Bakr was present throughout all that. 'Abdur Rahman told him about that and Abu Hurairah ﷺ said: "Did they tell you that?" He said: "Yes," so he said: "They know better."

Then Abu Huraiah attributed what he used to say concerning that to Al-Fadl bin Abbas, and Abu Hurairah said: "That is from Al-Fadl; I did not hear it from the Prophet (ﷺ)." So Abu Hurairah retracted what he used to say on this issue.

I said to Abdul Malik, "Did they say that with regard to Ramadān?" He said: "Yes, he (ﷺ) used to wake up *junub* without that being the result of a wet dream, then he would fast."[25]

'Āishah (ﷺ) narrated that a man came to the Prophet (ﷺ) and asked him a question, while she was listening from behind the door. The man said: "O Messenger of Allah, the time for prayer comes while I am *junub*; can I fast?" The Messenger of Allah (ﷺ) said: "Me too; the time for prayer comes while I am *junub*, and I fast." He said: "You are not like us, O Messenger of Allah, for Allah has forgiven you your past and future sins." He said: "By Allah, I hope that I am the one who fears Allah the most among you, and the most knowledgeable of that which I should guard against."[26]

'Āishah (ﷺ) narrated that the Prophet (ﷺ) used to spend the night in a state of sexual impurity, then Bilal would come to him and inform him

---

25. Muslim: 1109
26. Muslim: 1110

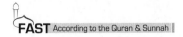

that it was time for prayer. So he would get up and take a bath, and I would see the water dripping from his head, then he go out and I would hear his voice during *Fajr* prayer."

(One of the narrators) Mutarrif said: "I said to Amir: Was that during Ramadān? He said: In Ramadān and at other times."[27]

Explanation

If a man has sexual intercourse with his wife during a night of Ramadān, he must take a bath in case he has sufficient time and then observe his fast. If the time is short, he may perform ablution and then fast. If he doesn't have time even for that, he must wash his face and hands, eat *sahur* and observe fast. Then he must take a bath immediately at dawn, in order to prepare for the *Fajr* prayer in congregation. Mutarrif asked his teacher the above question so that one should not be in doubt thinking that the religious law regarding voluntary fasting is lighter than that of obligatory fasting. Imām Sha'bi made clear that there is no difference in this issue, regardless whether it is obligatory or voluntary fasting.

---

27. Ibn Majah: 1703

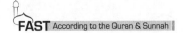

Conditions for the acceptance of a Fast

Being Muslim

Fasting is not accepted from a disbeliever because the fast is one of the pillars of Islam. Allah's Messenger (ﷺ) said:

بُنِيَ الْإِسْلَامُ عَلَى خَمْسٍ شَهَادَةِ أَنْ لَا إِلَهَ إِلَّا اللهُ وَأَنَّ مُحَمَّدًا رَسُولُ اللهِ وَإِقَامِ الصَّلَاةِ وَإِيتَاءِ الزَّكَاةِ وَالْحَجِّ وَصَوْمِ رَمَضَانَ

"Islam is based on (the following) five (Principles):

1.   To testify that *La ilaha illallah wa anna Muhammad-ar-rasul Allah* (none has the right to be worshiped but Allah and that Muhammad is the Messenger of Allah)

2.   Iqama-*as-salāt* (to perform the *salāt*)

3.   to pay *zakah*

4.   to perform Hajj

5.   to observe *saūm* during the month of Ramadān.[1]

Abu Hurairah ﷺ narrated that one day while the Prophet (ﷺ) was sitting out for the people, a man (the angel Jibril) came to him and asked: "What is faith?" Allah's Messenger (ﷺ) replied: "Faith is to believe in Allah, His angels, (the) meeting with Him, His Messengers, and to believe in the

---

1. Bukhari: 8

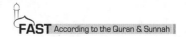

Resurrection." Then he asked: "What is Islam?" Allah's Messenger (ﷺ) replied: "To worship Allah, alone, and none else, to perform the *salāt*, to pay the *zakah* and to observe *saūm* during the month of Ramadān."[2]

Being of Sound Mind

Fasting is not accepted from one who is insane. It is reported on the authority of 'Āishah (ﷺ) from the Prophet (ﷺ) that he said:

رُفِعَ الْقَلَمُ عَنْ ثَلاَثَةٍ عَنِ النَّائِمِ حَتَّى يَسْتَيْقِظَ وَعَنِ الْـمُبْتَلَى حَتَّى يَبْرَأَ وَعَنِ الصَّبِيِّ حَتَّى يَكْبَرَ

"The pen has been lifted from three: From the sleeping person until he awakens, from the insane person until he comes to his senses, and from the child until he grows up."[3]

The Absence of any Obstacle

Fasting is not valid if a woman is menstruating or has postpartum bleeding. Allah's Messenger (ﷺ) said:

أَلَيْسَ إِذَا حَاضَتْ لَمْ تُصَلِّ وَلَـمْ تَصُمْ؟ فَذَلِكِ مِنْ نُقْصَانِ دِينِهَا

"Is it not a fact that if she is menstruating, she does not pray or fast? So this deficiency is in her religion."[4]

Knowledge of the Time

From the call to *Fajr* prayer until sunset. Allah says:

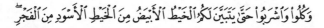
وَكُلُواْ وَٱشْرَبُواْ حَتَّىٰ يَتَبَيَّنَ لَكُمُ ٱلْخَيْطُ ٱلْأَبْيَضُ مِنَ ٱلْخَيْطِ ٱلْأَسْوَدِ مِنَ ٱلْفَجْرِ

---

2. Bukhari: 50
3. Abu Dawud: 4398
4. Bukhari: 304, 1951

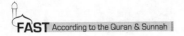

ثُمَّ أَتِمُّواْ الصِّيَامَ إِلَى الَّيْلِ

"And eat and drink until the white thread (light) of dawn appears to you distinct from black thread (darkness of night), then complete your *saūm* (fast) till the nightfall." (Al-Baqarah 2: 187)

An Abiding Intention

Fasting is not valid without an abiding intention.

Things which Invalidate Saum

Eating or drinking intentionally

Fasting is invalidated by eating or drinking intentionally and there is no difference of opinion on this point. As for (eating and drinking due to) forgetfulness, it does not invalidate the fast, based upon the *hadith* of Abu Hurairah ﷺ, who reported from the Prophet (ﷺ) that he said:

إِذَا نَسِيَ فَأَكَلَ وَشَرِبَ فَلْيُتِمَّ صَوْمَهُ فَإِنَّمَا أَطْعَمَهُ اللهُ وسَقَاه

"If somebody eats or drinks forgetfully then he should complete his *saūm* (fast), for what he has eaten or drank, has been given to him by Allah."[1]

The Severe Threat for one who Intentionally breaks His Fast

Abu Hurairah ﷺ narrated that the messenger of Allah (ﷺ) said:

مَنْ أَفْطَرَ يَوْمًا مِنْ رَمَضَانَ مِنْ غَيْرِ رُخْصَةٍ رَخَّصَهَا اللهُ لَهُ لَمْ يَقْضِ عَنْهُ صِيَامُ الدَّهْرِ

"Whoever breaks his fast during a day of Ramadān, without any permission granted by Allah, it will nev-

---

1. Bukhari: 1933

er be made up, even if he fasted for his entire life."[2]

Explanation

This narration is not authentic but there is no difference of opinion on this topic that breaking the fast intentionally without solid reason is a great sin. If a person abandons a fast of Ramadān or breaks it without any religiously valid excuse, he can then keep fasting his whole life but he cannot achieve the reward and virtuousness of the missed fast of Ramadān; his sin and offence will not be forgiven by just severe repentance.

Ibn Masud also narrated the same narration. Sa'id bin Al-Musaiyab, Ash-Sha'bi, Ibn Jubair, Ibrahim, Qatadah and Hammad said: "He should observe *saūm* one day in lieu of that missed day." *Imam* Bukhari described it under the chapter: Whoever has a sexual intercourse with his wife in Ramadān, (intentionally, he has to pay expiation).

Whoever Intentionally Break His Fast and its Expiation

Abu Hurairah ﷺ narrated: While we were sitting with the Prophet (ﷺ) a man came and said: "O Allah's Messenger! I have been ruined." Allah's Messenger (ﷺ) asked what was the matter with him. He replied: "I had sexual intercourse with my wife while I was observing *saūm*." Allah's Messenger (ﷺ) asked him: "Can you observe *saūm* for two months?" He replied in the negative. The Prophet (ﷺ) asked him: "Can you afforded to feed sixty poor person?" He replied in the negative. The Prophet (ﷺ) kept silent and while we were in that state, a big basket full of dates was brought to the Prophet (ﷺ). He asked: "Where is the questioner?" He replied: "I (am here)." The Prophet (ﷺ) said (to him): "Take this (basket of Dates) and give it in charity." The man said: "Should I give it to a person poorer than I? By Allah; There is no family between its (i.e. Al-Madina's) two mountains who are poorer than I." The Prophet (ﷺ) smiled till his premolar teeth became visible and then said, "Feed your family with it."[3]

---

2. Abu Dawud: 2396
3. Bukhari : 1936

Explanation

1- This *Hadith* is acted upon according to the people of knowledge regarding one who breaks his fast on purpose during Ramadān by sexual intercourse. As for one who breaks his fast on purpose by eating and drinking, then the people of knowledge differ over it. Some of them said that he has to make it up and atone for it. They likened eating and drinking to sexual intercourse in this regard.

This is the saying of Sufyan Ath-Thawri, Ibn Mubarak, and Ishaq. Some of them said: He has to make it up, but there is no atonement required of him, because atonement was only mentioned from the Prophet (ﷺ) in the case of sexual intercourse and was not mentioned by him for eating and drinking. And they say that the eating and drinking is not like sexual intercourse. This is the saying of Ash-Shafi'i and Ahmad.

Ash-Shafi'i said: "The saying of the Prophet (ﷺ) to the man who had broken his fast and who had told to give charity: "Take it to feed your family," carries this meaning; it implies that the atonement is required from the one who is capable of it. This man was not capable of the atonement, so when the Prophet (ﷺ) gave him something and he possessed it, then the man said: "There is no one that is more in need of it than us." So the Prophet (ﷺ) said: "Take it to feed your family." This is because atonement can only take place after he has surplus from his provisions." Ash-Shafi'i preferred that whoever has a case similar to this, then he is to eat from it and the atonement will be a debt upon him, so whenever he is able to make the atonement, he should make it.[4]

2- That person was Salmah bin Sakhr.

3- This *hadith* also tells us that a woman is not liable to be subjected to *kaffara* (the payment of expiation). The majority of scholars do not approve it. Some hold that if both the man and the woman mutually agree to have sexual intercourse, they are both liable to make the payment of expiation. In case a man does it forcibly, he

---

4. Tirmidhi: 724

alone is required to make such a payment and not the woman.

4- The same ruling applies in cases of *zina* (adultery or fornication), homosexuality and bestiality. We should remember that these are major sins in Islam and are even more forbidden when done during the days of Ramadān.

5- If a man wants to have intercourse with his wife but he breaks his fast by eating first, his sin is more serious, because he has violated the sanctity of the month on two counts by eating and by having intercourse. It is even more certain in this case that expiation is obligatory, and if he tries to get out of it, that only makes matters worse. He must repent sincerely.[5]

The Secretion of Al-Mani

The secretion of *mani* invalidates the fast; this is because it is ordinarily accompanied by feelings of desire and ejaculation, whether this was caused by the wife's caressing him, by masturbation or by thinking (of sexual matters) and looking (at some object of desire).

Allah's Messenger (ﷺ) said:

كُلُّ عَمَلِ ابْنِ آدَمَ لَهُ الْحَسَنَةُ بِعَشْرِ أَمْثَالِهَا إِلَى سَبْعِمَائَةِ ضِعْفٍ قَالَ اللهُ: إِلَّا الصِّيَامَ فَهُوَ لِي وَأَنَا أَجْزِي بِهِ يَدَعُ الطَّعَامَ مِنْ أَجْلِي وَيَدَعُ الشَّرَابَ مِنْ أَجْلِي وَيَدَعُ لَذَّتَهُ مِنْ أَجْلِي، وَيَدَعُ زَوْجَتَهُ مِنْ أَجْلِي، وَلَخَلُوفُ فَمِ الصَّائِمِ أَطْيَبُ عِنْدَ اللهِ مِنْ رِيحِ الْمِسْكِ، لِلصَّائِمِ فَرْحَتَانِ، فَرْحَةٌ حِينَ يُفْطِرُ وَفَرْحَةٌ عِنْدَ لِقَاءِ رَبِّهِ

"Every action of the sons of Adam is for him, and the reward of good deeds in multiplied from ten to seven hundred times; Allah says: Except for fasting, that is for Me and I shall reward it. He leaves food for my sake, he leaves drink for My sake, he leaves

---

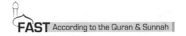

his desire for My sake and he heaves his wife for My sake. Verily, the fragrance from the mouth of a fasting person is sweeter in Allah's sight than the scent of musk. The fasting person will be happy on two occasions: once when he breaks his fast and once when he meets his Lord."[6]

Explanation

The words of the Prophet (ﷺ) in the *hadith*: "He leaves his desire for My sake" includes all matters of pleasure and desire, because the words "His pleasure" and "his desire" are in the singular form, which in Arabic means they are general. So a fasting person is required to abandon all forms of desire and pleasure, though what is referred here is sexual desire, which includes the ejaculation of *mani* by any means; if *mani* is ejaculated, his fast is invalidated.

The secretion by masturbation is not permissible during Ramadhān or outside of Ramadhān, it is considered a sin and a crime. It is certainly written as an evil deed if Allah does not pardon the person for it. Its expiation is true repentance and performing good deeds, which remove evil deed. Since it occurred during the daytime of Ramadān, the sin is even greater in evil. Thus, it needs sincere repentance, the performance of righteous deeds, increasing in acts that bring one nearer to Allah and acts of obedience, and preventing the soul from forbidden lusts. Also, that fast, which was corrupted by masturbation, must be made up.[7]

Intentional Vomiting

Abū Ad-Dardā' ؓ narrated: "The Messenger of Allah (ﷺ) vomited, and broke his fast." I met Thawban, the freed slave of the Messenger of Allah (ﷺ) in a Masjid in Damascus, and said to him: "Abū Ad-Dardā' narrated to me that the Messenger of Allah (ﷺ) vomited and broke his fast. He said: "He spoke the truth, and I Poured water for him for his *wudū*." [8]

6. Ibn Khuzaimah: 1897
7. Fatawa Islamiyah: 3/259
8. Abu Dawud: 2381

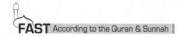

Abu Hurairah & narrated that the Messenger of Allah (ﷺ) said:

مَنْ ذَرَعَهُ قَيْءٌ وَهُوَ صَائِمٌ فَلَيْسَ عَلَيْهِ قَضَاءٌ وَإِنِ اسْتَقَاءَ فَلْيَقْضِ

"Whoever is overcome with vomiting, then there is no making up on him, but if he vomits intentionally then he must make it up."[9]

Menstruation and Postnatal Bleeding

Abu Az-Zinad said, "Very often the *Sunnah* (legal ways) and the truth go against the opinions, and for the Muslims there is no way out except to follow the truth and the *Sunnah* (legal ways) of the Prophet (ﷺ). An example of that is that a menstruating woman should observe *saūm* in lieu of her missed *saūm*, but she is not to offer the *salāt* in lieu of her missed *salāt*."

Abu Sa'īd & narrated that the Prophet (ﷺ) said;

أَلَيْسَ إِذَا حَاضَتْ لَمْ تُصَلِّ وَلَمْ تَصُمْ؟ فَذَلِكِ مِنْ نُقْصَانِ دِينِهَا

"Isn't it true that a woman does not offer *salāt* and does not observe the *saūm* while menstruating? And that is the defect (a loss) in her religion."[10]

'Āishah (ﷺ) narrated:

كُنَّا نَحِيضُ عِنْدَ رَسُوْلِ اللهِ (ﷺ) ثُمَّ نَطْهُرُ فَيَأْمُرُنَا بِقَضَاءِ الصِّيَامِ وَلَا يَأْمُرُنَا بِقَضَاءِ الصَّلَاةِ

"We would menstruate during the time of the Messenger of Allah (ﷺ), then when we became pure we were ordered to make up the fasts, but we were not ordered to make up the *salāt*."

---

9. Abu Dawud: 2380, Ibn Abi Shaiba: 9188
10. Bukhari: 1951

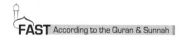

Abu 'Eisa said. This is acted upon according to the people of knowledge, and we do not know of any disagreement among them; the menstruating woman makeups the fasts but she does not makes up the *salāt*.[11]

Some important issues regarding the menstruating woman and the woman with Post-childbirth bleeding

Delaying the Bathing

If the woman sees that she has become pure before the time of *Fajr*, then she must fast and there is no harm in her delaying the bathing until after the time of *Fajr* enters. However, she must bathe and pray before sunrise.[12]

If the Woman Becomes Pure After Fajr

If the blood stops flowing from her during the time that *Fajr* comes in or a little before it, her fast is correct and she is credited with fulfillment of that obligation, even if she did not bathe until after it became morning. However, if the blood did not stop until after it was clearly morning (i.e, the time for *Fajr* had entered), then she abstains during that day, but it is not accepted from her (as a fast); rather, she makes up for that day after Ramadān.[13]

Using Pills that Prevent the Menses

The woman should not do this and she should remain upon what Allah decreed and wrote upon the daughters of Adam. For verily, Allah has a wisdom in making this monthly cycle. This wisdom suits the nature of the woman. If this natural occurrence is prevented, there is no doubt that there will be a harmful reaction upon the woman's body. Indeed the Prophet (ﷺ) said:

لَا ضَرَرَ وَلَا ضِرَارَ

---

11. Tirmidhi: 787
12. Fatawa Islamiyah: 3/299
13. Fatawa Islamiyah: 3/297

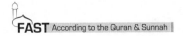

"There is no harming nor is there reciprocating of harm." [14]

This is without consideration of what these pills cause of harms to the womb, as the doctors have mentioned. Thus, my opinion concerning this matter is that the woman should not use these pills and all praise is due to Allah for his decree and His wisdom. When the menses comes to her, she abstains from fasting and prayer, and when she becomes pure, she returns to fasting and prayer. Then, when Ramadān ends, she makes up for whatever she missed of fasting. [15]

Post-Childbirth Bleeding

Whenever the woman with post-childbirth bleeding becomes pure and that which she knows to be a sign of purity becomes apparent to her, which is the white pad or total cleanliness, then she fasts and prays. It makes no difference if it is even a day or a week after giving birth. For verily, there is no limit for the minimum amount of postnatal bleeding. Some women do not see any blood at all after giving birth. Reaching a period of 40 days is not a condition. If the women with postnatal bleeding becomes pure within 40 days and she fasts some days, then her bleeding returns during the 40 days, she must leave off fasting during the days that her bleeding returned – because it is postnatal bleeding – until she becomes pure or completes the 40 days, then she must bathe, even if she does not think she is pure, because the 40 days is the end of the postnatal bleeding according to the correct view between the two opinions of the scholars. [16]

If a pregnant woman has a miscarriage and the fetus has taken shape or has a discernible outline of any part of the body, such as a head or hand, then her blood is considered nifās (postpartum). If, however, she passes something that looks like a blood clot (ʿalaq) or a chewed piece of meat (*mudghah*) that has no discernible human features, her bleeding is istihadah. If she is able, she must fast, otherwise she can break her fast and

14. Ibn Majah: 2340
15. Fatawa Islamiyah: 3/296, 297
16. Fatawa Islamiyah: 3/298

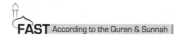

make it up later on.[17]

Cupping: Letting out Blood Medically

Ibn Abbas (ﷺ) narrated:

اِحْتَجَمَ النَّبِيُّ (ﷺ)وَهُوَ صَائِمٌ

"The Prophet (ﷺ) was cupped while he was observing *saūm*."[18]

Anas bin Malik ﷺ was asked whether they disliked the cupping for a person observing *saūm*. He replied in the negative and said, "Only if it causes weakness."

Ibn 'Umar (ﷺ) used to be cupped while he was observing *saūm* but later he abandoned it and began to be cupped at night. Abu Mūsā was cupped at night. It is narrated that Sa'd, Zaid bin Arqam and Umm Salamah were cupped while observing *saūm*. Umm Alqama said: "We used to be cupped (during observing *saūm*) in Aishah's presence and she did not object. Al-Hasan and others narrate on the authority of the Prophet (ﷺ): "The cupping and the cupped persons break their *saūm* if they practice this while observing the *saūm*."

Imam Bukhari mentioned it under the chapter: Cupping and vomiting of a person.

Thawban narrated that the Prophet (ﷺ) said:

أَفْطَرَ الْحَاجِمُ وَالْمَحْجُومُ

"The one who cups and the one who is cupped have broken their fast."[19]

Explanation

There seems to be an apparent contradiction here but in fact it is not so.

---

17. Fatawa al-Lajnah ad-Dā'imah: 10/224
18. Bukhari: 1939
19. Abu Dawud: 2367

This *hadith* narrated by Shaddad bin Aus stands abrogated due to the narration of Abdullah bin Abbass 🕮, 'Abdullāh bin 'Abbas described the same to have transpired during the year of the conquest of Makkah and during the year of the Hajjatul-Wada (the last pilgrimage performed by the Prophet 🕮). As to the matter of undesirability, the cupping does not invalidate fasting according to the majority of Ulama but the same is undesirable, and that too is in consideration of the fact that the bleeding may cause weakness, which in turn may force someone to break their fast. But in case someone is strong enough to withstand any such weakness or drowsiness resulting from the cupping, then the ruling concerning its undesirability is ineffective.

The ruling on the fasting person donating blood

If a person donates blood and a large amount of it is taken from him, this invalidates his fast based on an analogy with cupping. This is by blood being drawn from him through the veins to save a sick person or to preserve the blood for emergencies. However, if the amount that is taken from him is a small amount, then it does not break the fast. This is like the amount that is taken by way of needles and syringes to do blood tests and examinations.[20]

Some Important Issue Regarding Medical Treatment During Ramadān

Taking medicines and pills by mouth, injections of nourishing substances, or blood transfusions break the fast.

Injections that are not given to replace food and drink but are used to administer medications such as penicillin and insulin, tonics, or vaccinations do not break the fast regardless of whether they are intramuscular or intravenous.[21] But as a precaution, all these injections should be given during the night.

- Kidney dialysis, whereby blood is taken out, cleaned, and put back

---

20. Fatawa Islamiah: 3/275
21. Fatawa Ibn Ibrahīm: 4/189

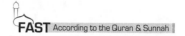

with some chemicals or nourishing substances such as sugars and salts, is considered to break the fast.[22]

- Having a blood sample taken does not break the fast and is permissible because it is something that is needed.[23]

- Medicines used by gargling do not break the fast so long as they are not swallowed. If a person has a tooth filled and feels the taste of it in his throat, this does not break his fast.

- According to the most correct view, suppositories, eye-drops, eardrops, having a tooth extracted and treating wounds do not break the fast.

- Even though there is a difference of opinion between the people of knowledge concerning eye drops (and eardrops). Some of them have said that if its taste reaches the throat, then it breaks the fast. However, the correct view is that it does not break the fast at all, because the eye is not an entrance to the body. But if the person makes up the day of fasting to be safe and avoids the difference of opinion that if He tastes its taste in his throat while fasting, there is no harm in that. Yet, the correct view in that it does not break the fast regardless of whether the drops were placed in the eye or the ear.[24]

- Puffers used for asthma do not break the fast, because this is just compressed gas that goes to the lungs – it is not food or drink nor does it resemble them. It only resembles that which is dropped in the outer opening of the urethra and that which is used to treat *ma'mumah* (head injury down to the skull) and *ja'ifah* (injury to the inside of stomach). It is also similar to kohl and anal inductions (i.e. a suppository) and similar things from all that reaches the brain or inner body through other than the mouth or nose. The scholars differ in these matters as to whether the fasting person breaks his fast by using them. Among them are those who say that the fasting person breaks his fast by using any of these things.

22. Fatawa al-Lajnah Ad-Da'imah: 10/190
23. Fatawa Ad-Da'wah, by Shaykh Ibn Baz, No: 979
24. Fatawa Islamiah: 3/267

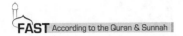

Also, there are those among them who say that the fasting person does not break his fast by using some of these things, but not others. However, there is an agreement among all of the scholars that none of these things are called food or drink. Yet, the scholars who declare the fast broken by using these things or some of them, give them the ruling of food and drink by the common factor that all of that riches the interior of the body by choice. They also base their position on what is confirmed from the Prophet's statement:

وَبَالِغْ فِي الِاسْتِنْشَاقِ إِلاَّ أَنْ تَكُونَ صَائِمًا

"And be excessive in inhaling water (for *wudhu*) unless you are fasting"[25]

Thus, the Prophet (ﷺ) made an exception for the fasting person regarding this due to fear that the water may reach his throat or his stomach by him being excessive in inhaling water, and thereby corrupt his fast. Hence, this proves that every thing that reaches the interior of the body by choice breaks the fast.

Those scholars who do not rule that the fast is corrupted by such things, like Shaykhul Islam Ibn Taimiyyah and those who agree with him, do not hold that comparing these things with food and drink is correct. For verily, there is nothing in the evidences that dictates that what breaks the fast is everything that reaches the brain or the inner body or whatever enters the body by an opening or reaches the inner body. There is no established evidence of the Islamic law for making any of these characteristics attached to the ruling of the fasting person breaking his fast. There is no evidence that is religiously correct for attaching this ruling to any of these characteristics. Also, giving this (such characteristics) the meaning of what reaches the throat or the stomach of water due to exaggerating in inhaling it is not correct, as there is a difference. For verily the water nourishes, so when it reaches the throat or the stomach, it corrupts the fast regardless of whether it entered the mouth or the nose, as each of them is only a path. For this reason the fast is not corrupted by simply rinsing the mouth or inhaling water if it is done without excessiveness

---

25. Abu Dawud: 2366

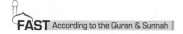

and that has not been prohibited. Hence, the fact that the mouth is a path is a discarded description that has no effect (in the matter). Therefore, if water or something similar reaches the interior of body through the nose, it has the same ruling as it reaching the interior of the body through the mouth. Thus the nose and the mouth are the same. That which is apparent is that using this medicine through inhaling, due to what has preceded, does not break the fast. This is because it does not have the same ruling as food and drink in any way.[26]

Useless Activities

Among the things that can destroy one's good deeds and cause bad deeds to be recorded is allowing oneself to be distracted by quiz shows, soap operas, movies and sports matches, idle gatherings, hanging about in the streets with evil people and time wasters, driving around for no purpose, and crowding the streets and sidewalks. The month of *tahajjud*, *dhikr* and worship for many people becomes a month in which they sleep during the day – so as to avoid feeling hunger – and spend their nights in entertainment and indulging in their desires. This further causes them to miss their prayers and the opportunity to pray them in congregation. Some people even greet this month with feelings of annoyance, thinking only of the pleasures they will miss out on. In Ramadān, some people even travel to the lands of the disbelievers to enjoy a holiday! Even the mosques are not free from such evils, as women come to it wearing makeup and perfume. Even the Sacred House of Allah (Ka'bah) is not free of these ills. Some people make this month a season for begging, even though they are not in need. Some entertain themselves with dangerous fireworks and the like, and some of them waste their time in the markets, wandering around the shops, or having new clothes stitched and following fashions. Some shop owners introduce new products and new styles in their stores during the last ten days of the month, thus keeping people away from earning rewards and good deeds.

A person should not allow himself to be provoked, because the Prophet (ﷺ) said:

---

26. The permanent committee, Fatawa Islamiyah: 3/271, Rulings Pertaining to Ramadān

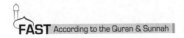

"If someone fights him or insults him, he should say: 'I am fasting, I am fasting.'"

One reason for this is remind himself, and the other reason is to remind the one who is provoking him. But anyone who looks at the conduct of many of those who fast will see something quite different. It is essential to exercise self-control and to be calm, but we see the opposite among the crazy drivers who speed up when they hear the *Adhaan* for *Magrhib*.[27]

---

27. Rulings Pertaining to Ramadān, pg. 20, 21

Things Which Do Not Invalidate Saum

Eating or Drinking Forgetfully

Abu Hurairah ◈ narrated that the Prophet (ﷺ) said:

إِذَا نَسِيَ فَأَكَلَ وَشَرِبَ فَلْيُتِمَّ صَوْمَهُ فَإِنَّمَا أَطْعَمَهُ اللهُ وسَقَاه

"If somebody eats or drinks forgetfully then he should complete his *saūm*, for what he has eaten or drank, has been given to him by Allah."[1]

Abu Huraira ◈ said: "O Messenger of Allah! I ate and drank out of forgetfulness while I was fasting." He said:

أَطْعَمَكَ اللهُ وَسَقَاكَ

"Allah fed you and gave you drink." [2]

Explanation

Whoever eats or drinks forgetfully while he is fasting, then his fast is correct. However, when he remembers he must stop. If a morsal of food or some drink is in his mouth, he must spit it out. The proof of the completion of his fast is above statements of the Prophet.

---

1. Bukhari: 1933
2. Abu Dawud: 2398

This is also because a person is not punished for forgetfully doing a prohibited action. This is due to the statement of Allah, the Most High:

$$رَبَّنَا لَا تُؤَاخِذْنَا إِنْ نَسِينَا أَوْ أَخْطَأْنَا$$

"Our lord, do not punish us if we forget or fall into error." (Al-Baqarah 2:286)

Allah, the Most High, said: "I have done so (i.e. pardoned it)"

If a person sees another fasting person forgetfully eating, it is obligatory upon him to remind him that he is fasting, because this is a part of changing an evil. Verily, the Prophet (ﷺ) said:

$$مَنْ رَأَى مِنْكُمْ مُنْكَرًا فَلْيُغَيِّرْهُ بِيَدِهِ فَإِنْ لَـمْ يَسْتَطِعْ فَبِلِسَانِهِ فَإِنْ$$
$$لَـمْ يَسْتَطِعْ فَبِقَلْبِهِ$$

"Whoever among you sees an evil, then let him change it with his hand, and if he is not able, then with his tongue, and if he is not able, then with his heart.[3]

There is no doubt that the fasting person's eating and drinking while fasting is a form of evil, but he is pardoned for it if he does so forgetfully, and there is no punishment for it. However, concerning the person who sees him doing so, has no excuse from stopping him.[4]

The Ruling on Tasting Food

There is no harm in tasting the food if there is a need for it. This is done by the person placing it on the tip of his tongue so that he may know its sweetness and saltiness; however, he should not swallow any of it. Rather, he should spit it out or expel it from his mouth and his fast will not be corrupted by that.[5]

But we should remember that it is disliked to taste food unnecessarily

---

3. Muslim: 49
4. Fatawa Islamiyah: 3/265, 266
5. Fatawa Islamiyah: 3/265

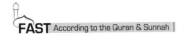

because this carries the risk of the fast being broken. Example of cases where it is necessary to taste food includes a mother chewing food for an infant when she has no other way to feed him. It was reported that Ibn Abbas (ﷺ) said: "There is nothing wrong with tasting vinegar or anything that one wishes to buy."[6]

Exaggeration in Sniffing Water into the Nose

Laqit bin Sabrah ؓ narrated that he said: "O Messenger of Allah! Inform me about *wudū*." So he said:

$$أَسْبِغِ الْوُضُوءَ وَخَلِّلْ بَيْنَ الأَصَابِعِ وَبَالِغْ فِي الاِسْتِنْشَاقِ إِلاَّ أَنْ تَكُونَ صَائِمًا$$

"Perform *Wudū*, and go between the fingers, and perform istinshaq extensively except when fasting."[7]

Use of Siwak or Toothbrush, and Tooth Paste

'Abdullāh bin Amir bin Rabiah narrated from his father who said: "I saw the Prophet (ﷺ) (a number of times), such that I was not able to count, using the *Siwak* while he was fasting."[8]

Explanation

Refraining from using the tooth stick during the daytime in Ramadān or during other days outside of Ramadān when a person in fasting is baseless. This is because using the tooth stick is *Sunnah*.

It is as has been mentioned in the authentic *hadith*:

$$السِّوَاكُ مَطْهَرَةٌ لِلْفَمِ مَرْضَاةٌ لِلرَّبِّ$$

"*Siwak* is a means of purification for the mouth and is

---

6. Fathul Bari: 4/197, Irwa' al-Ghaleel: 7/86
7. Tirmidhi: 788
8. Tirmidhi: 725

pleasing to the Lord."[9]

It is legislated especially during *wudū* (ablution), for the prayer, when getting up from sleep, upon entering the house when one first enters, while fasting and at other times. It does not corrupt the fast unless the tooth stick has a taste and an effect upon the spit. In that case you should not swallow its taste. Likewise, if some blood comes out from the gums when using the tooth stick, you should not swallow it. If you cautiously avoid this, then there is no harm in rubbing the teeth with water, the tooth stick and the tooth brush after beginning the fast. Some scholars have declared using the tooth stick disliked for the fasting person after mid-day, because it removes the foul taste in the mouth of the fasting person. However, the correct view is that it is recommended to use the tooth stick at the beginning of the day and its end, and that its use does not remove the bad taste in the mouth. It only cleans the teeth and mouth from odors, smells and leftover particles of food.

In reference to using paste, it seems most evident that it is disliked due to what it contains of fragrance and because it has a taste that mixes with the spit, and one cannot be certain that he won't swallow it. Therefore, whoever needs it should use it after *sahur* and before the time for abstaining from food. If a person uses it during the daytime and makes sure he does not swallow any of it, there is no harm in using it if there is a need for it. If a light amount of blood comes from the teeth while the person is rubbing them with the brush or the toothstick, it does not break the fast.[10]

Nosebleed and gums bleed

If a person suffers from a nosebleed, his fast is still valid, because this is something that is beyond his control.[11]

If he has gum ulcers or his gums bleed after using the *Siwak* (tooth stick), it is not permissible for him to swallow the blood; he must spit it out. However, if some of the blood enters his throat by accident and he did

9. Nasai: 5

10. Fatawa Islamiyah: 3/261-263

11. Fatawa al-Lajnah ad-Da'imah: 10/264

not mean for that to happen, there is no need to worry. Similarly, if vomit rises in his throat and then goes back down to his stomach without him intending for this to happen, his fast is still valid.[12]

Pouring Water Due to Thirst

Abu Bakr ibn Abdur Rahman narrated from someone from the Companions of the Prophet (ﷺ): "I saw the Prophet (ﷺ) ordering people, while traveling during the year of the conquest of Makkah, to break the fast. He said: 'Energize for your enemy.' The Messenger of Allah (ﷺ) himself fasted. Abu Bakr said: 'The one who narrated to me said:

$$\text{لَقَدْ رَأَيْتُ رَسُولَ اللهِ (ﷺ) بِالْعَرْجِ يَصُبُّ عَلَى رَأْسِهِ الْمَاءَ وَهُوَ}$$
$$\text{صَائِمٌ مِنَ الْعَطَشِ أَوْ مِنَ الْحَرِّ}$$

"I saw Allah's Messenger (ﷺ) at Al-'Araj pouring water over his head while he was fasting, due to thirst or heat.'""[13]

Swimming is disliked because it might make one break the fast by swallowing water. If a person's work involves diving and he can be sure that he will not get water in his mouth, there is nothing wrong with this.

Explanation

In order to fight extreme heat or thirst, a fasting person is allowed to pour water on his head or body, or take a shower, or put a wet cloth on his body.

Kohl for the Fasting Person

Al-A'mash reported: "I did not see any of our companions dislike using kohl for a fasting person. Ibrahim permitted the use of Kohl with aloe for a fasting person."[14]

---

12. Fatawa al-Lajnah ad-Da'imah: 10/254
13. Abu Dawud: 2365
14. Abu Dawud: 2379

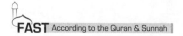

It was reported from Ubaidullah bin Abi Bakr bin Anas from Anas bin Malik that he used to apply kohl while fasting.[15]

Kissing or Caressing one's Wife

'Āishah (رضى الله عنها) narrated:

$$كَانَ النَّبِيُّ (ﷺ) يُقَبِّلُ وَيُبَاشِرُ وَهُوَ صَائِمٌ وَكَانَ أَمْلَكَكُمْ لِإِرْبِهِ$$

"The Prophet (ﷺ) used to kiss and embrace (his wives) while he was observing *saūm*, and he had more power to control his desires than any of you."

Jabir bin Zaid said: "If a man gets a sexual discharge as a result of casting a look (at his wife), he should complete his *saūm*." [16]

'Āishah (رضى الله عنها) narrated: "Allah's Messenger (ﷺ) used to kiss some of his wives while he was observing *saūm*." And then she smiled.[17]

"Amr bin Abi Salamah narrated that he asked the Messenger of Allah (ﷺ): "May the fasting person kiss (his wife)?" The Messenger of Allah (ﷺ) said: "Ask this one," meaning Umm Salamah. She told him that the messenger of Allah (ﷺ), did that. He said: "O Messenger of Allah, Allah has forgiven you your past and future sins."

The messenger of Allah (ﷺ) said to him:

$$أَمَا وَاللهِ إِنِّى لَأَتْقَاكُمْ للهِ وَأَخْشَاكُمْ لَهُ$$

"By Allah, I am the one who is the most pious and fears Allah the most among you." [18]

Jabir bin 'Abdullāh narrated that Umar bin al-Khattab said: "I got excited, so I kissed [my wife] while I was fasting. I said: 'O Messenger of Allah! I have done a horrible thing today; I kissed while I was fasting.'" He said: "What do you think If you sense your mouth with water while

---

15. Abu Dawud: 2379
16. Bukhari: 1927
17. Bukhari: 1928
18. Muslim: 1108

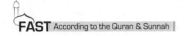

fasting?" In his narration, Eisa bin Hammad (one of the narrators) said: "I ('Umar) said: 'There would be no harm in that,'" then both of them were in accord- "He said: Then what?"[19]

It is Disliked in the Case of Young Person

Abu Hurairah ◈ narrated that a man asked the Prophet (◈) about embracing (a woman) while fasting? The Prophet (◈) allowed him. Another one came and asked him [the same thing] and the Prophet (◈) prohibited it for him. The one whom he allowed was an old man, and the one whom he prohibited was a young man.[20]

Ibn Abbas said: "A concession was granted to those who are older with regard to touching while fasting, but it was disliked on the part of those who are young."[21]

Sexual relation with your wives on the night of the *Saūm*

Allah says:

أُحِلَّ لَكُمْ لَيْلَةَ ٱلصِّيَامِ ٱلرَّفَثُ إِلَىٰ نِسَآئِكُمْ هُنَّ لِبَاسٌ لَّكُمْ وَأَنتُمْ لِبَاسٌ لَّهُنَّ عَلِمَ ٱللَّهُ أَنَّكُمْ كُنتُمْ تَخْتَانُونَ أَنفُسَكُمْ فَتَابَ عَلَيْكُمْ وَعَفَا عَنكُمْ فَٱلْـَٰنَ بَٰشِرُوهُنَّ وَٱبْتَغُوا۟ مَا كَتَبَ ٱللَّهُ لَكُمْ

"It is made lawful for you to have sexual relations with your wives on the night of As-*Saūm*. They are *libas* for you and you are the same for them. Allah knows that you used to deceive yourselves, so he turned to you (accept your repentance) and forgave you. So now have sexual relations with them and seek that which Allah has ordained for you (offspring)." (Al-Baqarah 2: 187)

Imam Ibn Kathīr says: These verses contain a relief from Allah for the

19. Abu Dawud: 2385
20. Abu Dawud: 2387
21. Ibn Majah: 1688

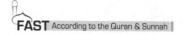
Muslims by ending the practice that was observed in the early years of Islam. At that time, Muslims were allowed to eat, drink and have sexual intercourse only until the *'Ishā'* (Night) prayer, unless one sleeps before the *'Ishā'* prayer. Those who slept before *'Ishā'* or offered the *'Ishā'* prayer, were not allowed to drink eat or sexual intercourse sex until the next night. The Muslims found that to be difficult for them.

The *ayāt* used the word *rafath* to indicate sexual intercourse, according to Ibn 'Abbas, 'Atā' and Mujāhid similar *tafsir* was offered by Sa'id bin Jubayr, Tawus, Salim bin 'Abdullāh, 'Amr bin Dinar, Al-Hasan, Qatadah, Az-Zuhri, Ad-Dahhak, Ibrahim An-Nakhai, As-Suddi, Ata Al-Khurasani and Muqati bin Hayyan.

Allah said:

$$هُنَّ لِبَاسٌ لَكُمْ وَأَنْتُمْ لِبَاسٌ لَهُنَّ$$

"They are *libas* (i.e., body-cover, or screen) for you
and you are *libas* for them."

Ibn 'Abbas, Mujahid, Sa'īd bin Jubayr, Al-Hasan, Qatadah, As-Suddi and Muqatil bin Hayyan said that this *ayah* means: "Your wives are a resort for you and you for them." Ar-Rabi' bin Anas said: "They are your cover and you are their cover." In short, the wife and the husband are intimate and have sexual intercourse with each other, and this is why they were permitted to have sexual activity during the nights of Ramadān, so that matters are made easier for them.

Al-Bukhari reported this *hadith* by Abu Ishaq who related that he heard Al-Barā' say: When fasting Ramadān was ordained, Muslims used to refrain from sleeping with their wives the entire month, but some men used to deceive themselves. Allah Revealed:

$$عَلِمَ اللهُ أَنَّكُمْ كُنْتُمْ تَخْتَانُونَ أَنْفُسَكُمْ فَتَابَ عَلَيْكُمْ وَعَفَا عَنْكُمْ$$

"Allah knows that you used to deceive yourselves, so
he turned to you and forgave you."[22]

---

22. Fathul Bari: 8/30

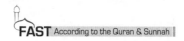

Ali bin Abu Talhah narrated that Ibn Abbas (ﷺ) said: "During the month of Ramadān after Muslims would pray *'Ishā'* they would not touch their women and food until the next night. Then some Muslims, including Umar bin AL-Khattab ﷺ touched (had sex with) their wives and had some food during Ramadn after *'Ishā'*. They complained to Allah's Messenger (ﷺ). Then Allah sent down above mentioned verse.[23]

Having a wet Dream during the Day in Ramadān

Zaid bin Aslam narrated from a man from his companions, from a man among the companions of the Prophet (ﷺ) who said: "The fast is not broken for one who vomited, had a sexual dream, or been cupped."[24]

Explanation

Wet dreams do not invalidate the fast, because it is not done by choice of the fasting person. He must perform a complete bath as he would for sexual impurity.

Some Important Medical Aspects

The following things do not break the fast:

- Having the ears syringed, nose drops and nasal sprays - so long as one avoids swallowing anything that reaches the throat.

- Tablets that are placed under the tongue to treat angina and other conditions - so long as one avoids swallowing anything that reaches the throat.

- Anything inserted into the vagina, such as passerines, douches, scopes or fingers for the purpose of a medical examination.

- Insertion of a scope or inter-uterine device (IUD or coil) and the like into the uterus.

  Insertion into the urethra – for males or females – of a catheter, opaque dye for diognostic imaging medication or solutions for

23. Tabari: 3/506-507
24. Abu Dawud: 2376

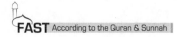
cleaning the bladder.

- Dental fillings, tooth extraction, cleaning of the teeth, so long as one avoids swallowing anything that reaches the throat.

- Rinsing, gargling or applying topical mouth sprays so longs as one avoids swallowing anything that reaches the throat.

- Subcutaneous, intramuscular or intravenous injections – except for those used to provide nourishment.

- Oxygen

  Anesthetic gases – so long as the patient is not given nourishing solutions.

- Medication absorbed through the skin, such as creams and patches used to administer medicine and chemicals.

  Insertion of a catheter into veins for diagnostic imaging or treatment of blood vessels in the heart or other organs.

- Use of a laparoscope (instrument inserted through a small incision in the abdomen) to examine the abdominal cavity or to perform operations.

- Taking biopsies or samples from the liver or other organs – so long as this is not accompanied by the administration of solution.

- Gastrascopy – so long as this is not accompanied by the administration of solution or other substances.

- Introduction of any instrument or medication to the brain or spinal column.[25]

If some water enters the throat of a fasting person during rising his mouth or cleaning his nose with water, this does not break his fast because he did not do so intentionally. This is due to Allah's Statement:

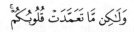

"But what your hearts purposefully intended." (Al-

---

25. Seventy matters related to Fasting by Sheikh Salih Al-Munajjid: 47, 48

Ahzab 33:5)

Swallowing Saliva

Saliva does not harm the fast because it is only spit. If the person swallows it, there is no harm in that and if he spits it out, there is no harm. In reference to phelegm, which is that which comes up from the chest or the nose and it is also called mucus, and this thick phlegm which the person sometimes gets from the chest and sometimes from the head, the man and women must spit it out. It is obligatory to expel it and refrain from swallowing it for the fasting person.

Concerning normal saliva, which is spit there is no problem with it and it does not harm the fasting person, whether a man or a woman.[26]

Using body Oil, Henna and Incense

There is no harm in using body oil while fasting when there is a need for it. Verily, the oil only moistens the outer skin and it does not affect the inside of the body. Even if it is possible for it to enter the pores of the skin, it is still not considered as something that breaks the fast.

Applying henna while fasting does not break the fast nor does it have any effect on the fasting person. This is just like kohl, eardrops, and eyedrops. All of that does not harm the fasting person nor does it break the fast.

It is also permissible during the day time in Ramadān to use perfume like 'Uud oil, cologne and incense under the condition that one does not inhale the incense smoke.[27]

The basic ruling concerning all of these originally permissible matters is that they are still permissible. If they were forbidden for the fasting person, Allah or His Messenger (ﷺ) would have clarified that. Allah says:

$$ وَمَا كَانَ رَبُّكَ نَسِيًّا $$

"...Your Lord is never forgetful." (Maryam 19:64)

---

26. Fatawa Islamiyah: 3/260
27. Fatawa Islamiyah: 3/264, 265

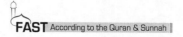

The Emission of Prostatic Fluid

The emission of prostatic fluid (*madhi*) does not invalidate the fast according to the most correct view of the two opinions held by the scholars. It make no difference whether that was caused by kissing the wife or any thing else that arouses the lust.[28]

---

28. Fatawa Islamiyah: 3/277

Prevention
During Saum

Speaking Falsehood and Acting in Accordance to it

Abu Hurairah ﷺ narrated that the Prophet (ﷺ) said:

مَنْ لَـمْ يَدَعْ قَوْلَ الزُّورِ وَالْعَمَلَ بِهِ فَلَيْسَ لِلهِ حَاجَةٌ فِي أَنْ يَدَعَ
طَعَامَهُ وَشَرَابَهُ

"Whoever does not give up lying speech (false statements) and acting on those lies and evil actions etc, Allah is not in need of his leaving his food and drink."[1]

Explanation

This *hadith* exhorts those observing *saūm* to fulfill all the requirements of fasting. One should not conduct himself in such a manner that on the one side he observes *saūm* and on the other he is fearless of Allah. To save himself from Allah's wrath and to get the reward of the fasts, one must abstain from all sorts of vices, such as cheating, lying, backbiting, and using obscene language. The threat held against such people in this *hadith* should make them fear that their *saūm* will go waste and they would be deprived of its reward. It does not mean that such people

1. Bukhari: 1903

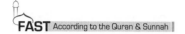

should start eating and drinking during *saūm* but what is intended is that they should save themselves from all kinds of sins so that they may earn the reward of *saūm*.

If Somebody Fights with Him

Abu Hurairah ﷺ narrated that Allah's Messenger (ﷺ) said:

$$ الصِّيَامُ جُنَّةٌ فَلَا يَرْفُثْ وَلَا يَجْهَلْ وَإِنِ امْرُؤٌ قَاتَلَهُ أَوْ شَاتَـمَهُ فَلْيَقُلْ $$
$$ إِنِّي صَائِمٌ $$

"*Saūm* is a shield. So, the person observing *saūm* should avoid sexual relation with his wife and should not behave foolishly and impudently and if some-body fights with him or abuses him, he should say to him twice: 'I am observing *Saūm*.'"[2]

Explanation

We learn from it that during *saūm* not only food, drink and sex are pro-hibited but also the improper use of the tongue and the other organs of the body as well. When one is observing *saūm*, he should neither use abusive language nor talk foolishly nor tell lies nor make obscene con-versation nor indulge in backbiting nor quarrel with anyone. If some one provokes him, he should keep himself quiet and remember that he is observing *saūm* and has to abstain from such things. As for as possible, he should keep his tongue engaged in the remembrance of Allah and recitation of the Qur'an.

Backbiting

A fasting person should fear Allah and realize His Might and Magnifi-cence at all times and in all circumstances, preserving his fasting and avoiding the things that would nullify it, so as to ensure its validity and acceptability. Furthermore, a fasting person should keep remembering

2. Bukhari: 1894

Allah, reciting the Qur'an, and performing as many supererogatory acts of worship as possible. The *salaf*, for example, used to keep to mosques while fasting so as to preserve their fasting and avoid backbiting, as they used to say. In addition, the Prophet (ﷺ) said:

"Whoever does not give up evil speech and related deeds Allah is in no need of his leaving his food and drink (i.e. Allah will not accept his fasting)."[3]

This is because seeking Allah's pleasure and drawing near to Him through abstaining from lawful desires (during fasting) must be preceded by generally abstaining from unlawful ones, such as lying, oppression, and aggression against people's lives, properties, and honor. It was narrated on the authority of Abu Hurairah, as a *marfu' hadith* that the Prophet (ﷺ) said:

$$\text{الصَّائِمُ فِي عِبَادَةٍ مَا لَمْ يَغْتَبْ مُسْلِمًا أَوْيُؤْذِهِ}$$

"The fasting person is in a state of worship as long as he does not backbite or hurt a Muslim."[4]

Additionally, it was narrated on the authority of Anas (ﷺ) that the Prophet (ﷺ) said:

$$\text{مَا صَامَ مَنْ ظَلَّ يَأْكُلُ لُحُومَ النَّاسِ}$$

"He does not observe fasting who continues eating the flesh of people (through backbiting them)."[5]

Backbiting is a great Sin

Allah says:

$$\text{يَٰٓأَيُّهَا ٱلَّذِينَ ءَامَنُوا۟ ٱجْتَنِبُوا۟ كَثِيرًا مِّنَ ٱلظَّنِّ إِنَّ بَعْضَ ٱلظَّنِّ إِثْمٌ وَلَا تَجَسَّسُوا۟}$$
$$\text{وَلَا يَغْتَب بَّعْضُكُم بَعْضًا أَيُحِبُّ أَحَدُكُمْ أَن يَأْكُلَ لَحْمَ أَخِيهِ مَيْتًا}$$

---

3. Bukhari: 1903
4. Ad-Dailmi, Ibn Adi: 1/302, Ibn Abi Shaibah: 8889
5. Ibn Abi Shaibah: 8890

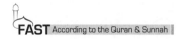
فَكَرِهْتُمُوهُ وَاتَّقُوا اللَّهَ إِنَّ اللَّهَ تَوَّابٌ رَّحِيمٌ ﴿١٢﴾

"O you who believe! Avoid much suspicions, indeed some suspicious are sins. And spy not, neither backbite one another. Would one of you like to eat the flesh of his dead brother? You would hate it (so hate backbiting). And fear Allah. Verily, Allah is the One who accepts repentance, Most Merciful." (Al-Hujurāt 49:12)

Anas (ﷺ) narrated that the Messenger (ﷺ) said:

لَـمَّا عُرِجَ بِى مَرَرْتُ بِقَوْمٍ لَهُمْ أَظْفَارٌ مِنْ نُحَاسٍ يَخْمِشُونَ وُجُوهَهُمْ وَصُدُورَهُمْ فَقُلْتُ مَنْ هَؤُلَاءِ يَا جِبْرِيلُ قَالَ هَؤُلَاءِ الَّذِينَ يَأْكُلُونَ لُحُومَ النَّاسِ وَيَقَعُونَ فِى أَعْرَاضِهِمْ

"During the *mi'raj* (the Night of Ascension), I saw a group of people who were scratching their chests and face with their copper nails. I asked: 'Who are these people, O Jibrīl?' Jibrīl replied: 'These are the people who ate flesh of others (by backbiting) and trampling people's honour.'"[6]

In a word, since a fasting person abstains from unlawful things during fasting, he should, with greater reason, abstain from those things which are unlawful at all times, so as to be among the true observers of fasting.[7]

---

6. Abu Dawud: 4878
7. Al-Mulakhasul Fiqhi with addition: 1/385, 386

Al-Iftar

Time of Iftar

Umar bin Al-Khattab (ﷺ) narrated that Allah's Messenger (ﷺ) said:

إِذَا أَقْبَلَ اللَّيْلُ مِنْ هَا هُنَا وَأَدْبَرَ النَّهَارُ مِنْ هَا هُنَا وَغَرَبَتْ الشَّمْسُ فَقَدْ أَفْطَرَ الصَّائِمُ

"When night falls from this side and the day vanishes from this side and the sun sets, then the person observing *Saūm* should break his *Saūm*."[1]

'Abdullāh bin Abi Aūfā (ﷺ) narrated that we were in the company of the Prophet (ﷺ) on a journey and he was observing *saūm*, and when the sun set, he addressed somebody: "O so-and-so, get up and mix *sawiq* with water for us." He replied: "O Allah's Messenger! (Will you wait) until evening?" The Prophet (ﷺ) said: "Get down and mix *sawiq* with water for us." He replied: "O Messenger of Allah! (If you wait) until it is evening." The Prophet (ﷺ) said again: "Get down and mix *sawiq* with water for us." He replied: "It is still daytime." The Prophet (ﷺ) said again: "Get down and mix *sawiq* with water for us." He got down and mixed *sawiq* for them. The Prophet (ﷺ) drank it and then said: "When you see night falling from this side, the fasting person should break his *saūm*."[2]

1. Bukhari: 1954
2. Bukhari: 1956

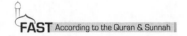

Recommendation of Hastening to break the Fast

Sahl bin Sa'd (ﷺ) narrated that Allah's Messenger ﷺ said:

لَا يَزَالُ النَّاسُ بِخَيْرٍ مَا عَجَّلُوا الْفِطْرَ

"The people will remain on the right path as long as they hasten the Iftār."[3]

Abu 'Atiyyah narrated: "*Masrūq* and I entered upon 'Āishah and said: 'O mother of the Believers, there are two men among the Companions of Muhammad (ﷺ); one of them hastens to break the fast and hasten to offer *salāt*, and the other delays the breaking the fast and delays the prayer.' She said: 'Who is the one who hastens to break the fast and hastens to offer *salāt*?' We said: 'Abdullāh bin Mas'ud.' She said: 'That is what the Messenger of Allah (ﷺ) used to do.'"

Abu Kuraib added: "The other one was Abū Mūsā."[4]

Abu Hurairah (ﷺ) narrated that the Prophet (ﷺ) said:

لاَ يَزَالُ الدِّينُ ظَاهِرًا مَا عَجَّلَ النَّاسُ الْفِطْرَ لِأَنَّ الْيَهُودَ وَالنَّصَارَى
يُؤَخِّرُونَ

"The religion (of Islam) will continue to be manifest as long as people hasten to break their fast (at its earlier time) because the Jews and Christians delay it."[5]

Explanation

"The people will remain on the right path" here means welfare of the religion as well as that of this world. Breaking the *saūm* early does not mean that it is terminated before the prescribed time. What it really means is without any delay after the sunset. One should not delay it for the mere reason that the rigour one has gone through in the *saūm* should be enhanced further, as is done by some Sufis. There is no merit is such things

---

3. Bukhari: 1957
4. Muslim: 1099
5. Abu Dawud: 2353

because the real merit lies in following the *Sunnah* of the Prophet (ﷺ). Welfare of the Muslims will, therefore, come in the share of the Muslims because of their following the Prophet's *Sunnah* of breaking the *saūm* in the early moments of the prescribed time.

If Somebody Breaks the Fast before Sunset

Asma bint Abi Bakr (﵂) said: "We broke our fast during the lifetime of the Prophet (ﷺ) on a cloudy day and then the sun appeared." Hisham was asked, "Were they ordered to observe fasting in lieu of that day?" He replied, "It had to be made up for."[6]

Breaking The fast without legitimate excuse

Whoever breaks the fast duing Ramadān without a legitimate excuse has committed a serious major sin, The Prophet (ﷺ) said, when describing a dream that he had seen:

"....until I was at a mountain where I heard loud voices. I asked: 'What are these voices?' They said: 'This is the houling of the people of Hell-fire.' Then I was taken (to another place), and I saw people hanging from their harmstrings with the corners of their mouths torn and dripping with blood. I said: 'Who are these?' They said:

$$ أَلَّذِيْنَ يُفْطِرُونَ قَبْلَ تَـحِلَّةَ صَوْمِهِمْ $$

'The people who broke their fast before it was the proper time to do so, (i.e., before the time of breaking fast).'"[7]

What to use to Break One's Fast

Ar-Rabbab narrated from Salmān bin 'Āmir from her paternal uncle who said that the Messenger of Allah (ﷺ) said:

---

6. Bukhari: 1959
7. Saheeh At-Targheeb: 1/588

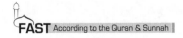

إِذَا كَانَ أَحَدُكُمْ صَائِمًا فَلْيُفْطِرْ عَلَى التَّمْرِ فَإِنْ لَمْ يَجِدِ التَّمْرَ فَعَلَى الْمَاءِ فَإِنَّ الْمَاءَ طَهُورٌ

"When one of you fasts, then let him break his fast with dates, and if he does not find dates, then with water, for water is indeed purifying."[8]

Anas bin Malik (رضي الله عنه) narrated:

كَانَ رَسُولُ اللهِ (ﷺ) يُفْطِرُ عَلَى رُطَبَاتٍ قَبْلَ أَنْ يُصَلِّيَ فَإِنْ لَمْ تَكُنْ رُطَبَاتٌ فَعَلَى تَمَرَاتٍ فَإِنْ لَمْ تَكُنْ حَسَا حَسَوَاتٍ مِنْ مَاءٍ.

"The Messenger of Allah (ﷺ) would break his fast with fresh dates before praying, if there were no fresh dates, then with dried dates, if he did not have dried dates, then he would take some mouthful of water."[9]

The Saying at the Time of Breaking the Fast

Ibn Umar (رضي الله عنه) narrated that the Prophet (ﷺ) used to say when breaking his fast:

ذَهَبَ الظَّمَأُ وَابْتَلَّتِ الْعُرُوقُ وَثَبَتَ الْأَجْرُ إِنْ شَاءَ اللهُ

"Dhahabaz Zamā'u wabtallatil 'Uruqu wa thabatal ajru inshā'Allāh."

(The thirst is gone, and the veins are quenched, and the reward is assured, if Allāh wills).[10]

'Abdullāh bin 'Amr bin 'Ās narrated that the Messenger of Allah (ﷺ) said:

إِنَّ لِلصَّائِمِ عِنْدَ فِطْرِهِ لَدَعْوَةٌ مَا تُرَدُّ

---

8. Abu Dawud: 2355
9. Abu Dawud: 2356
10. Abu Dawud: 2355

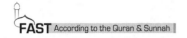

"When the fasting person breaks his fast, his supplication is not turned back."

Ibn Abi Mulaikah said: "When he broke his fast, I heard 'Abdullāh bin 'Amir say:

$$ اَللَّهُمَّ إِنِّي أَسْأَلُكَ بِرَحْمَتِكَ الَّتِي وَسِعَتْ كُلَّ شَيْءٍ أَنْ تَغْفِرَ لِي $$

Allaahumma innee as'aluka bi-rahmatikal-latee wasi'at kulla shai'in an taghfira lee.

'O Allah! I ask You by Your mercy, which encompasses all things, to forgive me.'"[11]

Abu Hurairah (ﷺ) narrated that the Messenger of Allah (ﷺ) said:

$$ ثَلَاثَةٌ لَا تُرَدُّ دَعْوَتُهُمْ الإِمَامُ الْعَادِلُ وَالصَّائِمُ حَتَّى يُفْطِرَ وَدَعْوَةُ $$

$$ الْـمَظْلُومِ يَرْفَعُهَا اللهُ دُونَ الْغَمَامِ يَوْمَ الْقِيَامَةِ وَتُفْتَحُ لَهَا أَبْوَابُ السَّمَاءِ وَيَقُولُ بِعِزَّتِي لَأَنْصُرَنَّكِ وَلَوْ بَعْدَ حِينٍ $$

"There are three whose supplications are not turned back: A just ruler, a fasting person until he breaks his fast, and the supplication of one who has wronged is raised by Allah up to the clouds on the Day of Resurrection, and the gates of heaven are opened for it, and Allah says, 'By My might I will help you (against the wrongdoer) even if it is after a while."[12]

The moment of breaking the fast is a time for the acceptance of supplication, so it is appropriate to supplicate for oneself, for the family and the fulfillment of needs.

In fact a muslim should know about the rulings related to fasting and breaking the fast in terms of both the correct time and manner of performance, so as to observe it in the proper legal way that agrees with the

---

11. Ibn Majah: 1753
12. Ibn Majah: 1752

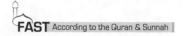
Sunnah of the Prophet (صلى الله عليه وسلم). In this way – by following in the Prophet's footsteps when observing the fast – one's fast is likely to be valid and one's good deeds during fasting are likely to be accepted, if Allah wills; this is a very important issue. Allah, Exalted be He, says:

لَّقَدۡ كَانَ لَكُمۡ فِى رَسُولِ ٱللَّهِ أُسۡوَةٌ حَسَنَةٌ لِّمَن كَانَ يَرۡجُواْ ٱللَّهَ وَٱلۡيَوۡمَ ٱلۡأٓخِرَ وَذَكَرَ ٱللَّهَ كَثِيرًا ﴿٢١﴾

"Indeed in the Messenger of Allah (Muhammad صلى الله عليه وسلم) you have a good example to follow for him who hopes in (the Meeting with) Allah and the Last Day and remembers Allah much. (Al-Ahzab 33:21)

For Whom is
Fasting Mandatory

Muslim

Because Fast is a third pillar of Islam.

Sane

Allah's Messenger (ﷺ) said:

رُفِعَ الْقَلَمُ عَنْ ثَلَاثَةٍ عَنِ النَّائِمِ حَتَّى يَسْتَيْقِظَ وَعَنِ الْـمُبْتَلَى حَتَّى
يَبْرَأَ وَعَنِ الصَّبِيِّ حَتَّى يَكْبَرَ

"The pen has been lifted from three: From the sleeping person until he awakes, from the insane person until he comes to his senses, and from the child until he grows up."[1]

The insane are not held responsible for their actions; but if a person is insane at times and sane at other times, he must fast during his periods of sanity and is excused during his period of insanity. If he becomes insane during the day, this does not invalidate his fast, similar to the case of someone who becomes unconscious because of illness or some other reason, for he had the intention of fasting when he was sane.[2]

---

1. Abu Dawud: 4398
2. Majalas Shahr Ramadān, by Ibn 'Uthaymīn: 28

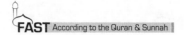

Must Reach Puberty

As described in the above mentioned *hadith*; but it is permissible for children to observe *saūm*.

Saūm of Children

Umar (﷜) once said to a drunk during the month of Ramadān: "Woe to you! Even our children are observing *saūm* (and you are drunk)." He then gave him the legal punishment.

Ar-Rubaī' bint Mu'awwidh narrated: The Prophet (ﷺ) sent a messenger to the village of the Ansār in the morning of the day of 'Āshūra' (10th of Muharram) to announce:

مَنْ أَصْبَحَ مُفْطِرًا فَلْيُتِمَّ بَقِيَّةَ يَوْمِهِ وَمَنْ أَصْبَحَ صَائِمًا فَلْيَصُم

"Whoever has eaten something should not eat but complete the *saūm*, and whoever is observing the *saūm* should complete it".

She further said: "Since then we used to observe *saūm* on that day regularly and also make our children observe the fast. We used to make toys of wool for the children and if anyone of them cried for food, he was given those toys until it was the time of *iftar*."[3]

Imam Bukhari mentioned this narration and the saying of Umar (﷜) under the Chapter: "The *Saūm* of Children." Obligatory and voluntary *saūm*s are same in this matter.

Children should be instructed to fast at the age of seven if they are able, and some scholars say, similar to the case of the *salāt*, a child may be physically disciplined at the age of ten if he does not fast. Children will be rewarded for fasting, and their parents will be rewarded for bringing them up properly and guiding them to do righteous deeds. Al-Rubayyi' bin Mu'awwidah (﷜) said, speaking about Ramadān when it was made obligatory:

"We used to make our children fast, and we would make them a toy

---

3. Bukhari: 1960

made out of wool. If any one of them started to cry for food, we would give them that toy to play with until it was time to break the fast." Allah says:

$$\text{يَـٰٓأَيُّهَا ٱلَّذِينَ ءَامَنُوا۟ قُوٓا۟ أَنفُسَكُمْ وَأَهْلِيكُمْ نَارًا وَقُودُهَا ٱلنَّاسُ وَٱلْحِجَارَةُ عَلَيْهَا مَلَـٰٓئِكَةٌ غِلَاظٌ شِدَادٌ لَّا يَعْصُونَ ٱللَّهَ مَآ أَمَرَهُمْ وَيَفْعَلُونَ مَا يُؤْمَرُونَ ٦}$$

"O you who believe! Ward of from youselves and your families a Fire (Hell) whose fuel is men and stones, over which are (appointed) angels stern (and) severe, who disobey not, (from executing) the Commands they receive from Allah, but do that which they are commanded." (Al-Tahreem 66:6)

Extra attention must be given to the matter of girls when they have just reached the age of maturity, for they may fast, out of shyness, during their menses and not make them up later.

Must be Healthy

Allah says:

$$\text{وَمَن كَانَ مَرِيضًا أَوْ عَلَىٰ سَفَرٍ فَعِدَّةٌ مِّنْ أَيَّامٍ أُخَرَ يُرِيدُ ٱللَّهُ بِكُمُ ٱلْيُسْرَ وَلَا يُرِيدُ بِكُمُ ٱلْعُسْرَ وَلِتُكْمِلُوا۟ ٱلْعِدَّةَ وَلِتُكَبِّرُوا۟ ٱللَّهَ عَلَىٰ مَا هَدَىٰكُمْ وَلَعَلَّكُمْ تَشْكُرُونَ ١٨٥}$$

"Whoever is ill or on a journey, the same number of days (which one did not observe *saūm* must be made up) from other days. Allah intends for you ease, and He does not want to make things difficult for you. (He wants that you) must complete the same number (of days), and that you must magnify Allah for having guided you so that you may be grateful to Him."

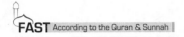

(Al-Baqarah 2:185)

This verse indicates that ill persons who are unable to fast or fear harm by fasting are allowed to break the fast. When one does not fast in this case, he is obliged to fast other days instead. This verse also indicates that Allah allowed this for such persons out of His Mercy and to make matters easy for them.[4]

Fasting for the Sick Person

It is legislated for the sick person to break the fast during the month of Ramadān if the fast is harmful to him or difficult upon him, or he needs to take some medicine during the day. This medicine can be various types of pills, syrups and so forth, from that which is eaten or drunk. Whoever is unable to fast due to an illness that he is not expected to recover from, then he breaks his fast and feeds a poor person for each day.

Allah said:

وَعَلَى الَّذِينَ يُطِيقُونَهُ فِدْيَةٌ طَعَامُ مِسْكِينٍ

"And upon those who are able to do so, i.e., fast, (but with difficulty,) there is a ransom of feeding a poor person." (Al-Baqarah 2:184)

It is also due to the Prophet's statement:

إِنَّ اللهَ يُحِبُّ أَنْ تُؤْتَى رُخَصُهُ كَمَا يَكْرَهُ أَنْ تُؤْتَى مَعْصِيَّتُهُ

"Verily, Allah loves that His concession be taken just as He hates that His disobedience be done."[5]

In another narration he said:

كما يحب أن تؤتى عزائمه

"...just as He likes for His Decisions to be

4. Ibn Khatir: 1/441
5. Ahmad: 2/108

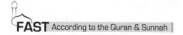

followed."[6]

The aim of this religion is not be burden people to a point that they will be physically incapable of carrying out the duties manadated by Allah. This why when there is clear evidence that fasting will result in the opposite of the intended result, namely endangering the sanctity of life itself, the Lawgiver, makes room for the believer. By physical disability ('al-'ajiz), we mean the old person who is mentally sound but physically weak, and observation of the fast would further weaken his body. Also, at this point the fast is not mandatory upon the old person because he is unable to do so. In the case of the terminally ill, like a person suffering from cancer or AIDS, whose fasting may worsen their condition, Allah says:

$$فَٱتَّقُوا۟ ٱللَّهَ مَا ٱسْتَطَعْتُمْ$$

"...So fear Allah as much as you can." (Al-Qur'ān 64:16)

Also,

$$لَا يُكَلِّفُ ٱللَّهُ نَفْسًا إِلَّا وُسْعَهَا$$

"On no soul does Allah place a burden greater than it can bear..." (Al-Qur'ān 2:286)

These verses indicate when the body is no longer able to executing the prescribed duties, then the pen that records the deeds ceases to record. These people who have been allowed to break their fast of Ramadān, would have to compensate for each and every day that they do not fast by feeding one poor person.

Before the fasting of Ramadān was prescribed to the believers, everyone was given a choice between fasting or feeding. This is what the Qur'ān refers to in chapter "Al-Baqarah":

$$وَعَلَى ٱلَّذِينَ يُطِيقُونَهُ فِدْيَةٌ طَعَامُ مِسْكِينٍ$$

"...for those who can do it (with hardship) is a ran-

---

6. Ibn Hibban: 913, 914

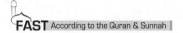

som, the feeding of indigent…" (Al-Qur'ān 2:184)

This verse was abrogated by the verse of Ramadān.

When a believer is incapable of fasting due to the reasons mentioned above, feeding the poor becomes a substitute.

If the aliment is minor, such as a cough or a headache, then it is not considered a valid reason to break the fast.

If there is medical proof, if a person knows from his usual experience, or he is certain that fasting will make his illness worse or will delay his recovery, he is permitted to break his fast. Rather, it is disliked (makrooh) for him to continue fasting in such cases. If a person is seriously ill, he is not obligated to have the intention during the night to fast the following day, even if there is a possibility that he may be well in the morning, because what counts is the present moment.

If fasting will cause unconsciousness, he should break his fast and make it up later. If a person becomes unconscious during the day and recovers before *maghrib* or after it, his fast is still valid as long as he was fasting in the morning. If he becomes unconscious from the time of *Fajr* until *maghrib*, then according to the majority of scholars his fast is not valid. According to the majority of scholars, it is obligatory for a person who falls unconscious to make up his fast later, no matter how long he was unconscious for. Some scholars have issued fatawas (verdicts) to the effect that a person who falls unconscious, takes sleeping pills, or receives a general anesthetic for a genuine reason and becomes unconscious for three days or less must make up the fasts later, for he is regarded as being like one who sleeps. If he is unconscious for more than three days, he does not have to make up the fasts because he is regarded as being like the one who is insane.

The *Fidyah* (Expiation) for Breaking the Fast for the Old

Al-Bukhari reported that 'Atā heard Ibn Abbās (ﷺ) recite:

وَعَلَى ٱلَّذِينَ يُطِيقُونَهُۥ فِدْيَةٌ طَعَامُ مِسْكِينٍ

"And as for those who can fast with difficulty, (e.g.,
an old man), they have (a choice either to fast or) to
feed a Miskīn (poor person) (for every day)."

Ibn Abbās (ﷺ) then commented, this *ayah* was not abrogated. It is for
the old man and woman who are able to fast with difficulty, but choose
instead to feed a poor person for every day.[7]

Others reported that Saʿīd bin Jubayr mentioned this from Ibn Abbās
(ﷺ). So the abrogation here applies to the healthy person, who is not
travelling and who has to fast, as Allah said:

$$فَمَن شَهِدَ مِنكُمُ ٱلشَّهْرَ فَلْيَصُمْهُ$$

"So whoever of you sights (the crescent on the first
night of) the month (Ramadān, i.e., is present at his
home), he must observe *saūm* that Month."

As for the old man (or woman) who cannot fast, he is allowed to abstain
from fasting and does not have to fast another day instead, because he is
not likely to improve his condition and be able to fast other days. So he is
required to pay a *fidyah* for every day missed. This is the opinion of Ibn
Abbās (ﷺ) and several others among the *salaf* who read the *ayah*:

$$وَعَلَى ٱلَّذِينَ يُطِيقُونَهُ$$

"And as for those can fast with difficulty, (e.g., an
old man)."

To mean those who find it difficult to fast, just as Ibn Masʿūd (ﷺ) stated.
This is also the opinion of Al-Bukhari who said: "As for the old person
who cannot fast, (he should do like) Anas (ﷺ) who, for one or two years
after he became old fed some bread and meat to a poor person for each
day he did not fast."[8]

This point, which Al-Bukhari attributed to Anas (ﷺ) without a chain of
narrators was collected with a continuous chain of narrators by Abu Yaʿla

7. Fath Al-Bari: 8/28
8. Fath Al-Bari: 8/179

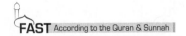

Mawsuli in his Musnad, that Ayyub bin Abu Tamimah said: "Anas could no longer fast. So he made a plate of tharīd (broth, bread and meat) and invited thirty poor persons and fed them."[9]

Pregnant and Nursing Mothers

Anas bin Mālik narrated, a man from Banū 'Abdullāh bin Ka'b said: "Some cavalry men of Messenger of Allah (ﷺ) came galloping upon us, so I came to the Messenger of Allah (ﷺ) and found him having a lunch. He said: 'Come and eat.' I said, 'I am fasting.' So he said: 'Come and I will narrate to you about the fast – or fasting. Indeed Allah Most High lifted (the fast and) half of the *salāt* from the traveler, and (He lifted) that fast – or fasting – from the pregnant or from the nursing mother.' And By Allah! The Prophet (ﷺ) said both of them or one of them. So woe to me, for I did not eat from the meal of the Prophet (ﷺ)."[10]

Imam Tirmidhi mentioned under this *hadith*: "Some of the people of knowledge say that the pregnant and breast-feeding persons break the fast, makes up for it, and feeds. This is the view of Sufyān, Malik, Ash-Shāfi'i, and Ahmad. Some of them said: They break the fast and feed, but they are not required to make it up, and if they wish they can make it up and not feed others."

Explanation

If the pregnant and breast-feeding women fear that fasting will harm the child, then they may break the fast, but they must make it up later, because their situation is similar to a sick person, about whom Allah says:

$$وَمَن كَانَ مَرِيضًا أَوْعَلَىٰ سَفَرٍ فَعِدَّةٌ مِّنْ أَيَّامٍ أُخَرَ يُرِيدُ اللَّهُ$$
$$بِكُمُ الْيُسْرَ وَلَا يُرِيدُ بِكُمُ الْعُسْرَ$$

"....and whoever is ill or on a journey, the same number (of days which one did not observe *saūm* must be made up from other days. Allah intends for

9. Musnad Abu Yala: 7/204, Ibn Kathir: 1/439
10. Trimidhi: 715

you ease, and He does not want to make things difficult for you." (Al-Baqarah 2:185)

Once the danger is past, they must make up for it, either during the winter, when the days are shorter and the weather is cooler, or, if she is unable to do it in the winter, then in the following year. But as for the feeding (poor people), it is not permissible except in a situation where the thing which prevents her from fasting or the excuse for not fasting is continuous, and it is not expected that it will be removed; in these circumstances, she may feed (poor people) instead of fasting.

The Traveler

The Preference to Break the Fast while on a Journey

Jabir bin ʿAbdullāh (🙵) narrated that Allah's Messenger (🙵) was on a journey and saw a crowd of people, and a man was being shaded (by them). He said: "What is the matter?" They said: "He (the man) is observing *saūm.*" The Prophet (🙵) said:

$$لَيْسَ مِنْ الْبِرِّ الصَّوْمُ فِي السَّفَرِ$$

"It is not from Al-Birr (righteousness) to observe *saūm* on a journey."[11]

Jabir bin ʿAbdullāh (🙵) narrated that the Messenger of Allah (🙵) set out for Makkah in Ramadān during the year of the conquest, and he fasted until he reached Kurāʿ al-Ghamīm, and the people fasted. Then he called for a vessel of water, which he lifted up so that the people could see it, and then he drank it. After that it was said to him that some of the people were still fasting. He said: "Those are the disobedient ones, those are disobedient ones." [12]

Jabir bin ʿAbdullāh (🙵) narrated that the Messenger of Allah (🙵) passed by a man in the shade of a tree on whom water was sprinkled. He said: "What is the matter with your companions?" They said: "O Messenger

11. Bukhari: 1946
12. Muslim: 1114

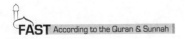

of Allah, he is fasting." He said:

$$إِنَّهُ لَيْسَ مِنَ الْبِرِّ أَنْ تَصُومُوا فِى السَّفَرِ وَعَلَيْكُمْ بِرُخْصَةِ اللهِ الَّتِى رَخَّصَ لَكُمْ فَاقْبَلُوهَا$$

"It is not righteousness to fast when traveling. Take to the concession which Allāh has granted you, accept it."[13]

Whoever preferred to Fast while on a journey

'Āishah (﷽) narrated that Hamza bin 'Amr Al-Aslamī asked the Prophet (﷽): "Should I observe *saūm* while traveling," as he used to fast regularly. So the Messenger of Allah (﷽) replied:

$$إِنْ شِئْتَ فَصُمْ وَإِنْ شِئْتَ فَأَفْطِرْ$$

"You may observe *saūm* if you wish, and you may break the *saūm* if you wish."[14]

Abū Ad-Dardā' (﷽) narrated: "We set out with Allah's Messenger (﷽) on one of his journeys on a very hot day, and it was so hot that one had to put his hand over his head because of the severity of heat. None of us was observing *saūm* except the Prophet (﷽) and Ibn Rawāha."[15]

Hamzah bin 'Amr Al-Aslami said: "O Messenger of Allah, I find that I have the strength to fast when travelling; is there any sin on me for that?" The Messenger of Allah (﷽) said:

$$هِيَ رُخْصَةٌ مِنَ اللهِ فَمَنْ أَخَذَ بِهَا فَحَسَنٌ وَمَنْ أَحَبَّ أَنْ يَصُومَ فَلاَ جُنَاحَ عَلَيْهِ$$

"It is a concession from Allah, so whoever avails himself of it has done well, and whoever wants to

---

13. Nasa'i: 2260
14. Tirmidhi: 711
15. Bukhari: 1943

fast, there is no blame on him."[16]

Ibn Abbas (رضي الله عنه) said:

لاَ تَعِبْ عَلَى مَنْ صَامَ وَلاَ عَلَى مَنْ أَفْطَرَ قَدْ صَامَ رَسُولُ اللهِ (ﷺ)
فِي السَّفَرِ وَأَفْطَرَ

"Do not criticize the one who fasts or the one who does not fast, for the Messenger of Allah (ﷺ) fasted when travelling, and he (also) did not fast (when travelling)."[17]

Whoever is determined to travel in Ramadān should not have the intention of breaking his fast until he is actually traveling because something may happen to prevent him from setting out on his journey.[18]

The Companions of the Prophet (ﷺ) did not Criticize each Other

Anas bin Malik (رضي الله عنه) narrated:

كُنَّا نُسَافِرُ مَعَ النَّبِيِّ (ﷺ) فَلَمْ يَعِبْ الصَّائِمُ عَلَى الْمُفْطِرِ وَلَا
الْمُفْطِرُ عَلَى الصَّائِمِ

"We used to travel with the Prophet (ﷺ) and neither did the person observing the saūm criticize those who were not observing the saūm, nor did those who were not observing the saūm criticize the ones who were observing the saūm."[19]

Abu Sa'eed Al-Khudri (رضي الله عنه) narrated: "We went out on a campaign with the Messenger Allah (ﷺ) during Ramadān, and some of us were fasting and some not. Those who were fasting did not find fault with those who were not, and those who were not fasting did not find fault with

---

16. Muslim: 1121 (107)
17. Muslim: 1113 (89)
18. Tafseer al-Qurtubi: 2/278
19. Bukhari: 1947

those who were. They thought that for those who found the strength and fasted, that was good; and thought that for those who found themselves weak and did not fast, that was good too."[20]

Humaid said: "I went out while I was fasting. They said to me: 'Repeat it'. I said: 'Anas told me that the Companions of the Messenger of Allah (ﷺ) used to travel, and those who fasted did not criticize those who did not, and those who did not fast did not criticize those who did.'"

Then I met Ibn Abi Mulaikah and he narrated something similar to me from 'Āishah (ﷺ).[21]

Anas (ﷺ) narrated: "We were with the Prophet (ﷺ) on a journey, and some of us were fasting and some were not. We made a stop on a hot day, and those of us who had the best shade were those who had garments with which to shade themselves, and some of us shielded themselves from the sun with their hands. Those who were fasting fell down, (in exhaustion to rest), and those who were not fasting set up the tents and watered the mounts. The Messenger of Allah (ﷺ) said:

$$\text{ذَهَبَ الْمُفْطِرُونَ الْيَوْمَ بِالْأَجْرِ}$$

'Today those who are not fasting have taken all the reward.'"[22]

Explanation

It is permissible for the traveller who is travelling on a journey in which it is permissible for him to shorten his prayers to break his fast during his journey. It makes no difference whether he is walking or riding, and it makes no difference whether he is riding in a car or on an airplane or something else. It also makes no difference whether he becomes fatigued on his journey to such an extent that he cannot bear fasting or he is not fatigued. It does not matter whether he is suffering from hunger and thirst or he is not affected by any of that. This is because the Islamic law has

---

20. Muslim: 116 (96)
21. Muslim: 1118 (99)
22. Muslim: 1119

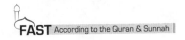

unrestrictedly given permission to break the fast for the traveller who is travelling on a journey in which it is permissible for him to shorten his prayers, and other similar things from the concessions of travelling.[23]

Length of Journey for Breaking the Fast

Mansūr Al-Kalbi narrated that once Dihyah bin Khalifah left from a village of Damascus a distance as much as is between the village of 'Aqabah and Al-Fustāt in Ramadān, and that is three miles. He broke his fast, and some people broke their fast along with him, but some of them did not like to break their fast. When he returned to his village, he said: "By Allah! Today I saw something which I never dreamt of seeing. Some people detested the guidance of the Messenger of Allah (ﷺ) and his Companions," addressing it to those who fasted. He then said: "O Allah! Take me to you!"[24]

As mentioned above breaking the fast is permissible while on a journey in which it is permissible to shorten the prayer. About that length Yaha bin Yazid Al-Hunai reported: I asked Anas bin Mālik (ﷺ) about shortening the prayer and he said:

$$كَانَ رَسُولُ اللهِ (ﷺ) إِذَا خَرَجَ مَسِيرَةَ ثَلَاثَةِ أَمْيَالٍ أَوْ ثَلَاثَةِ فَرَاسِخَ$$
$$- شُعْبَةُ الشَّاكُّ$$

"When the Messenger of Allah (ﷺ) had covered a distance of three miles or three *farsakh* (Shu'bah, one of the narrators, had some doubt about the wording), he performed two *rak'ahs*."

Explanation

(i)   A *farsakh* is equal to three miles.

(ii)   A doubt lurks in the above mentioned narration whether it is three miles or three *farsakh*. The original *hadith* does not state it, but it

---

23. Fatawa Islamiah: 3/290, 291
24. Ibn Majah: 2413

is the doubt of the reporter of the chain of narrators, as to whether Anas (﷽) used the words 'three miles' or 'three *Farsakh*'. We must know that no distance has been specified in any *hadith* which would make a person eligible to perform a two rak'ah prayer. This concession, like performing Tayammum during travel, has been kept open to the effect that it is permissible to perform a two-rak'ah prayer during any journey. It appears from the *hadith* that a 'three mile travel' is indeed a journey, but as long as Shu'bah doubt it, the scholars have given a ruling that the distance should be three *farsakh* (i.e. nine miles). Some put the figure to 48 miles whereas other suggest 52 miles. But these are mere conjectures and are substantiated by any evidence.[25]

A person is not considered a traveler until he has left the city. If he is still within the city, he is regarded as a resisdent and is not permitted to shorten his prayers or break his fast. His journey should also not have been one undertaken for some sinful purposes (according to the majaorty of scholars).

A traveler should not break his fast until he has passed beyond the inhabited houses of his town; once he has passed the city limits, he may break his fast. Similarly if he is flying, once the plane has taken off and has gone beyond the city limits, he may break his fast. If the airport is outside his city, he can break his fast there, but if the airport is within his city or attached to it, he should not break his fast in the airport because he is still within the bounds of his own city.

If the sun sets and he breaks his fast on the ground, and then the plane takes off and he sees the sun, he does not have to stop eating. He has already completed his day's fasting, and there is no way to repeat an act of worship once it has already been completed. If the plane takes off before sunset and he wants to complete that day's fast during the journey, he should not break his fast until the sun has set from wherever he is in the air. The pilot is not permitted to bring the plane down to an altitude from which the sun cannot be seen just for the purposes of breaking the fast, for this would just be a kind of trickery. If the pilot were to bring the plane down lower for a genuine reason though, and the disk of the sun

---

25. Ittifaful Kiram

disappears as a result, he may break his fast.[26]

Nāfi' narrated: "Ibn Umar used to leave to go to Al-Ghābah (a place near Al-Madīnah). He would neither break his fast, nor shorten his *salāt*?"

The Fast of Bus Drivers

The ruling of travel is applied to the drivers. They may shorten and combine the prayers and break the fast. If someone says, "When do they fast since their work is continuous?" We answer, "They fast during the days of winter, because its days are short and cool." In reference to drivers who work inside of the cities, they do not have the ruling of the traveler and it is obligatory on them to fast.[27]

Same ruling applies to pilots, and airline employees even if their travel is daily. The same applies to sailors who have a home on land. But if the sailor has his wife and all he needs with him on the ship and is constantly traveling, then he is not allowed to break his fast or shorten his prayers. If nomadic Bedouins are traveling from their winter home to their summer home or vice versa, they are allowed to break their fast and shorten their prayers. Once they have settled in either their summer home or their winter home though, they should not break their fast or shorten their prayers, even if they are following their flocks.[28]

If the Traveller Arrives in the Land

If the traveler passes through a land that is not his land and he is not fasting, he does not have to abstain (from eating and drinking etc.) if his stay is going to be for four days or less.

Abdur Rehman bin Humaid Zuhri narrated: I asked As-Saib bin Yazid: "What did you hear from Allah's Messenger (ﷺ) about staying in Makkah?" He said: I heard Allah's Messenger (ﷺ) saying:

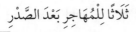

ثَلَاثًا لِلْمُهَاجِرِ بَعْدَ الصَّدْرِ

---

26. Fatawa of Shaykh Ibn Baz as quoted in Rulings pertaining to Ramadān, pg. 31, 32
27. Fatawa Islamiah: 3/296
28. Majmō' Al-Fatawa Ibn Taymiyah: 25/213 as quoted in Rulings pertaining to Ramadān, p. 33

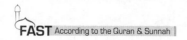

"Three days are permissible after entering."[29]

If he decided to stay in that land for more than four days, then he completes (the fast of) that day during which he arrived and he makes up for it (after Ramadān). He is also obliged to fast the rest of the days, because with this intention of his that has been mentioned, he has the same ruling as the residents and he does not have the ruling of the travelers according to the majority of the scholars.

Moreover if any person has settled firmly in the land and he stays in an air-conditioned hotel or in fancy castle or a building or anything similar, and his needs and luxurious accommodations are fulfilled while he enjoys what the residents enjoy of furnishings, beds, food, air conditioners are complete service, then in this situation he is considered a resident. He is not truly considered on a journey, which is a piece of the torment:

Abu Hurairah (ﷺ) narrated that the Prophet (ﷺ) said:

$$السَّفَرُ قِطْعَةٌ مِنْ الْعَذَابِ يَمْنَعُ أَحَدَكُمْ طَعَامَهُ وَشَرَابَهُ وَنَوْمَهُ فَإِذَا$$
$$قَضَى نَهْمَتَهُ فَلْيُعَجِّلْ إِلَى أَهْلِهِ$$

"Traveling is a kind of torture as it prevents one from eating, drinking and sleeping (properly). So, when one's needs are fulfilled, one should return quickly to one's family."[30]

I do not think that this type of person may break his fast or shorten the prayer. Rather, he is like the resident.[31]

If any person starts Ramadān in one city and then travels to another city where the people started fasting before him or after him, he should follow the ruling governing the people to whom he has traveled. He should only end Ramadān when they end Ramadān, even if it means that he is fasting more than thirty days, because the Prophet (ﷺ) said:

"Fast when everyone is fasting and break your fast when everyone is

---

29. Ibn Majah: 1073
30. Bukhari: 1804
31. Fatawa Islamiah: 3/294, 295

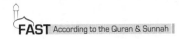

breaking their fast."

If this means that his fast is less than twenty nine days, he must make it up after Eid, because the *hijri* month cannot be less than twenty nine days.[32]

The Permission for the One at War to Break the Fast

Qaza'ah narrated to me: "I came to Abu Sa'eed Al-Khudri (☀) while he was surrounded by people. When the people dispersed from around him, I said: 'I am going to ask you about what these people were asking.' I asked him about fasting while travelling. He said: 'We travelled with the Messenger of Allah (☀) to Makkah when we were fasting. We made a stop and the Messenger of Allah (☀) said:

$$ إِنَّكُمْ مُصَبِّحُو عَدُوِّكُمْ وَالْفِطْرُ أَقْوَى لَكُمْ فَأَفْطِرُوا $$

"You have drawn near to your enemy, and breaking the fast will make you stronger, so break the fast."

This was a concession, so some of us fasted and some did not. Then we made another stop and he said: "In the morning you are going to meet your enemy. And breaking the fast will make you stronger, so break the fast." He emphasized it (the second time), so we broke the fast. Then he said: "I remember we fasted with the Messenger of Allah (☀) after that, when travelling.""[33]

Student's Exams are no excuse

Student's exams are no excuse for a person breaking the fast during Ramadān, and it is not permissible to obey one's parents in breaking the fast because of having exams. There is no obedience to any created being if it involves disobedience to the creator.[34]

---

32. Fatawh as-*Siyām* by Shaykh Ibn Baz, pg.15, 16
33. Muslim: 1120
34. Fatawa al-Lajnah ad-Da'imah: 10/241

If a person feels extreme hunger or thirst

If a person feels extreme hunger or thirst, and fears that he may die or that some of his faculties may be irreparably damaged, and he has credible grounds for believing this to be so, he may break his fast and make up for it later on, as saving one's life is obligatory. It is not permissible though, to break one's fast because of bearable hardship or because one feels tired or is afraid of some imagined illness. People who work in physically demanding jobs are not permitted to break their fast, and they must have the intention at night of fasting the following day. If they cannot stop working and they are afraid that some harm may befall them during the day, or they face some extreme hardship that causes them to break their fast, then they should eat only what is enough to help them bear the hardship, then they should refrain from eating until sunset, but they must make the fast up later. Workers in physically demanding jobs, such as working with furnaces and smelting metals, should try to change their hours so that they work at night or take their holidays during Ramadān. They should do so even if their leave is unpaid, but if this is not possible, then they should look for another job where they can combine their religious and worldly duties.

"And whoever fears Allah and keeps his duty to Him,
He will make a way for him to get out (from every
difficulty). And He will provide him from (sources)
he could never imagine." (Al-Talaaq 65:2-3)[35]

---

35. Fatawa al-Lajnah ad-Da'imah: 10/233-235, Rulings pertaining to Ramadān: pg. 36, 37

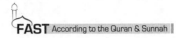

Some Related Issues to Ramadan

Umrah During Ramadān

Umm Maʿqil narrated that the Prophet (ﷺ) said:

$$عُمْرَةٌ فِي رَمَضَانَ تَعْدِلُ حَجَّةً$$

"Umrah during Ramadān is equal to Hajj."[1]

Explanation

"Equal to Hajj" means the return and reward to which Hajj is eligible. It does not mean that it will serve as a substitute for Hajj and absolve one from the need to perform it. This distinction of ʿUmrah in the month of Ramadān is perhaps for the reasons, that in this way two acts of worship are combined at one time.

Giving Food to a Fasting Person

Zaid bin Khalid Al-Juhani narrated that the Messenger of Allah (ﷺ) said:

$$مَنْ فَطَّرَ صَائِماً كَانَ لَهُ مِثْلُ أَجْرِهِ غَيْرَ أَنَّهُ لاَ يُنْقِصُ مِنْ أَجْرِ الصَّائِمِ شَيْئاً$$

---

1. Tirmidhi: 939

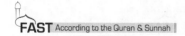

"Whoever provides food for a fasting person to break
his fast with, then for him is the same reward as his
(the fasting person's fast), without anything being di-
minished from the reward of the fasting person."[2]

'Abdullāh bin Zubair (ﷺ) narrated that the Messenger of Allah (ﷺ) broke
his fast with Sa'd bin Mu'adh and said:

أَفْطَرَ عِنْدَكُمُ الصَّائِمُونَ وَأَكَلَ طَعَامَكُمُ الْأَبْرَارُ وَصَلَّتْ عَلَيْكُمُ
الْـمَلَائِكَةُ

*"Aftara indakumus-saimun, wa akala ta'amakumal-
adbrar, was sallat 'alaikumul-mala'ika*

May fasting people break their fast with you, may
the righteous eat your food, and may the angels send
blessing upon you."[3]

The Prophet (ﷺ) used to be More Generous in the Month of Ramadān

Ibn 'Abbas (ﷺ) narrated:

كَانَ النَّبِيُّ (ﷺ) أَجْوَدَ النَّاسِ بِالْخَيْرِ وَكَانَ أَجْوَدُ مَا يَكُونُ فِي
رَمَضَانَ حِينَ يَلْقَاهُ جِبْرِيلُ

"The Prophet (ﷺ) was the most generous amongst
the people, and he used to be more so in the month of
Ramadān when Jibril used to visit him during every
night of Ramadān until the end of the month."

وَكَانَ جِبْرِيلُ عَلَيْهِ السَّلَام يَلْقَاهُ كُلَّ لَيْلَةٍ فِي رَمَضَانَ حَتَّى يَنْسَلِخَ
يَعْرِضُ عَلَيْهِ النَّبِيُّ (ﷺ) الْقُرْآنَ فَإِذَا لَقِيَهُ جِبْرِيلُ عَلَيْهِ السَّلَام كَانَ

---

2. Tirmidhi: 807
3. Ibn Majah: 1747

$$أَجْوَدَ بِالْخَيْرِ مِنَ الرِّيحِ الْـمُرْسَلَةِ$$

"The Prophet (ﷺ) used to recite the Noble Qur'ān to Jibril, and when Jibrīl met him, he used to be more generous than the fair wind [sent by Allah with glad tidings (rain) in readiness and haste to do charitable deeds]."[4]

Imam Ahmad records this *hadith* with the additional words at its end, "He was not asked for anything except that he would give it."

Giving and generosity are attributes that Allah likes for Muslims to have, this is because Allah is the most Generous and Giving of all.

Allah's Messenger (ﷺ) said:

$$إِنَّ اللهَ جَوَادٌ يُـحِبُّ الْـجُوْدَ$$

"Indeed Allah is Generous and He Loves generosity."[5]

At another place Allah's Messenger (ﷺ) said that Allah says:

$$وَلَوْ أَنَّ أَوَّلَكُمْ وَآخِرَكُمْ وَحَيَّكُمْ وَمَيِّتَكُمْ وَرَطْبَكُمْ وَيَابِسَكُمْ اجْتَمَعُوا فِي صَعِيدٍ وَاحِدٍ فَسَأَلَ كُلُّ إِنْسَانٍ مِنْكُمْ مَا بَلَغَتْ أُمْنِيَّتُهُ فَأَعْطَيْتُ كُلَّ سَائِلٍ مِنْكُمْ مَا سَأَلَ مَا نَقَصَ ذَلِكَ مِنْ مُلْكِي إِلاَّ كَمَا لَوْ أَنَّ أَحَدَكُمْ مَرَّ بِالْبَحْرِ فَغَمَسَ فِيهِ إِبْرَةً ثُمَّ رَفَعَهَا إِلَيْهِ ذَلِكَ بِأَنِّي جَوَادٌ مَاجِدٌ أَفْعَلُ مَا أُرِيدُ عَطَائِي كَلاَمٌ وَعَذَابِي كَلاَمٌ إِنَّمَا أَمْرِي لِشَيْءٍ إِذَا أَرَدْتُهُ أَنْ أَقُولَ لَهُ كُنْ فَيَكُونُ$$

"If the first of you and the last of you, the living among you, and the dead among you, the fresh among you and the dry among you were placed together upon one plateau, and each person among them were to ask

4. Bukhari: 1902
5. Tirmidhi: 2799

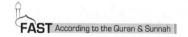

for his utmost desire, and I were to give each what he asked for, that would not diminish from My sovereignty, except as if one of were to pass by an ocean and dip a needle into it then remove it. That is because I am the Most Liberal without need, the Most Generous, doing as I will. I give by My speech and I punish by My speech, whenever I will something I only say: "Be" and it shall be."[6]

The act of fasting provides the fortunate, wealthy members of society to experience for a time the pain and suffering which millions of people go through everyday without food, water and other basic necessities of life. Fasting bridges the gap between the rich and the poor, the sustained and the impoverished, the fulfilled and the needy. This experience should then inspire compassion and mercy, which is *mani*fest by generosity of wealth and time to help those in need. Muslims are encouraged especially during this month to go out and feed the hungry and to spend their wealth on good causes.

Abu Hurairah (	&) narrated that the Prophet (	&) said:

مَا مِنْ يَوْمٍ يُصْبِحُ الْعِبَادُ فِيهِ إِلَّا مَلَكَانِ يَنْزِلَانِ فَيَقُولُ أَحَدُهُمَا اللَّهُمَّ أَعْطِ مُنْفِقًا خَلَفًا وَيَقُولُ الْآخَرُ اللَّهُمَّ أَعْطِ مُـمْسِكًا تَلَفًا

"Every day two angels came down (from the heaven) and one of them says: 'O Allah! Compensate every person who spends in Your Cause,' and the other (angel) says: 'O Allah! Destroy every miser.'"

In another narration Allah's Messenger (	&) said:

"The example of an alms-giver and a miser is like the example of two persons wearing two iron cloaks from their breasts to their collar bones; and when the alms-giver gives in charity, the cloak becomes capacious till it covers his whole body to such an extent

6. Tirmidhi: 2495

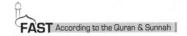

that it hides his fingertips and covers his footprints (obliterates his tracks). When the miser wants to spend, it (the iron cloak) sticks and (its) every ring gets stuck to its place, he tries to widen it, but it does not become wide."

Abu Hurairah (ﷺ) narrated that the Prophet (ﷺ) said:

سَبْعَةٌ يُظِلُّهُمْ اللهُ تَعَالَى فِي ظِلِّهِ يَوْمَ لَا ظِلَّ إِلَّا ظِلُّهُ إِمَامٌ عَدْلٌ وَشَابٌّ نَشَأَ فِي عِبَادَةِ اللهِ وَرَجُلٌ قَلْبُهُ مُعَلَّقٌ فِي الْمَسَاجِدِ وَرَجُلَانِ تَحَابَّا فِي اللهِ اجْتَمَعَا عَلَيْهِ وَتَفَرَّقَا عَلَيْهِ وَرَجُلٌ دَعَتْهُ امْرَأَةٌ ذَاتُ مَنْصِبٍ وَجَمَالٍ فَقَالَ إِنِّي أَخَافُ اللهَ وَرَجُلٌ تَصَدَّقَ بِصَدَقَةٍ فَأَخْفَاهَا حَتَّى لَا تَعْلَمَ شِمَالُهُ مَا تُنْفِقُ يَمِينُهُ وَرَجُلٌ ذَكَرَ اللهَ خَالِيًا فَفَاضَتْ عَيْنَاهُ

"Seven people will be shaded by Allah under His shade on the Day (of Resurrection) when there will be no shade except His. They are:

1. A just ruler.
2. A young man who has been brought up in the worship of Allah, (i.e. worships Allah Alone sincerely from his childhood).
3. A man whose heart is attached to the mosques [who offers the five compulsory congregational *salāt* (prayers) in the mosques].
4. Two persons who love each other only for Allah's sake and they meet and part in Allah's cause only.
5. A man who refuses the call of a charming woman of noble birth for illegal sexual intercourse with her and says: 'I am afraid of Allah.'
6. A person who practices charity so secretly that his left hand does not know what his right hand has given (i.e. nobody knows how much he has given in charity).

7.	A person who remembers Allah in seclusion and his eyes become flooded with tears."[7]

The Virtues for the Fasting Person when others are Eating in his Presence

Umm 'Umarah (🙏) narrated that the Messenger of Allah (🙏) came to us and we brought food for him. Some of those who were with him were fasting, and the Messenger of Allah (🙏) said:

الصَّائِمُ إِذَا أُكِلَ عِنْدَهُ الطَّعَامُ صَلَّتْ عَلَيْهِ الْـمَلاَئِكَةُ

"If food is eaten in the presence of one who is fasting, the angels send blessing upon him."[8]

The Middle Night of Sha'bān

'Āishah (🙏) narrated: "I could not find the Messenger of Allah (🙏) one night. So I left and found him at Al-Baqī'. He said: 'Did you fear you had been wronged by Allah and His Messenger?' I said: 'O Messenger of Allah! I thought that you had gone to one of your wives.' So he said: 'Indeed Allah, Mighty and Sublime is He, descends to the lowest Heavens during the night of the middle of Sha'bān to grant forgiveness to more than the number of hairs on the sheep of (Banū) Kalb.'"[9]

Abu Mūsā Al-Ash'ari (🙏) narrated that the Messenger of Allah (🙏) said: "Allah looks down on the night of the middle of Sha'bān and forgives all His creation, apart from the idolater and the mushahin (opponent)."[10]

'Ali bin Abu Talib (🙏) narrated that the Messenger of Allah (🙏) said: "When it is the night of the middle of Sha'bān, spend its night in prayer and observe a fast on the day. For Allah descends at sunset on that night to the lowest heaven and says: 'Is there no one who will ask Me for forgiveness, that I may forgive him? Is there no one who will ask Me for

---

7. Bukhari: 1442, 1443
8. Ibn Majah: 1748
9. Tirmidhi: 739
10. Ibn Majah: 1390

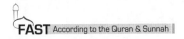

provision, that I may provide for him? Is there no one who is afflicted by trouble, that I may relieve him?' And so on, until dawn comes."[11]

These three *hadith*s are very famous among the people and many orators narrate them in their speeches and sermons, but we should remember that these narrations are unauthentic. Imām Suyuti, Abu Talib Makki, *Imam Ghazali* and Shaikh Abdul Qadir Jilani quoted many weak and denounced narrations in favour of the virtue of the fifteenth night of Sh'ban, and all these narrations are baseless.[12]

Some Weak Narrations about Ramadān

We mentioned here some weak and unauthentic narrations because in many books these narrations are mentioned without criticism. Many orators also narrate these narrations in their speeches and sermons. People believe them to be authentic.

'Āmir bin Mas'ūd narrated that the Prophet (ﷺ) said:

$$\text{الْغَنِيمَةُ الْبَارِدَةُ الصَّوْمُ فِي الشِّتَاءِ}$$

"Fasting during the winter is an easy reward."[13]

Abdur-Rahman bin 'Auf narrated that the Messenger of Allah (ﷺ) said:

$$\text{صَائِمُ رَمَضَانَ فِي السَّفَرِ كَالْـمُفْطِرِ فِي الْحَضَرِ}$$

"The one who fasts during Ramadān while travelling is like the one who breaks his fast when not travelling."[14]

Ibn Abbas (ﷺ) narrated that the Prophet (ﷺ) said:

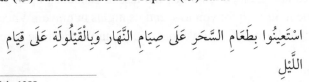

$$\text{اسْتَعِينُوا بِطَعَامِ السَّحَرِ عَلَى صِيَامِ النَّهَارِ وَبِالْقَيْلُولَةِ عَلَى قِيَامِ اللَّيْلِ}$$

---

11. Ibn Majah: 1388
12. Ma'ārif As-Sunan: 5/319
13. Tirmidhi: 797
14. Ibn Majah: 1666

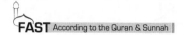

"Seek help by eating suhur for fasting that day and by taking a brief rest (at midday) for praying at night."[15]

Abu Hurairah (ﷺ) narrated that the Messenger of Allah (ﷺ) said:

$$لِكُلِّ شَيْءٍ زَكَاةٌ وَزَكَاةُ الْجَسَدِ الصَّوْمُ$$

"For everything there is *zakah*, and the *zakah* of the body is fasting."

(A narrator in one of the chains) Mukriz added in his narration: "And the Messenger of Allah (ﷺ) said: 'Fasting is half of patience.'"[16]

'Āishah (ﷺ) narrated that the Prophet (ﷺ) said:

$$إِذَا نَزَلَ الرَّجُلُ بِقَوْمٍ فَلاَ يَصُومُ إِلاَّ بِإِذْنِهِمْ$$

"If a man stays among a people, he should not fast without their permission."[17]

Abdul-Rahman bin An-Nu'man bin Ma'bad bin Hawdhah narrated from his father from his grandfather from the Prophet (ﷺ) that he ordered scented *ithmid* be used at the time of sleep and said: "A person fasting should abstain from it."[18]

Anas bin Malik (ﷺ) narrated that he used to apply kohl while fasting.[19]

An-Nadr bin Shaiban said: I said to Abu Salmah bin 'Abdur-Rahman: "Tell me something that you heard from your father which he heard from the Messenger of Allah (ﷺ) with no one in between your father and the Messenger of Allah (ﷺ) concerning the month of Ramadān." He said: "Yes; my father said: The Messenger of Allah (ﷺ) said: 'Allah, may He be Blessed and Exalted, enjoined the fast of Ramadān upon you, and I have made it *Sunnah* for you to spend its nights in prayer. Whoever fasts it and spends its nights in prayer out of faith and in the hope of reward, he

---

15. Ibn Majah: 1693
16. Ibn Majah: 1745
17. Ibn Majah: 1763
18. Abu Dawud: 2377
19. Abu Dawud: 2378

will emerge from his sins as on the day his mother bore him.'"[20]

Abu Firas narrated that he heard 'Abdullāh bin 'Amr say: "I heard the Messenger of Allah (ﷺ) say:

صَامَ نُوحٌ الدَّهْرَ إِلاَّ يَوْمَ الْفِطْرِ وَيَوْمَ الأَضْحَى

'(Prophet) Nuh fasted for a lifetime, except for the Days of Fiter and Adha'.'"[21]

Umm Hani' (ﷺ) narrated that the Messenger of Allah (ﷺ) entered upon her and asked for some drink, and he drank. Then he offered it to her and she drank it. Then she said: "O Messenger of Allah! I was fasting." So the Messenger of Allah (ﷺ) said:

الصَّائِمُ الْمُتَطَوِّعُ أَمِينُ نَفْسِهِ إِنْ شَاءَ صَامَ وَإِنْ شَاءَ أَفْطَرَ

"The one fasting a voluntary fast is the trustee for himself; if he wishes he fasts, and if he wishes he breaks."[22]

In another narration Allah's Messenger (ﷺ) asked her: "Were you making up something?" She said: "No" He said: "If it is voluntary, it will not harm you."[23]

'Āishah (ﷺ) narrated: "Hafsah and I were both fasting when we were presented some food that we really wanted, so we ate from it. The Messenger of Allah (ﷺ) came and Hafsah beat me to him – she was the daughter of her father – and she said: 'O Messenger of Allah (ﷺ) we were both fasting when we were presented with some food that we wanted, so we ate from it.' He said: 'Make up another day in its place.'"[24]

---

20. Nasā'i: 2212
21. Ibn Majah: 1714
22. Tirmidhi: 732
23. Abu Dawud: 2456
24. Tirmidhi: 735

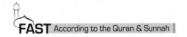

Making Up for Ramadan

Salmah bin Al-Akwa' (&) narrated: "When the following verse was revealed:

$$وَعَلَى الَّذِينَ يُطِيقُونَهُ فِدْيَةٌ طَعَامُ مِسْكِينٍ$$

'.....And as for those who can fast with difficulty, (e.g. and old man), they have (a choice either to fast or) to feed a Miskīn (poor person) for every day....' Those who wanted to break the fast and pay the *fidyah* (did so), until this verse was revealed:

$$فَمَنْ شَهِدَ مِنْكُمُ الشَّهْرَ فَلْيَصُمْهُ$$

'....So whoever of you sights (the crescent on the first night of) the month (of Ramadān i.e. is present at his home), he must observe *Saūm* that month....'"[1]

It is desirable for one to hasten to make up for the missed fasts of Ramadān so as not to be accountable for it. It is also desirable to make up for the missed days of fasting consecutively. Morever, it is also permissible for one to delay the make up fast, as its compensation time is flexible.

Abū Salamah narrated: "I heard 'Āishah say: 'I would owe Ramadān fasts, and I would not be able to make them up until Sha'bān. Because of being busy with the Messenger of Allah (&) or for the Messenger of Allah (&).'"[2]

---

1. Muslim: 1145 (150)
2. Muslim: 1146

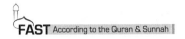

If one delays making up for the missed days of Ramadān until the next Ramadān begins, one is to observe fasting of the present Ramadān and to make up for the missed days afterwards. As for a person who has delayed making up for such unperformed fasting due to a legal excuse that prevented him from doing so, he does not have to do anything except making up for it (i.e. there is no expiation for it). Yet, if a person has delayed making up for fasting for no legal excuse, he is to make up for the missed days in addition to the feeding of a poor person for each day he missed, with a quantity of half a Sā' of food in expiation for each day.[3]

Whoever died and ought to have observed *Saūm*

'Āishah (🙏) narrated that Allah's Messenger (🙏) said:

مَنْ مَاتَ وَعَلَيْهِ صِيَامٌ صَامَ عَنْهُ وَلِيُّهُ

"Whoever died and he ought to have observed *saūm* (the missed days of Ramadān) then his guardians must observe *saūm* on his behalf."[4]

Ibn Abbas (🙏) narrated: A man came to the Prophet (🙏) and said, "O Allah's Messenger! My mother died and she ought to have observed one month (for her missed Ramadān). Shall I observe *saūm* on her behalf?" The Prophet (🙏) replied in the affirmative and said:

فَدَيْنُ اللهِ أَحَقُّ أَنْ يُقْضَى

"Allah's debts have more right to be paid."[5]

'Abdullāh bin Buraidah narrated that his father said: "While I was sitting with the Messenger of Allah (🙏) a woman came to him and said: 'I gave a slave woman in charity to my mother, then she died.' He said: 'Your reward is assured, and she (the slave woman) has been returned to you as inheritance.' She said: 'O Messenger of Allah, she owned one month of fasting, should I fast on her behalf?' He said: 'Fast on her behalf.' She

---

3. Al-Mulakhsul Fiqhi
4. Bukhari: 1952
5. Bukhari: 1953

said: 'She never went for Hajj, should I perform Hajj on her behalf?' He
said: 'Perform Hajj on her behalf.'"[6]

Explanation

A sick person who hopes to recover should wait until he gets better, and
then make up for the fasts he has missed. He is not allowed to merely
feed the poor. The person who is suffering from a chronic illness and has
no hope of recovery and an elderly person who is unable to fast should
feed a poor person with half a Sa' of the staple food of the country for
every day that he missed. (Half a Sa' is roughly equivalent to one and a
half kilograms of rice.) It is permissible for him to do this all at once on
one day at the end of the month, or he may feed one poor person every
day. He must do this by given actual food due to the wording of the *ayah*
and he cannot do it by giving money to the poor[7].

He may however, give money to a trustworthy person or charitable or-
ganization to buy food and distribute it to the poor on his behalf.

If a sick person does not fast in Ramadān while waiting to recover in
order that he can make the days up later, and then finds out that his sickness is chronic, he must feed a poor person for every day that he did not
fast.[8]

If a person is waiting to recover from his illness and hopes to get better
but then dies, there is no "debt" owned by him or his heirs. If a person's
sickness is considered to be chronic and he does not fast but feeds the
poor instead, then medical advances result in the discovery of a remedy
which he is administered and then recovers, he does not have to make up
the fasts he missed, because he did what he had to do at that time.[9]

If a sick person recovers and is able to make up the missed fasts but does
not do so before he dies, money should be taken from his estate to feed
a poor person for every day that he missed. If any of his relatives wants
to fast on his behalf, then this is fine, for it was reported in Bukhari and

---

6. Muslim: 1149

7. Fatawa al-Lajnah Ad-Daa'imah, 10/198

8. From the Fatawa of Shaykh Ibn 'Uthaymeen

9. Fatawa al-Lajnah ad-Daa'imah, 10/195

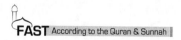

Muslim that the messenger of Allah (ﷺ) said:

"Whoever dies owing some fasts let his heir fast on his behalf."[10]

---

10. Rulings pertaining to Ramadān: pg. 37, 38

Fasting as an Atonement

These verses speak of fasting as an atonement for things such as shaving the head while in a state of *ihram*, when one is permitted to do so, due to illness or some harm to the head, because of the inability to provide a sacrificial animal, killing a person by mistake who is protected by a treaty, breaking one's oath, killing game while in a state of *ihram* and *zihar*. Allah Most High says:

وَأَتِمُّوا الْحَجَّ وَالْعُمْرَةَ لِلَّهِ فَإِنْ أُحْصِرْتُمْ فَمَا اسْتَيْسَرَ مِنَ الْهَدْيِ وَلَا تَحْلِقُوا رُءُوسَكُمْ حَتَّى يَبْلُغَ الْهَدْيُ مَحِلَّهُ فَمَن كَانَ مِنكُم مَّرِيضًا أَوْ بِهِ أَذًى مِّن رَّأْسِهِ فَفِدْيَةٌ مِّن صِيَامٍ أَوْ صَدَقَةٍ أَوْ نُسُكٍ فَإِذَا أَمِنتُمْ فَمَن تَمَتَّعَ بِالْعُمْرَةِ إِلَى الْحَجِّ فَمَا اسْتَيْسَرَ مِنَ الْهَدْيِ فَمَن لَّمْ يَجِدْ فَصِيَامُ ثَلَاثَةِ أَيَّامٍ فِي الْحَجِّ وَسَبْعَةٍ إِذَا رَجَعْتُمْ تِلْكَ عَشَرَةٌ كَامِلَةٌ ذَلِكَ لِمَن لَّمْ يَكُنْ أَهْلُهُ حَاضِرِي الْمَسْجِدِ الْحَرَامِ وَاتَّقُوا اللَّهَ وَاعْلَمُوا أَنَّ اللَّهَ شَدِيدُ الْعِقَابِ ﴿١٩٦﴾

"And perform properly (i.e. all the ceremonies according to the ways of Prophet Muhammad), the Hajj and 'Umrah (i.e. the pilgrimage to Makkah) for Allah. But if you are prevented (from completing them), sacrifice a *hadi* (animal, i.e. a sheep, a cow, or a camel, etc.) such as you can afford, and do not shave your heads until the *hadi* reaches the place of sacrifice. And whosoever of you is ill or has an ailment in his scalp (necessitating shaving), he must pay *Fi-*

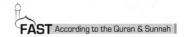

dyah (ransom) of either observing *Saūm* (three days) or giving sadaqah (charity – feeding six poor persons) or offering sacrifice (one sheep). Then if you are in safety and whosoever performs the 'Umrah in the months of Hajj, before (performing) the Hajj (i.e. Hajj At-Tamattu'), he must slaughter a *hadi* such as he can afford, but if he cannot afford it, he should observe *Saūm* three days during the Hajj and seven days after his return (to his home), making ten days in all. This is for him whose family is not presented at Al-Masjid Al-Haram (i.e. non-resident of Makkah). And fear Allah much and know that Allah is severe in punishment." (Al-Baqarah 2:196)

Killing a Person by Mistake

Allah Most High says:

$$\text{وَإِن كَانَ مِن قَوۡمٍ بَيۡنَكُمۡ وَبَيۡنَهُم مِّيثَٰقٌ فَدِيَةٌ}$$
$$\text{مُّسَلَّمَةٌ إِلَىٰٓ أَهۡلِهِۦ وَتَحۡرِيرُ رَقَبَةٍ مُّؤۡمِنَةٍ فَمَن لَّمۡ يَجِدۡ}$$
$$\text{فَصِيَامُ شَهۡرَيۡنِ مُتَتَابِعَيۡنِ تَوۡبَةً مِّنَ ٱللَّهِ وَكَانَ ٱللَّهُ عَلِيمًا}$$
$$\text{حَكِيمًا}$$

"And if he belonged to a people with whom you have a treaty of mutual alliance, compensation (blood money – diyah) must be paid to his family and a believing slave must be freed. And whosoever finds this (the penance of freeing a slave) beyond his means, he must fast for two consecutive months in order to seek repentance from Allah. And Allah is ever All-Knowing, Most Wise. (An-Nisā' 4:92)

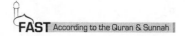

Breaking One's Oath

Allah Most High says:

لَا يُؤَاخِذُكُمُ ٱللَّهُ بِٱللَّغْوِ فِيٓ أَيْمَٰنِكُمْ وَلَٰكِن يُؤَاخِذُكُم بِمَا عَقَّدتُّمُ ٱلْأَيْمَٰنَ فَكَفَّٰرَتُهُۥٓ إِطْعَامُ عَشَرَةِ مَسَٰكِينَ مِنْ أَوْسَطِ مَا تُطْعِمُونَ أَهْلِيكُمْ أَوْ كِسْوَتُهُمْ أَوْ تَحْرِيرُ رَقَبَةٍۖ فَمَن لَّمْ يَجِدْ فَصِيَامُ ثَلَٰثَةِ أَيَّامٍۚ ذَٰلِكَ كَفَّٰرَةُ أَيْمَٰنِكُمْ إِذَا حَلَفْتُمْۚ وَٱحْفَظُوٓاْ أَيْمَٰنَكُمْۚ كَذَٰلِكَ يُبَيِّنُ ٱللَّهُ لَكُمْ ءَايَٰتِهِۦ لَعَلَّكُمْ تَشْكُرُونَ ﴿٨٩﴾

"Allah will not punish you for what is unintentional in your oaths, but He will punish you for your deliberate oaths; for its expiation (a deliberate oath) feed ten masakeen (poor persons), on a scale of the average of that with which you feed your own families; or clothe them; or manumit a slave. But whosoever cannot afford (that), then he should fast for three days. That is the expiation for oaths when you have sworn. And protect your oaths (i.e. do not swear much). Thus Allah makes clear to you His Ayat (Proofs, evidence, verses) that you may be grateful." (Al-Ma'dah 5:89)

Killing Game while in a State of Ihram

Allah Most High says:

يَٰٓأَيُّهَا ٱلَّذِينَ ءَامَنُواْ لَا تَقْتُلُواْ ٱلصَّيْدَ وَأَنتُمْ حُرُمٌۚ وَمَن قَتَلَهُۥ مِنكُم مُّتَعَمِّدًا فَجَزَآءٌ مِّثْلُ مَا قَتَلَ مِنَ ٱلنَّعَمِ يَحْكُمُ بِهِۦ ذَوَا عَدْلٍ مِّنكُمْ هَدْيًۢا بَٰلِغَ ٱلْكَعْبَةِ أَوْ كَفَّٰرَةٌ طَعَامُ مَسَٰكِينَ أَوْ عَدْلُ ذَٰلِكَ صِيَامًا لِّيَذُوقَ وَبَالَ أَمْرِهِۦۗ عَفَا ٱللَّهُ عَمَّا سَلَفَۚ وَمَنْ عَادَ فَيَنتَقِمُ ٱللَّهُ مِنْهُۗ وَٱللَّهُ عَزِيزٌ ذُو ٱنتِقَامٍ ﴿٩٥﴾

O, you who believe! Kill not game while you are in

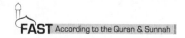

a state of *Ihram* for Hajj or "Umrah (Pilgrimage) and whosoever of you kills it intentionally, the penalty is an offering, brought to the Ka'bah of an eatable animal (i.e. sheep, goat, cow, etc.) equivalent to the one he killed, as adjudged by two just men among you; or, for expiation, he should feed Masakeen (poor persons), or its equivalent in *Saūm*, that he may taste the heaviness (punishment) of his deed. Allah has forgiven what is past, but whosoever commits it again, Allah will take retribution from him. And Allah is Al-mighty, Most Able in Retribution." (Ma'idah 5:95)

Zihar

Allah Most High says:

وَٱلَّذِينَ يُظَٰهِرُونَ مِن نِّسَآئِهِمْ ثُمَّ يَعُودُونَ لِمَا قَالُواْ فَتَحْرِيرُ رَقَبَةٍ مِّن قَبْلِ أَن يَتَمَآسَّا ۚ ذَٰلِكُمْ تُوعَظُونَ بِهِۦ ۚ وَٱللَّهُ بِمَا تَعْمَلُونَ خَبِيرٌ ۝ فَمَن لَّمْ يَجِدْ فَصِيَامُ شَهْرَيْنِ مُتَتَابِعَيْنِ مِن قَبْلِ أَن يَتَمَآسَّا ۖ فَمَن لَّمْ يَسْتَطِعْ فَإِطْعَامُ سِتِّينَ مِسْكِينًا ۚ ذَٰلِكَ لِتُؤْمِنُواْ بِٱللَّهِ وَرَسُولِهِۦ ۚ وَتِلْكَ حُدُودُ ٱللَّهِ ۗ وَلِلْكَٰفِرِينَ عَذَابٌ أَلِيمٌ ۝

"And those who make unlawful to them (their wives) (by Az-*Zihar*) and wish to free themselves from what they uttered, (the penalty) in that case (is) the free-ing of a salve before they touch each other. That is an admonition to you (so that you may not return to such an ill thing). And Allah is fully Aware of what you do. And he who finds not (the money for freeing a slave) must fast two successive months before they both touch each other. And for him who is unable to do so, he should feed sixty of *Miskeen* (poor). That is in order that you may have perfect faith in Allah

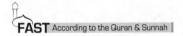

and His Messenger. These are the limits set by Allah. And for disbelievers, there is a painful torment." (Mujādilah 58:3, 4)

Zihar (الظهار) is derived from the word zahr meaning back, making resemblance between one's wife and the mother's back. This is a figure of speech in Arabic language which means that you are like my mother and unlawful for me in marriage. According to the terminology of the Shari'ah, *zihar* means comparing one's wife to one's mother, and making her unlawful for oneself. It is not considered a divorce in the Shari'ah but one has to make expiation for it before returning to his wife. Its expiation is to free a slave or fast for sixty days consecutively or to feed sixty poor persons. It is compulsory to bear one of these punishments.

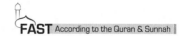

Days During Which the Fast in Prohibited

Not to observe *Saūm* for a day or two ahead of Ramadān

Abu Hurairah (ﷺ) narrated that the Messenger of Allah (ﷺ) said:

لاَ تَقَدَّمُوا رَمَضَانَ بِصَوْمِ يَوْمٍ وَلاَ يَوْمَيْنِ إِلاَّ رَجُلٌ كَانَ يَصُومُ صَوْمًا فَلْيَصُمْهُ

"Do not start fasting one or two days before Ramadān, except a man who (observes a regular) fast, then let him fast it."[1]

Al-Wisal

In Arabic *wisal* is a term used with reference to a person who does not break his fast in the evening but goes on observing it continuously on to the second day with no eating or drinking in between. This kind of fasting was only allowed to the Prophet (ﷺ).

Anas (ﷺ) narrated that the Prophet (ﷺ) said: "Do not practise *al-wisal*. The people said to the Prophet (ﷺ): "But you practise *al-wisal*?" The Prophet (ﷺ) replied:

لَسْتُ كَأَحَدٍ مِنْكُمْ إِنِّي أُطْعَمُ وَأُسْقَى أَوْ إِنِّي أَبِيتُ أُطْعَمُ وَأُسْقَى

1. Muslim: 1082

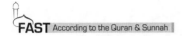

"I am not like any of you, for I am given food and drink (by Allah) during the night."[2]

Abū Sa'id (؈) narrated that he had heard the Prophet (؈) saying:

لاَ تُوَاصِلُوا فَأَيُّكُمْ أَرَادَ أَنْ يُوَاصِلَ فَلْيُوَاصِلْ حَتَّى السَّحَرِ

"Do not fast continuously (i.e., do not practise *al-wisal*), and if you intend to lengthen your *saūm* (fasting period), then carry it on only till the *sahar* (before the following dawn)."

The people said to him: "But you practise (*al-wisal*), O Allah's Messenger!" He replied:

إِنِّي لَسْتُ كَهَيْئَتِكُمْ إِنِّي أَبِيتُ لِي مُطْعِمٌ يُطْعِمُنِي وَسَاقٍ يَسْقِينِ

"I am not similar to you, for during the night I have One Who makes me eat and drink."[3]

In another narration:

نَهَى رَسُولُ اللهِ (؈) عَنْ الْوِصَالِ رَحْمَةً لَهُمْ

"Allah's Messenger (؈) forbade *Al-wisal* with mercy to them."

The Punishment for the Person who Practises Al-Wisal Very Often

Abu Hurairah (؈) narrated: Allah's Messenger (؈) forbade *Al-wisal* in observing *Saūm*. So one of the Muslim said to him, "But you practise *Al-wisal*, O Allah's Messenger!" The Prophet (؈) replied:

وَأَيُّكُمْ مِثْلِي إِنِّي أَبِيتُ يُطْعِمُنِي رَبِّي وَيَسْقِينِي

"Who amongst you is similar to me? I am given food

---

2. Bukhari: 1961
3. Bukhari: 1963

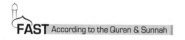

and drink during night by my Lord."

So when people refused to stop *al-wisal*, the Prophet (ﷺ) observed *saūm* day and night continuously along with them for a day and then another day and then they saw the crescent of the moon (of the month of Shawwāl). The Prophet (ﷺ) said to them (angrily):

لَوْ تَأَخَّرَ لَزِدْتُكُمْ كَالتَّنْكِيلِ لَهُمْ حِينَ أَبَوْا أَنْ يَنْتَهُوا

"If it (the crescent) had not appeared, I would have made you observe *saūm* for a longer period." That was as a punishment for them when they refused to stop (practicing *al-wisal*).[4]

Abu Hurairah (ﷺ) narrated that the Prophet (ﷺ) said twice: "(O you people) be cautious! Do not practise *al-wisal*." The people said to him: "But you practise *al-wisal*?" The Prophet (ﷺ) replied:

إِنِّي أَبِيتُ يُطْعِمُنِي رَبِّي وَيَسْقِينِ فَاكْلَفُوا مِنَ الْعَمَلِ مَا تُطِيقُونَ

"My Lord gives me food and drink during night. Do that much deeds which are within your ability."[5]

Anas (ﷺ) said: "The Messenger of Allah (ﷺ) performed *wisal* during the beginning of Ramadān and some of the Muslims performed *wisal*. News of that reached him and he said:

لَوْ مُدَّ لَنَا الشَّهْرُ لَوَاصَلْنَا وِصَالاً يَدَعُ الْمُتَعَمِّقُونَ تَعَمُّقَهُمْ إِنَّكُمْ لَسْتُمْ مِثْلِي - إِنِّى أَظَلُّ يُطْعِمُنِى رَبِّى وَيَسْقِينِى

"If the month is lengthened for us, we will fast continuously, so that those who go to extremes will give up their extreme ways. You are not like me – I am continually fed and given to drink by my Lord."[6]

---

4. Bukhari: 1965
5. Bukhari: 1966
6. Muslim: 1104 (60)

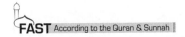

Observing *Saūm* Continuously throughout the Life

'Abdullāh bin 'Amr bin Al-'As said that the Messenger of Allah (ﷺ) was told that he ('Abdullāh) had said: "I shall most certainly spend my nights in standing (in prayer) and my days fasting for as long as I live." The Messenger of Allah (ﷺ) said: "Are you the one who said that?" I said to him: "I did say it, O Messenger of Allah." The Messenger of Allah (ﷺ) said:

فَإِنَّكَ لَا تَسْتَطِيعُ ذَلِكَ فَصُمْ وَأَفْطِرْ وَقُمْ وَنَمْ وَصُمْ مِنْ الشَّهْرِ
ثَلَاثَةَ أَيَّامٍ فَإِنَّ الْحَسَنَةَ بِعَشْرِ أَمْثَالِهَا وَذَلِكَ مِثْلُ صِيَامِ الدَّهْرِ

"You are not able to do that. Fast and break your fast, sleep and getup (to pray). Fast three days every month, for each deed brings a tenfold reward, and that will be like fasting for a lifetime."

I said: "I am able to do better than that." He said: "Fast one day and break your fast for two days." I said: "I am able to do better than that, O Messenger of Allah." He said: "Fast one day and break your fast one day (i.e., fast alternate days). That is the fast of Dawud, peace be upon him, and it is the best way of fasting." I said: "I am able to do better than that." The Messenger of Allah (ﷺ) said: "There is nothing better than that."

'Abdullāh bin 'Amr (ﷺ) said: "If I had accepted the three days that the Messenger of Allah (ﷺ) spoke of, that would have been dearer to me than my family and my wealth."[7]

'Abdullāh bin 'Amr bin Al-'Ās (ﷺ) narrated: The Prophet (ﷺ) said to me: "You observe *saūm* daily all the year and offer *salāt* (every night) all night?" I replied in the affirmative. The Prophet (ﷺ) said:

إِنَّكَ إِذَا فَعَلْتَ ذَلِكَ هَجَمَتْ لَهُ الْعَيْنُ وَنَفِهَتْ لَهُ النَّفْسُ لَا صَامَ
مَنْ صَامَ الدَّهْرَ صَوْمُ ثَلَاثَةِ أَيَّامٍ صَوْمُ الدَّهْرِ كُلِّهِ

"If you keep on doing this, your eyes will become

---

7. Muslim: 1159

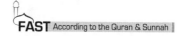

weak and your body will get tired. He who observe *saūm* all the year is like he who did not observe *saūm* at all. Observing *saūm* of three days will be equal to observing *saūm* of the whole year."

I replied I have the strength for more than this." The Prophet (ﷺ) said:

فَصُمْ صَوْمَ دَاوُدَ عَلَيْهِ السَّلَامِ وَكَانَ يَصُومُ يَوْمًا وَيُفْطِرُ يَوْمًا وَلَا يَفِرُّ إِذَا لَاقَى

"Then observe *saūm* like the fasting of Dawud (عليه السلام) who used to observe *saūm* on alternate days and would never flee from the battlefield on meeting the enemy."[8]

Abu Qatadah narrated that a man came to the Prophet (ﷺ) and said: "How do you fast?" The Messenger of Allah (ﷺ) got angry at his words, and when 'Umar (رضي الله عنه) saw that he was angry he said:

رَضِينَا بِاللهِ رَبًّا وَبِالإِسْلَامِ دِينًا وَبِمُحَمَّدٍ نَبِيًّا نَعُوذُ بِاللهِ مِنْ غَضَبِ اللهِ وَغَضَبِ رَسُولِهِ

"We are pleased with Allah as our Lord, with Islam as our religion and with Muhammad as our Prophet; we seek refuge with Allah from the wrath of Allah and the wrath of His Messenger."

'Umar (رضي الله عنه) started repeating these words until his anger went away, then 'Umar said: "O Messenger of Allah, what about the one who fasts all the time?" [He said:] "He has neither fasted nor broken the fast." 'Umar said: "What about one who fasts for two days, then breaks his fast for one day?" He said: "Is anyone able to do that?" He said: "What about the one who fasts one day and breaks his fast for day." He said: "That is the fast of Dawud (عليه السلام)." He ('Umar) said: "What about the one who fasts one day and breaks his fast for two days?" He said: "I wish that I were able

---

8. Bukhari: 1979

to do that." The Messenger of Allah (ﷺ) said: "Three days of each month and one Ramadān to the next, that is like fasting for an entire lifetime. Fasting on the day of Arafah, I ask Allah that it may expiate for (the sins of) the year that comes before it."[9]

Abu Qatabah (ﷺ) narrated that it was asked: "O Messenger of Allah! What is the case of the one who fasts daily?" He said:

$$ لاَ صَامَ وَلاَ أَفْطَرَ $$

"He did not fast nor break (the fast)."[10]

'Imran said that it was said: "O Messenger of Allah, so-and-so never broke his fast, even for one day for the rest of his life." He said: "He has neither fasted nor broken his fast."[11]

'Umar (ﷺ) said: "We were with the Messenger of Allah (ﷺ) and we passed by a man. They said: 'O Prophet of Allah, this man has not broken his fast for such and such a time.' He said: 'He has neither fasted nor broken his fast.'"[12]

'Amr bin Shurahbīl said: "A man came to the Messenger of Allah (ﷺ) and said: 'O Messenger of Allah (ﷺ), what do you say about a man who fasts for the rest of his life?' The Messenger of Allah (ﷺ) said: 'I wish that he would never eat for the rest of his life.' He said: 'Two-thirds (of his lifetime)?' He said: 'That is too much.' He said: 'Half?' He said: 'That is too much.' He said 'Shall I not tell you of that which will take away impurity from the heart?' He said: 'Yes.' 'He said: 'Fasting for three days each month."[13]

Observing *Saūm* on Friday

Muhammad bin 'Abbād bin Ja'far narrated: "I asked Jabir bin 'Abdullāh (ﷺ) while he was circumambulating the Ka'bah: 'Did the Messenger of

---

9. Muslim: 1162
10. Tirmidhi: 767
11. Nasā'i: 2381
12. Nasā'i: 2384
13. Nasā'i: 2388

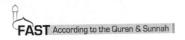

Allah (ﷺ) forbid fasting on Friday?' He said: 'Yes, by the Lord of this House.'"

Abu Hurairah (ؓ) narrated that the Messenger of Allah (ﷺ) said:

$$لاَ يَصُمْ أَحَدُكُمْ يَوْمَ الْجُمُعَةِ إِلاَّ أَنْ يَصُومَ قَبْلَهُ أَوْ يَصُومَ بَعْدَهُ$$

"None of you should fast on Friday, unless he fasts (a day) before it or after it."

Abu Hurairah (ؓ) narrated that the Messenger of Allah (ﷺ) said:

$$لاَ تَخْتَصُّوا لَيْلَةَ الْجُمُعَةِ بِقِيَامٍ مِنْ بَيْنِ اللَّيَالِي وَلاَ تَخُصُّوا يَوْمَ الْجُمُعَةِ$$
$$بِصِيَامٍ مِنْ بَيْنِ الأَيَّامِ إِلاَّ أَنْ يَكُونَ فِي صَوْمٍ يَصُومُهُ أَحَدُكُمْ$$

"Do not single out the night of Friday for fasting unless that coincides with a fast that one (habitually) observes."[14]

Jawairiyah bint Al-Harith (ؓ) narrated: The Prophet (ﷺ) visited her (Jawairiyah) on a Friday and she was observing *Saūm*. He asked her: "Did you observe *saūm* yesterday?" She said: "No." He said: "Do you intend to observe *saūm* tomorrow?" She said: "No" He said: "Then break your fast."[15]

It is undesirable to fix Frdiday for voluntary fast. One can, however, observe fating on it, if Friday occurs on the day when he habitually observes fast, or if one observes the fast of the Day of 'Arafah, or the Day of 'Āshura', and Friday occurs on that day, or if Friday occurs during the Ayyām Al-Beid, or Friday occurs when one is observing fasts of Nadhr (fasts one has vowed for). There is no harm in observing fast on Friday in all such cases but its special observance on Friday is not recommended.

Observing *Saūm* on the First day of 'Eīd-ul-Fitr

Abū 'Ubaid narrated: I witnessed the 'Eīd with 'Umar bin Al-Khattab

---

14. Muslim: 1143, 1144, (147, 148)
15. Bukhari: 1986

(ﷺ) who said: "Allah's Messenger (ﷺ) has forbidden people to observe *saūm* on the day on which you break fasting and the day on which you eat the meat of your scarifies (i.e., the first day of 'Eīd-ul-Fitr and 'Eīd-ul-Adha)."[16]

Abū Sa'īd (ﷺ) narrated:

$$نَهَى النَّبِيُّ (ﷺ) عَنْ صَوْمِ يَوْمِ الْفِطْرِ وَالنَّحْرِ وَعَنِ الصَّمَّاءِ وَأَنْ يَحْتَبِيَ الرَّجُلُ فِي ثَوْبٍ وَاحِدٍ$$

"The Prophet (ﷺ) forbade the *saūm* of 'Eīd-ul-Fitr and 'Eīd-ul-Adha (Two feast days) and also the wearing of as-sammā' (a single garment covering the whole body), and sitting with one's legs drawn up while being wrapped in one garment."[17]

Ziyād bin Jubair narrated: A man went to Ibn 'Umar (ﷺ) and said: "A man vowed to observe *saūm* one day (the sub narrator thinks that he said that the day was Monday), and that day happened to be the 'Eīd day." Ibn 'Umar (ﷺ) said: "Allah orders vows to be fulfilled and the Prophet (ﷺ) forbade, *saūm* on this day (i.e., 'Eīd)."[18]

Abū Sa'īd Al-Khudri (ﷺ) (who fought in twelve Ghazawat in the company of Allah's Messenger) narrated: I heard four things from the Prophet (ﷺ) and they won my admiration. He (ﷺ) said:

1. "No lady should travel on a journey of two days except with her husband or a Dhi-Mahram.

2. No *saūm* is permissible on the two days of 'Eīd-ul-Fitr and 'Eīd-ul-Adha.

3. "No *salāt* after the morning (compulsory) *salāt* until the sun rises; and no *salāt* after the 'Asr prayer till the sun sets.

4. "One should travel only for visiting three mosques: Masjid-al-Haram (Makkah), Masjid-Al-Aqsa, (Jerusalem), and this (my)

---

16. Bukhari: 1990
17. Bukhari: 1991
18. Bukhari: 1994

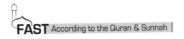

mosque (at Al-Madina)."[19]

Abū Sa'eed Al-Khudrī (ﷺ) narrated: "I heard a *hadith* from him that impressed me, so I said to him: 'Did you hear this from the Messenger of Allah (ﷺ).' He said: 'Would I attribute to the Messenger of Allah (ﷺ) something that I did not hear [from him]?' He said: 'I heard him say: "Fasting is not good on two days: The day of Al-Adha and the day of Al-Fitr (breaking the fast) after Ramadān."'"[20]

Observing *Saūm* on the Days of Tashriq

Bishr bin Suhaim narrated that the Messenger of Allah (ﷺ) delivered a sermon on the days of Tashriq (11th, 12th and 13th of Dhul-Hijjah) and said:

لاَ يَدْخُلُ الْجَنَّةَ إِلاَّ نَفْسٌ مُسْلِمَةٌ وَإِنَّ هَذِهِ الأَيَّامَ أَيَّامُ أَكْلٍ وَشُرْبٍ

"No one will enter Paradise but a Muslim soul, and these days are the days of eating and drinking."[21]

'Āishah and Ibn 'Umar narrated:

لَمْ يُرَخَّصْ فِي أَيَّامِ التَّشْرِيقِ أَنْ يُصَمْنَ إِلَّا لِمَنْ لَمْ يَجِدِ الْهَدْيَ

"Nobody was allowed to observe *saūm* on the days of Tashriq except those who could not afford the hady (Animals for sacrifice)."

Ibn Umar (ﷺ) said: "Observing *saūm* for those who perform Hajj-at-Tamattu' (in lieu of the Hady which they cannot afford) may be performed up to the day of 'Arafah. And if one does not have a hady and has not observed *saūm* (before the 'Eīd) then one should observe *saūm* during the days of Mina (11th, 12th and 13th of Dhul-Hijjah)."[22]

Abū Murrah narrated that he entered along with 'Abdullāh bin 'Amr upon his father 'Amr bin Āl-'As. He served the two of them some food,

19. Bukhari: 1995
20. Muslim: 827
21. Ibn Majah: 1720
22. Bukhari: 1997, 1998, 1999

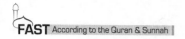

and said: "Eat." He said: "I am fasting." 'Amr said: "Eat, as these are the days in which the Messenger of Allah (ﷺ) ordered us to eat our meals and prohibited us from fasting." Malik said: "They were the days of Tashriq."[23]

The Prohibition of specifying Saturday for Fasting

'Abdullāh bin Burr As-Sulamī narrated from his sister, - (one of the narrators) Yazīd said: (His sister's name is) As-Sammā' that the Prophet (ﷺ) said:

$$لاَ تَصُومُوا يَوْمَ السَّبْتِ إلاَّ فِيمَا افْتُرِضَ عَلَيْكُمْ وَإِنْ لَـمْ يَجِدْ$$
$$أَحَدُكُمْ إلاَّ لِحَاءَ عِنَبَةٍ أَوْ عُودَ شَجَرَةٍ فَلْيَمْضُغْهُ$$

"Do not fast on Saturday, except what has been made obligatory on you. If one of you cannot find anything but a skin of grape, or a piece of wood from a tree then let him chew it."[24]

To maintain the uniqueness and distinction of Islam, imitating non-Muslims is prohibited, because the Jews respect Saturday and regard it holy so to single out just Saturday for fasting is to imitate them.

Fasting During the Second Half of Sha'bān

'Āishah (ﷺ) narrated that Allah's Messenger (ﷺ) used to observe *saūm* till one would say that he would never stop observing *saūm*, and he would abandon *saūm* till one would say that he would never observe *saūm*. I never saw Allah's Messenger (ﷺ) observing *saūm* for a whole month except the month of Ramadān, and did not see him fasting in any month more than in the month of Sha'bān.[25]

'Āishah (ﷺ) narrated that the Prophet (ﷺ) never observed *saūm* in any month more than in the month of Sha'bān. He used to say:

---

23. Abu Dawud: 2418
24. Abu Dawud: 2421
25. Bukhari: 1969

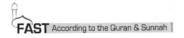

خُذُوا مِنَ الْعَمَلِ مَا تُطِيقُونَ فَإِنَّ اللَّهَ لَا يَمَلُّ حَتَّى تَمَلُّوا

"Do those deeds which you can do easily, as Allah
will not get tired (of giving rewards) till you get board
and tired (of performing religious deeds)."

The most beloved *salāt* to the Prophet (ﷺ) was the one that was done
regularly (throughout the life) even if it were little. And whenever the
Prophet (ﷺ) offered a *salāt* he used to offer it regularly.[26]

Abu Salamah said: "I asked 'Āishah (ﷺ) about the fasting of the Messenger of Allah (ﷺ) and she said: "He used to fast until we would say: 'He
has fasted,' and he used not to fast until we would say: 'He is not fasting.'
I never saw him fast more in any month then be fasted in Sha'bān. He
used to fast all of Sha'bān but a little."[27]

'Āishah (ﷺ) said that the Messenger of Allah (ﷺ) did not fast more in
any month of the year than he did in Sha'bān, and he used to say:

أَحَبُّ الْعَمَلِ إِلَى اللَّهِ مَا دَاوَمَ عَلَيْهِ صَاحِبُهُ وَإِنْ قَلَّ

"The dearest of deeds to Allah are those that a person
does regularly, even if they are small."[28]

Umm Salamah narrated: "I did not see the Prophet (ﷺ) fasting two consecutive months except for Sha'bān and Ramadān."[29]

Dislike to Fast during the Second Half of Sha'bān

Abu Hurairah (ﷺ) narrated that the Messenger of Allah (ﷺ) said:

إِذَا بَقِيَ نِصْفٌ مِنْ شَعْبَانَ فَلَا تَصُومُوه

"When a half of Sha'bān remains then do not fast."[30]

There is no harm if a person has been fasting since the beginning of the

---

26. Bukhari: 1970
27. Muslim: 1156 (176)
28. Muslim: 782 (177)
29. Tirmidhi: 736
30. Tirmidhi: 738

month, or it is a fast of making up and fulfilling a vow, or this coincides with his regular fast which he observes every month generally. However Muslims have been ordered to observe *saūm* in the first fortnight only, and not in the second in order to maintain their energy and vitality for the obligatory *saūm* (i.e. Ramadān). The Prophet (ﷺ) had greater spiritual strength and *saūm* did not cause him weakness due to his strength. Again by virtue of this strength he would sometimes even observe *saūm* which is termed *Saūm al-wisal* (صوم الوصال) observing *saūm* continuous without a break in the evening. But he has forbidden his followers from such fast.

Fasting Consecutive Days

'Abdullāh bin Shaqiq said: "I said to 'Āishah (ﷺ): 'Did the Prophet (ﷺ) fast an entire month other than Ramadān?' She said:

$$ وَاللهِ إِنْ صَامَ شَهْرًا مَعْلُومًا سِوَى رَمَضَانَ حَتَّى مَضَى لِوَجْهِهِ وَلاَ أَفْطَرَهُ حَتَّى يُصِيبَ مِنْهُ $$

'By Allah, he did not fast any entire month other than Ramadān, until he passed away, and he would not let any month pass without fasting some of it, until he died.'"[31]

In another narration: "He used to fast until we said: 'He has fasted, he has fasted,' and he would not fast until we said: 'He is not fasting, he is not fasting.'" She said:

$$ وَمَا رَأَيْتُهُ صَامَ شَهْرًا كَامِلاً مُنْذُ قَدِمَ الْـمَدِينَةَ إِلاَّ أَنْ يَكُونَ رَمَضَانَ $$

"And I did not see him fast an entire month, since he came to Al-Madinah, unless it was Ramadān."[32]

---

31. Muslim: 1156
32. Muslim: 1156 (174)

Voluntary Fasting

Fasting the Month of Muharram

'Āishah (🌸) narrated: "Allah's Messenger (🕌) ordered (The Muslims) to observe *saūm* on the day of Āshūra', and when fasting in the month of Ramadān was prescribed, it became optional for one to observe *saūm* on that day (of 'Āshūra').["1]

'Āishah (🌸) narrated that the Quraish use to observe *saūm* on the day of 'Āshūra' during the Pre-Islamic period of Ignorance, and Allah's Messenger (🕌) also observed the *saūm* on that day. When he came to Madinah, he observed *saūm* on that day and ordered others to observe *saūm* too. Later when the fasting of the month of Ramadān was prescribed, he gave up fasting on the day of 'Āshūra' and it became optional for one to observe that *saūm* or to leave it.[2]

Humaid bin Abdur-Rahman narrated that he heard Mu'awaiyah bin Abi Sufyan (🌸) on the day of 'Āshūra' during the year he performed the Hajj, saying on the pulpit: 'O people of Madinah! Where are your religious scholars? I heard Allah's Messenger (🕌) saying: 'This is the day of Āshūra'. Allah has not enjoined its *saūm* on you but I am fasting it. You have the choice either to observe *saūm* or not to observe *saūm* (on that day).'"[3]

Ibn Abbas (🌸) narrated that the Prophet (🕌) came to Madinah and saw the Jews observing a fast on the day of 'Āshūra'. He asked them about

---

1. Bukhari: 2001
2. Bukhari: 2002
3. Bukhari: 2003

that and they replied: "This is a good day; the day on which Allah rescued Bani Israel from their enemy. So, Mūsā observed *saūm* on this day." The Prophet (ﷺ) said:

فَأَنَا أَحَقُّ بِمُوسَى مِنْكُمْ

"We have more claim over Mūsā than you."

So the Prophet (ﷺ) observed *saūm* on that day and ordered (the Muslims) to observe *saūm* on that day.[4]

Abū Mūsā (ﷺ) narrated: The day of 'Āshūra' was considered as an 'Eīd day by the Jews. So the Prophet (ﷺ) ordered: "I recommend you (Muslims) to observe *saūm* on this day."[5]

Abū Mūsā (ﷺ) said that the people of Khaibar used to fast on the day of 'Āshūra, and they took it as a festival and dressed their women in their jewelry and finery on that day. Then the Messenger of Allah (ﷺ) said: "You (Muslims) should fast (on that day)."[6]

Salamah bin Al-Akwa' (ﷺ) narrated that the Prophet (ﷺ) ordered a man from the tribe of Bani Aslam to announce amongst the people that whoever had eaten should observe *saūm* for the rest of the day, and whoever has not eaten should continue fasting, as that day was the day of 'Āshūra'[7].

Ar-Rubayy' bint Mu'awwidh bin Afra' said: "On the morning of 'Āshūra', the Messenger of Allah (ﷺ) sent word to the village of the Ansar around Madinah saying: 'Whoever started the fasting, let him complete his fast, and whoever started the day not fasting let him complete the rest of the day (without food).'

After that, we used to fast on this day, and we would make our children fast too, even the little ones, if Allah willed. And we used to take them to the Masjid. We would make them toys out of wool, and if one of them cried for food, we would give (that toy) to him until it was time to break

---

4. Bukhari: 2004
5. Bukhari: 2005
6. Muslim 1131 (130)
7. Bukhari: 2007

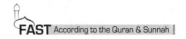

the fast."[8]

Jabir bin Samurah (ﷺ) narrated:

كَانَ رَسُولُ اللهِ (ﷺ) يَأْمُرُنَا بِصِيَامِ يَوْمِ عَاشُورَاءَ وَيُحُثُّنَا عَلَيْهِ
وَيَتَعَاهَدُنَا عِنْدَهُ فَلَمَّا فُرِضَ رَمَضَانُ لَـمْ يَأْمُرْنَا وَلَـمْ يَنْهَنَا وَلَـمْ
يَتَعَاهَدْنَا عِنْدَهُ

"The Messenger of Allah (ﷺ) used to enjoin us and
encourage us, to fast on the day of 'Āshūra', and he
used to check on us when that day came. When (fasting during) Ramadān was enjoined, he neither commanded us nor forbade us, and he did not check on
us."[9]

The Excellence of observing Saūm on the Day of 'Āshūra'

Ibn 'Abbas (ﷺ) narrated:

مَا رَأَيْتُ النَّبِيَّ (ﷺ) يَتَحَرَّى صِيَامَ يَوْمٍ فَضَّلَهُ عَلَى غَيْرِهِ إِلَّا هَذَا
الْيَوْمَ يَوْمَ عَاشُورَاءَ وَهَذَا الشَّهْرَ يَعْنِي شَهْرَ رَمَضَانَ

"I never saw the Prophet (ﷺ) seeking to observe
saūm on a day more (preferable to him) than this day,
the day of 'Āshūra, or this month, i.e., the month of
Ramadān."[10]

Abu Hurairah (ﷺ) narrated that the Prophet (ﷺ) was asked: "Which
prayer is best after the obligatory prayers, and which fasting is best after
the month of Ramadān?" He said:

أَفْضَلُ الصَّلَاةِ بَعْدَ الصَّلَاةِ الْـمَكْتُوبَةِ الصَّلَاةُ فِي جَوْفِ اللَّيْلِ
وَأَفْضَلُ الصِّيَامِ بَعْدَ شَهْرِ رَمَضَانَ صِيَامُ شَهْرِ اللهِ شَهْرِ الْـمُحَرَّمِ

---

8. Muslim: 1136
9. Muslim: 1128
10. Bukhari: 2006

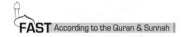

"The best prayer after the prescribed prayer is prayer in the middle of the night, and the best fasting after the month of Ramadān is fasting in the month of Muharram."[11]

Abu Qatadah (�radiallahu) narrated that the Messenger of Allah (ﷺ) said:

صِيَامُ يَوْمِ عَاشُورَاءَ إِنِّى أَحْتَسِبُ عَلَى اللَّهِ أَنْ يُكَفِّرَ السَّنَةَ الَّتِى قَبْلَهُ

"Fasting the day of 'Āshūra', I hope, will expiate for the sins of the previous year." [12]

This means that the minor sins are generally written off by the observance of the act of fasting, but the major sins can only be forgiven by repentance. As far as the people's rights, liabilities and monetary obligations, such as an indebted person, is concerned, their forgiveness depends entirely on the will of the people to whom it is owed.

Which Day Should be Fasted For 'Āshūra'?

Al-Hakam bin Al-A'raj narrated: "I came to Ibn 'Abbas (�radiallahu) while he was reclining on his rida' at Zamzam and said to him: 'Tell me about the fast of 'Āshūra.' He said: 'When you see the crescent of Muharram, then count, and fast on the ninth day.' I said: 'Is this how the Messenger of Allah (ﷺ) used to fast it?' He said: 'Yes.'"[13]

Abu Ghatafan bin Tarif Al-Murri said: "I heard 'Abdullāh bin 'Abbas (�radiallahu) say that when the Messenger of Allah (ﷺ) fasted on the day of Āshūra' and enjoined this fast, they said: 'O Messenger of Allah, it is a day that is venerated by the Jews and Christians.' The Messenger of Allah (ﷺ) said: 'Next year, if Allah wills, we will also fast on the nineth day.' He said: 'But the next year the Messenger of Allah (ﷺ) had passed away.'"[14]

---

11. Muslim: 1163 (203)
12. Ibn Majah: 1738, Muslim: 1162 (197)
13. Muslim: 133
14. Muslim: 1134

Explanation

Āshūra' (عاشوراء) is the 10th of Muharram. In one narration it is stated that when the Prophet (ﷺ) emigrated from Makkah to Madinah he saw that the Jews were fasting on this day. He asked them why they did this on that day, and they told him that Allah granted Prophet Mūsā emancipation from Pharaoh on this day, and so they observed *saūm* in token of their joy. On this he (ﷺ) said that in this happiness of Prophet Mūsā, Muslims have a greater right to observe *saūm* than the Jews. Consequently, he also observed *saūm* on the 10th of Muharram. Then he said that if he lived the following year, they would also observe it on the 9th thereby making themselves different from the Jews. According to another *hadith*, He (ﷺ) ordered the Muslims to observe *saūm* on Āshūra' and an additionally one on the 9th or the 11th of Muharram in opposition to the Jews.[15]

Thus observance of two *saūm* on this occasion is a *Sunnah* of the Prophet (ﷺ). These two *saūm*s can either be observed on 9th and 10th or 10th and 11th of Muharram. Some people think that: "If I remain alive till the next year, I shall also observe fast on the nineth of Muharram," means that he would have observed *saūm* on the 9th of Muharram only. But this interpretation does not agree with other *hadith*s. In order to oppose the Jews, he (ﷺ) resolved to observe one more *saūm* with that of 10th of Muharram and ordained it for the Muslims. In this connection, we have quoted above the authority from the Musnad of Ahmad. Hence, the meanings we have given in the translation of the text are correct.

Observing *Saūm* on the Day of 'Arafah

Abu Qatadah (ﷺ) narrated that the Prophet (ﷺ) said:

صِيَامُ يَوْمِ عَرَفَةَ أَحْتَسِبُ عَلَى اللهِ أَنْ يُكَفِّرَ السَّنَةَ الَّتِي بَعْدَهُ وَ السَّنَةَ الَّتِي قَبْلَهُ

"Fast the Day of 'Arafah, for indeed I anticipate that

---

15. Musnad Ahmad: 4/21 edited by Ahmad Shakir, Majma' Az-Zawaid: 3/188

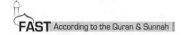

Allah will forgive (the sins) of the year before and after it."[16]

The ninth day of Dhull-Hajjah is called Yaum al-'Arafah (The Day of 'Arafah). On this day, the pilgrims stop and stand in prayers at 'Arafah which is the most important ritual of Hajj, so much so that Hajj is deemed incomplete without it. On that day, the pilgrims are engaged in the rememberance of Allah and prayers there are the most important worship on that day. For this reason, *saūm* is not desirable for them on that day; but for other people, *saūm* has a special merit on that day. The importance and merit of this *saūm* can be judged from the fact that it expiates sins of two consective years: the previous year and the current year. But these sins relate only to the minor sins, not the major ones; also it become a means of elevation of one's status.

Fasting on the Day of 'Arafah at 'Arafah

Umm Al-Fadl bint Al-Harith narrated: "While the people were with me on the day of 'Arafah they differed as to whether the Prophet (ﷺ) was observing *saūm* while other said that he was not observing *saūm*. So, I sent to him a bowl full of milk wile he was riding his camel and he drank it."

Maimunah (ﵻ) narrated: "The people doubted whether the Prophet (ﷺ) was observing *saūm* on the day of 'Arafah or not, so I sent milk while he was standing at 'Arafah, he drank it and the people were looking at him."[17]

'Ikrimah narrated: "We were in the house of Abu Hurairah when he narrated to us that the Messenger of Allah (ﷺ) prohibited fasting on the day of 'Arafat at 'Arafah."[18]

Ibn 'Abbas narrated: "The Prophet (ﷺ) broke (the fast) at Arafah; Umm Fadl sent him some milk to drink."

Ibn Abī Najih narrated from his father who said: "Ibn Umar was asked

---

16. Tirmidhi: 749, Muslim: 1162
17. Bukhari: 1988, 1989
18. Abu Dawud: 2440

about fasting (the day of) 'Arafah (at Arafat) and He said: 'I performed Hajj with the Prophet (ﷺ), and he did not fast during it; and with Abu Bakr, and he did not fast during it; and with 'Uthman, and he did not fast during it. I do not fast it, nor order it nor forbid it."[19]

Ibn 'Umar meant that the example and practice of the Messenger of Allah (ﷺ) and the caliphs was not to fast on the Day of Arafah in the valley of Arafat.

Fasting the First Ten Days of Dhull-Hijjah

Al-Hurr bin (As-Sayyāh) narrated from Hunaidah bin Khalid from his wife from one of wives of the Prophet (ﷺ) who said:

$$ يَصُومُ تِسْعَ ذِى الْحِجَّةِ وَيَوْمَ عَاشُورَاءَ وَثَلَاثَةَ أَيَّامٍ مِنْ كُلِّ شَهْرٍ أَوَّلَ اثْنَيْنِ مِنَ الشَّهْرِ وَالْخَمِيسَ $$

"The Messenger of Allah (ﷺ) used to fast (the first) nine days of Dhul-Hijjah, and the day of 'Āshūra, and three days every month: the first Monday of the month, and Thursday."[20]

Ibn 'Abbas (ﷺ) narrated that the Prophet (ﷺ) said:

$$ مَا الْعَمَلُ فِي أَيَّامٍ أَفْضَلَ مِنْهَا فِي هَذِهِ $$

"No good deeds done on other days are superior to those done on these (first ten days of Dhul-Hajjah)."

Then some Companions of the Prophet (ﷺ) said: "Not even Jihad?" He replied:

$$ وَلَا الْجِهَادُ إِلَّا رَجُلٌ خَرَجَ يُخَاطِرُ بِنَفْسِهِ وَمَالِهِ فَلَمْ يَرْجِعْ بِشَيْءٍ $$

"Not even Jihad, except that of a man who does it by putting himself and his property in danger (for Allah's

---

19. Tirmidhi: 750, 751
20. Abu Dawud: 2437

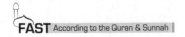

sake i.e., with his life and property), and does not return with any of those things (i.e., is martyred).[21]

a) The best days after the sacred month of Ramadān are the first ten days of Dhul-Hajjah.

b) Fasting for the first nine days of Dhul-Hajjah is from the best among the voluntary fasting; and fasting on the ninth of Dhul-Hajjah is the best among these days.

Fasting Six Days in Shawwāl

Abu Ayyub Ansāri (ﷺ) narrated that the Messenger of Allah (ﷺ) said:

مَنْ صَامَ رَمَضَانَ ثُمَّ أَتْبَعَهُ سِتًّا مِنْ شَوَّالٍ كَانَ كَصِيَامِ الدَّهْرِ

"Whoever fasts Ramadān then follows it with six days of [fasting in] Shawwāl, it is as if he fasted a lifetime."[22]

According to the formula there is a minimum ten-fold reward for every virtue, the *saūm* of one month of (Ramadān) is equivalent to the *saūm* of ten months. If one also observe the six days of *saūm* of Shawwāl, they will equal to *saūm* of two months. Thus, one becomes eligible for the reward of one full year's fast. He who makes it a permanent feature is like one who observes *saūm* throughtout his life. He will be considered by Allah as one who observes *saūm* permanently. Although voluntary in nature, they are highly important. One can observe these six-day *saūm* at a stretch or with intervals, but their observance one after the other at the beginning of the month is better. Similarly, if a person has missed some *saūm* of Ramadān due to illness, travelling etc., he should first make up the shortfall and then observe the voluntary six-day of Shawwāl. Thawban narrated that the Messenger of Allah (ﷺ) said:

مَنْ صَامَ سِتَّةَ أَيَّامٍ بَعْدَ الْفِطْرِ كَانَ تَمَامَ السَّنَةِ (مَنْ جَاءَ بِالْحَسَنَةِ فَلَهُ

---

21. Bukhari: 969
22. Muslim: 1164

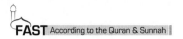

عَشْرُ أَمْثَالِهَا)

"Whoever fasts six days after the Fitr will have completed the year, for whoever does a good deed will have the reward of ten like it."[23]

Fasting three Days of the Month

Abu Dharr (ﷺ) narrated:

أَوْصَانِي حَبِيبِي (ﷺ) بِثَلَاثَةٍ لَا أَدَعُهُنَّ إِنْ شَاءَ اللهُ تَعَالَى أَبَدًا أَوْصَانِي بِصَلَاةِ الضُّحَى وَبِالْوِتْرِ قَبْلَ النَّوْمِ وَبِصِيَامِ ثَلَاثَةِ أَيَّامٍ مِنْ كُلِّ شَهْرٍ

"My beloved Prophet (ﷺ) advised me to do three things which I will never give up, if Allah wills. He advised me to pray duha, to pray *witr* before sleeping, and to fast three days of each month."[24]

Abu Hurairah (ﷺ) narrated:

أَمَرَنِي رَسُولُ اللهِ (ﷺ) بِثَلَاثٍ بِنَوْمٍ عَلَى وِتْرٍ وَالْغُسْلِ يَوْمَ الْجُمُعَةِ وَصَوْمِ ثَلَاثَةِ أَيَّامٍ مِنْ كُلِّ شَهْرٍ

"The Messenger of Allah (ﷺ) enjoined three things upon me: To sleep after praying *witr*, to perform *ghusl* on Friday, and to fast three days of each month."[25]

Abu Hurairah (ﷺ) narrated that I heard the Messenger of Allah (ﷺ) say:

شَهْرِ الصَّبْرِ وَثَلَاثَةِ أَيَّامٍ مِنْ كُلِّ شَهْرٍ صَوْمُ الدَّهْرِ

"The month of patience (Ramadān) and three days of

---

23. Ibn Majah: 1715
24. Nasa'i: 2406
25. Nasa'i: 2407

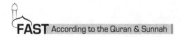

each month is fasting for a lifetime."[26]

'Uthman bin Abi Al-Ās said that he heard the Messenger of Allah (ﷺ) say:

صِيَامٌ حَسَنٌ ثَلَاثَةُ أَيَّامٍ مِنْ الشَّهْرِ

"It is good to fast three days of each month."[27]

Al-Hurr bin Sayyah narrated that he heard Ibn Umar (ﷺ) say:

كَانَ النَّبِيُّ (ﷺ) يَصُومُ ثَلَاثَةَ أَيَّامٍ مِنْ كُلِّ شَهْرٍ

"The Prophet (ﷺ) used to fast three days of eah month."[28]

Hafsah (ﷺ) narrated:

أَرْبَعٌ لَـمْ يَكُنْ يَدَعُهُنَّ النَّبِيُّ (ﷺ) صِيَامَ عَاشُورَاءَ وَالْعَشْرَ وَثَلَاثَةَ أَيَّامٍ مِنْ كُلِّ شَهْرٍ وَرَكْعَتَيْنِ قَبْلَ الْغَدَاةِ

"There are four things which the Prophet (ﷺ) never gave up: Fasting 'Āshūra, (fasting during) the ten days, (fasting) three days of each month, and praying two *rak'ahs* before *Fajr*."[29]

Mu'adhah Al-'Adawiyyah (ﷺ) narrated that she asked 'Āishah, the wife of the Prophet (ﷺ): "Did the Messenger of Allah (ﷺ) fast three days of every month?" She said: "Yes." She said to her: "Which three days did he fast?" She said: "He did not mind which days of the month he fasted."[30]

---

26. Nasa'i: 2410
27. Nasa'i: 2413
28. Nasa'i: 2413
29. Nasa'i: 2418
30. Muslim: 1160

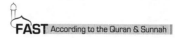

Observing Fast for the Three Days Preceeding the Night of the Full Moon

Jarir bin 'Abdullāh 🙵 narrated that the Prophet (🙵) said:

صِيَامُ ثَلَاثَةِ أَيَّامٍ مِنْ كُلِّ شَهْرٍ صِيَامُ الدَّهْرِ وَأَيَّامُ الْبِيضِ صَبِيحَةَ
ثَلَاثَ عَشْرَةَ وَأَرْبَعَ عَشْرَةَ وَخَمْسَ عَشْرَةَ

"Fasting three days of each month is fasting for a life-time, and the shining days of Al-Bīd, the thirteenth, fourteenth and fifteenth."[31]

'Imran bin Husain (🙵) narrated that the Prophet (🙵) said to him: "O so-and-so, did you fast in the middle of the month?" He said: "No." He said: "When you end the fast (of Ramadān), then fast two days."[32]

Observing the Fast in the Beginning of each Month

'Abdullāh bin Mas'ud (🙵) narrated:

كَانَ رَسُولُ اللهِ (🙵) يَصُومُ – يَعْنِي مِنْ غُرَّةِ كُلِّ شَهْرٍ – ثَلَاثَةَ
أَيَّامٍ

"The Messenger of Allah (🙵) used to fast – meaning from the *ghurrah* (beginning) of each month – three days."[33]

Fasting on Monday, Thursday and the Following Monday

Hafsah (🙵) narrated:

كَانَ رَسُولُ اللهِ (🙵) يَصُومُ ثَلَاثَةَ أَيَّامٍ مِنَ الشَّهْرِ الاثْنَيْنِ وَالْخَمِيسِ
وَالاثْنَيْنِ مِنَ الْجُمُعَةِ الأُخْرَى

---

31. Nasa'i: 2422
32. Muslim: 1161
33. Abu Dawud: 2450

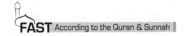

"The Messenger of Allah (ﷺ) used to fast three days every month; Monday and Thursday and Monday of the following week."[34]

Umm Salamah (ﷺ) narrated:

$$كَانَ رَسُولُ اللهِ (ﷺ) يَأْمُرُنِى أَنْ أَصُومَ ثَلَاثَةَ أَيَّامٍ مِنْ كُلِّ شَهْرٍ أَوَّلُهَا الِاثْنَيْنِ وَالْخَمِيسِ$$

'The Messenger of Allah (ﷺ) used to order me to fast three days every month, the first of them were Monday and Thursday."[35]

Fasting the Last Days of the Month

'Imran bin Husain (ﷺ) narrated that the Prophet (ﷺ) asked him, or asked a man and 'Imran was listening: "O Abu so-and-so! Have you observed fasting in the last days of this month?" The man replied: "No, O Allah's Messenger!" The Prophet (ﷺ) said to him: "When you finish your fast (of Ramadān) observe fast for two days (in Shawwāl)."[36]

The man whom the Prophet (ﷺ) asked seemed to have had the habit of observing the fast during the last days of every month, but he did not carry on this habit in the month of Sha'bān, for Allah's Messenger (ﷺ) had forbidden the fasting of the day immediately preceding Ramadān. In this narration the Prophet (ﷺ) ordered the man to make up for the days of Sha'bān, which he missed by observing fast on some days in Shawwāl, and that indicates that one should keep his habits of worshipping, and there is no harm if one observes the fast during the last days of Sha'bān if it is his habit to fast during the last days of every month.[37]

---

34. Abu Dawud: 2451
35. Abu Dawud: 2452
36. Bukhari: 1983
37. Fathul-Bari: 4/294

Fasting Monday and Thursday

'Āishah (﷽) narrated:

$$كَانَ النَّبِيُّ يَتَحَرَّى صَوْمَ الاِثْنَيْنِ وَالْخَمِيسِ$$

"The Prophet (﷽) used to try to fast on Mondays and Thursday."[38]

Abu Hurairah (﷽) narrated that the Prophet (﷽) used to fast on Mondays and Thursday. It was said: "O Messenger of Allah, why do you fast on Mondays and Thursday?" He said:

$$إِنَّ يَوْمَ الاِثْنَيْنِ وَالْخَمِيسِ يَغْفِرُ اللهُ فِيهِمَا لِكُلِّ مُسْلِمٍ إِلاَّ
مُتَهَاجِرَيْنِ يَقُولُ دَعْهُمَا حَتَّى يَصْطَلِحَا$$

"On Mondays and Thursday Allah forgives every Muslim except two who have forsaken one another. He says: 'Leave these two until they reconcile.'"[39]

Usamah bin Zaid said: "O Messenger of Allah, sometimes you fast, and you hardly ever break your fast, and some times you do not fast and you hardly ever fast, except two days which, if you are fasting, you include them in your fast, and if you are not fasting, then you fast them on your own." He said: "Which two days?" I said: "Monday and Thursday." He said:

$$ذَانِكَ يَوْمَانِ تُعْرَضُ فِيهِمَا الْأَعْمَالُ عَلَى رَبِّ الْعَالَمِينَ وَأُحِبُّ أَنْ
يُعْرَضَ عَمَلِي وَأَنَا صَائِمٌ$$

"Those are two days in which deeds are shown to the Lord of the worlds, and I like my deed to be shown (to Him) when I am fasting."[40]

Hafsah (﷽) narrated:

---

38. Tirmidhi: 745
39. Ibn Majah: 1740
40. Nasa'i: 2360

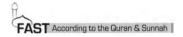

كَانَ رَسُولُ اللهِ إِذَا أَخَذَ مَضْجَعَهُ جَعَلَ كَفَّهُ الْيُمْنَى تَحْتَ خَدِّهِ
الأَيْمَنِ وَكَانَ يَصُومُ الاِثْنَيْنِ وَالْخَمِيسَ

"When the Messenger of Allah (ﷺ) would lie down,
he would place his right hand under his right cheek,
and he used to fast on Monday and Thursday."[41]

Comments:

a)   Voluntary fasting on Monday and Thursday should be observed.

b)   Fasting is a great deed whose blessing gives hope for forgiveness.

c)   Muslims being angry with each other without a reason is a big
sin.

d)   Showing anger due to a religious reason and for the admonishment
of one's family does not come under the warning mentioned in the
Hadith.

If someone Forces his Muslim Brother to Break his Voluntary fast

Abu Juhaifah narrated that the Prophet (ﷺ) made a bond of brotherhood
between Salman and Abu Ad-Dardā'. Salmān paid a vist to Abū Ad-
Dardā' and found Umm Ad-Dardā' dressed in shabby clothes and asked
her why she was in that state. She replied: "Your brother Abu Ad-Dardha
is not interested in the (luxuries of) this world." In the meantime Abū Ad-
Dardā' came and prepared a meal for Salmān. Salmān requested Abū Ad-
Dardā' to eat (with him), but Abū Ad-Dardā' said: "I am fasting." Salmān
said: "I am not going to eat unless you eat." So Abū Ad-Dardā' ate (with
Salmān). When it was night and (a part of the night passed), Abū Ad-
Dardā' got up (to offer the night prayer), but Salmān told him to sleep
and Abū Ad-Dardā' slept. After sometime Abū Ad-Dardā' again got up
[again], but Salmān told him to sleep. When it was the last hours of the
night, Salmān told him to get up, and they both offered prayer. Salmān

---

41. Nasa'i: 2369

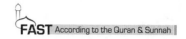

told Abū Ad-Dardā': "Your Lord has a right over you, you have a right over yourself, and your family has a right over you; so you should give the rights of all those who have a right on you." Abū Ad-Dardā' came to the Prophet (ﷺ) and narrated the whole story and the Prophet (ﷺ) said: "Salmān has spoken the truth."[42]

The Right of the Body, the Family and the Guests in Observing the Fast

'Abdullāh bin 'Amr bin Al-'As (ﷺ) narrated that Allah's Messenger (ﷺ) said to him: "O 'Abdullāh! Have I not been informed that you observe saūm during the day and offer salāt (prayer) the entire night." 'Abdullāh replied: "Yes, O Allah's Messenger!" The Prophet (ﷺ) said: "Don't do that; observe saūm for few days and then give it up for few days, offer salāt and also sleep at night, as your body has a right over you, and your wife has a right over you, and your guest has a right over you. It is sufficient for you to observe saūm three days in a month, as the reward of a good deed is multiplied ten times, so it will be like fasting throughout the year." I insisted (on fasting) and so I was given a hard instruction. I said: "O Allah's Messenger! I have strength." The Prophet (ﷺ) said: "Observe, saūm (fast) like the fasting of the Prophet Dawud (David) and do not observe fast more than that." I asked: "How was the fasting of the Dawud, the Prophet of Allah." He said: "Half of the year," (i.e., he used to observe fast on every alternate day).

Afterwards, when 'Abdullāh became old, he used to say: "It would have been better for me if I had accepted permission of the Prophet (ﷺ)."[43]

The Fast of the Prophet Dawud

'Abdullāh bin 'Amr bin Al-'As (ﷺ) narrated that the Prophet (ﷺ) said to him: "You observe fast daily all year round and offer prayer all night long?" I replied in the affirmative. The Prophet (ﷺ) said: "If you keep on doing this, your eyes will become weak and your body will get tired. He who observes the fast all year round is as if he who did not observe the

42. Bukhari: 1968
43. Bukhari: 1975

fast at all. Fasting three days (a month) will be equal to fasting the entire year." I replied: "I have the strength for more than this." The Prophet (ﷺ) said:

$$فَصُمْ صَوْمَ دَاوُدَ عَلَيْهِ السَّلَام كَانَ يَصُومُ يَوْمًا وَيُفْطِرُ يَوْمًا وَلَا يَفِرُّ إِذَا لَاقَى$$

"Then observe the *saūm* like the fasting of Dawud who used to fast on alternate days and would never flee from the battle field on meeting the enemy."

'Abdullāh bin 'Amr said that the Messenger of Allah (ﷺ) said to him:

$$أَحَبَّ الصِّيَامِ إِلَى اللهِ صِيَامُ دَاوُدَ وَأَحَبَّ الصَّلَاةِ إِلَى اللهِ صَلَاةُ دَاوُدَ عَلَيْهِ السَّلَامُ كَانَ يَنَامُ نِصْفَ اللَّيْلِ وَيَقُومُ ثُلُثَهُ وَيَنَامُ سُدُسَهُ وَكَانَ يَصُومُ يَوْمًا وَيُفْطِرُ يَوْمًا$$

"The most beloved fast to Allah is fast of (Prophet) Dawud, and the most beloved prayer to Allah is the prayer of Dawud, he used to sleep half of the night, then pray for one third, and sleep one sixth; and he would go without fasting for one day, and fast the next day."[44]

Whoever Visited Some People and did not break his Optional Fast

Anas (ﷺ) narrated that the Prophet (ﷺ) paid a visit to Umm Sulaim and she palced before him dates and ghee. The Prophet (ﷺ) said: "Replace the ghee and dates, in their respective containers for I am fasting." Then he stood somewhere in her house and offered an optional prayer, and then he invoked Allah to bless Umm Sulaim and her family. Then Umm Sulaim said: "O Allah's Messenger! I have a special request (today)." He said: "What is it?" She replied: "(Please invoke for) your servant Anas."

---

44. Abu Dawud: 2448

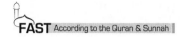

So, Allah's Messenger (ﷺ) did not leave anything good in this world or in the Hereafter which he did not invoke (Allah to bestow) on me. He said:

اللَّهُمَّ ارْزُقْهُ مَالًا وَوَلَدًا وَبَارِكْ لَهُ

"O Allah! Give him (i.e. Anas) property and children and bless him."

Thus, I am one of the richest among the Ansar and my daughter Umaina told me that when Al-Hajjaj came to Basrah, more than 120 of my off-spring had been buried.[45]

Abu Hurairah (ﷺ) narrated that the Prophet (ﷺ) said:

إِذَا دُعِىَ أَحَدُكُمْ إِلَى طَعَامٍ وَهُوَ صَائِمٌ فَلْيَقُلْ إِنِّى صَائِمٌ

"If one of you is invited to eat when he is fasting, let him say: 'I am fasting.'"[46]

Can Someone Select a Special Day for Fasting

'Alqamah narrated that he asked 'Āishah (ﷺ): "Did Allah's Messenger (ﷺ) use to do extra deeds of worship on some certain days?" She replied: "No, but his deeds were regular and costant. Who amongst you can endure what Allah's Messenger (ﷺ) used to endure?"[47]

The Prophet's Fasts at Times other than Ramadān

Ibn Abbas (ﷺ) narrated that the Prophet (ﷺ) never fasted a full month except the month of Ramadān, and he used to fast until one would say: "By Allah, he will never stop fasting." And he would abandon fasting until one would say: "By Allah, he will never fast."[48]

Anas (ﷺ) narrated that Allah's Messenger (ﷺ) used to leave the fast in

---

45. Bukhari: 1982
46. Muslim: 1150
47. Bukhari: 1987
48. Bukhari: 1971

a certain month until we thought that he would not observe the *saum* in that month; and he used to fast in another month until we thought that he would not stop observing the *saum* at all in that month. And if one wanted to see him offering prayer at night, one could see him (in that condition), and if one wanted to see him sleeping at night, one could see him (in that condition) too.[49]

Humaid narrated: I asked Anas (﴿) about the *saum* of the Prophet (﴿). He said: "Whenever I like to see the Prophet (﴿) observing the *saum* in any month, I could see that, and whenever I liked to see him not observing the *saum*, I could see that too; if I liked to see him offering the *salat* in any night, I could see that, and if I liked to see him sleeping, I could see that, too." Anas further said: "I never touched silk or velvet softer than the hand of Allah's Messenger (﴿) and never smelled musk or perfume more pleasant than the smell of Allah's Messenger (﴿)."[50]

A Woman Fasting without the Permission of Her Husband

Hammam bin Munabbih said: This is what Abu Hurairah (﴿) narrated from Muhammad the Messenger of Allah (﴿)" – and he quoted a number of *hadith*s, including the following:

The Messenger of Allah (﴿) said:

$$لاَ تَصُمِ الْـمَرْأَةُ وَبَعْلُهَا شَاهِدٌ إِلاَّ بِإِذْنِهِ وَلاَ تَأْذَنْ فِي بَيْتِهِ وَهُوَ$$
$$شَاهِدٌ إِلاَّ بِإِذْنِهِ وَمَا أَنْفَقَتْ مِنْ كَسْبِهِ مِنْ غَيْرِ أَمْرِهِ فَإِنَّ نِصْفَ$$
$$أَجْرِهِ لَهُ$$

"No woman should fast (superoragative Fasting) while her husband is present without his permission, and she should not allow anyone to enter his house while he is present without his permission; and whatever she spends from his earnings without instructions from him, half of the reward will go to him."[51]

---

49. Bukhari: 1972
50. Bukhari: 1973
51. Muslim: 1026

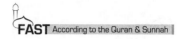

a)   There is no need for asking anyone's permission to perform an obligation.

b)   Voluntary fast by a woman in the presence of her husband may jeopardize his right, particularly when a woman observes voluntary fasts frequently. Therefore a woman should seek her husband's permission for observing a voluntary fast.

A Fasting Person who is Invited to a Feast

Abu Hurairah (☙) narrated that the Messenger of Allah (☙) said:

> إِذَا دُعِيَ أَحَدُكُمْ فَلْيُجِبْ فَإِنْ كَانَ مُفْطِرًا فَلْيَطْعَمْ وَإِنْ كَانَ
> صَائِمًا فَلْيُصَلِّ

> "If one of you is invited (for a meal) then let him accept (the invitation). If he is not fasting, then let him eat, and if he is fasting, then let him pray."

Hisham said: "And the prayer means to supplicate (for the host)."[52]

Abu Hurairah narrated that the Messenger of Allah (☙) said: "If one of you is fasting, and is invited to a meal, then let him, say: 'I am fasting.'"

Jabir (☙) narrated that the Messenger of Allah (☙) said:

> إِذَا دُعِيَ أَحَدُكُمْ فَلْيُجِبْ فَإِنْ كَانَ صَائِمًا فَلْيُصَلِّ وَإِنْ كَانَ مُفْطِرًا
> فَلْيَطْعَمْ

> "Whoever is invited to eat when he is fasting, let him accept the invitation; if he wants, then let him eat, and if he wants, then let him not eat."[53]

---

52. Abu Dawud: 2460
53. Ibn Majah: 1751

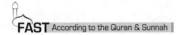

The Night Prayer
in Ramadan

In Arabic, the night prayer has many names. It is called *qiyām* (literally: standing) or *qiyām-ul-layl* (standing at night), *salātul layal* (the night prayer), tahhajud (from hajada: to remain awake at night), *witr* or *tarawīh* (resting). In this section, we choose to use the term tarawīh. Most schalors allow the usage of this term, but some have reservations because it carries the implication that one must rest after every four *rak'ahs* of the tarawīh, something which has no basis in the *Sunnah*. According to Muhammad Saraqah:

"The reason for this name is due to the long recitation [within it], and the people would rest after every four *rak'ah*. This rest became a necessary element of tarawīh, even with very short recitations, which led people to think that this was the correct name revealed to Allah's Messenger (ﷺ).

It is important to clarify that this name is wrong both textually and in meaning. As for textually, it is not known that the Prophet (ﷺ) taught his Companions to rest after every four *rak'ah*.

Thus, it should be brought to the attention of the people that this is a novel name. It is better to use the name that the Prophet (ﷺ) used for this prayer, which is *qiyām*.

One might ask: 'Is it wrong to rest after finishing two or four *rak'ah*?' My answer is: If the *imam* gets tired, or feels that the people praying behind him are tired from long standing and recitation, he may allow

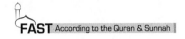

some rest."[1]

The Virtue of Performing the Night Prayer in Ramadān

Abu Hurairah (ؓ) narrated that Allah's Messenger (ﷺ) said:

مَنْ قَامَهُ إِيمَانًا وَاحْتِسَابًا غُفِرَ لَهُ مَا تَقَدَّمَ مِنْ ذَنْبِهِ

"Whoever performs *Salāt* at night in the month of Ramadān with sincere faith and hoping for a reward from Allah, then all his past sins will be forgiven"[2]

Abu Hurairah (ؓ) narrated that Allah's Messenger (ﷺ) used to urge (the people) to perform *tahajjud* at night during the month of Ramadān. He did not order them or make it obligatory on them. He (ﷺ) said:

مَنْ قَامَهُ إِيمَانًا وَاحْتِسَابًا غُفِرَ لَهُ مَا تَقَدَّمَ مِنْ ذَنْبِهِ

"Whoever performs *salāt* at night in the month of Ramadān with sincere faith and hoping for a reward from Allah, then all his past sins will be forgiven."[3]

'Amr bin Murrah Al-Juhani (ؓ) narrated that a man from the tribe of Quda'ah said to the Messenger (ﷺ): "What would be my status if I would testify that there is no (true) god except Allah and that you are Allah's Messenger, pray the five prayers, fast and [perform] *qiyām* in Ramadān, and give *zakah*?" The Prophet (ﷺ) said:

مَنْ مَاتَ عَلَى هَذَا كَانَ مِنَ الصِّدِّيقِينَ وَالشُّهَدَآءِ

"Any one dying upon this will be (in Jannah) among the most truthfull and the martyrs."[4]

---

1. Irshadus-Sari: 75-77, The Night Prayer by Sheikh Albani and Muhammad Al-Jibali: 8
2. Bukhari: 2008
3. Muslim: 759
4. Sahih At-Targhīb: 355, 745, 989

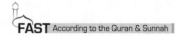
The Legality of performing the Night prayer in Congregation

Allah says in the Qur'ān:

إِنَّ رَبَّكَ يَعْلَمُ أَنَّكَ تَقُومُ أَدْنَىٰ مِن ثُلُثَيِ ٱلَّيْلِ وَنِصْفَهُۥ وَثُلُثَهُۥ وَطَآئِفَةٌ مِّنَ ٱلَّذِينَ مَعَكَ

"Verily, your Lord knows that you do stand (to pray at night) a little less than two thirds of the night, or half the night, or a third of the night, and also a party of those with you." (Al-Muzzammil 73:20)

'Urwah narrated that he was informed by 'Āishah (ﷺ) that Allah's Messenger (ﷺ) went out in the middle of the night and performed *salāt* in the mosque and some men performed *salāt* behind him. In the morning, the people spoke about it and then a large number of them gathered and performed *salāt* (prayer) behind him (on the second night). The next morning the people again talked about it and on the third night the mosque was full with a large number of people. Allah's Messenger (ﷺ) came out and the people performed *salāt* (prayer) behind him. On the fourth night the mosque was overwhelmed with people and could not accommodate them, but the Prophet (ﷺ) came out only for the morning *salāt* (prayer). When the morning *salāt* (prayer) was finished, he recited *tashah-hud* and (addressing the people) said: "Your presence was not hidden from me but I was afraid lest the night *salāt* should be enjoined on you and you might not be able to carry it on." So, Allah's Messenger (ﷺ) died and the situation remained like that (i.e., people offered the night prayers individually)."[5]

Ibn Shihab narrated that Abdur Rahman bin 'Abdul Qari said: "I went out in the company of 'Umar bin Al-Khattab one night in Ramadān to the mosque and found the people performing *salāt* (Prayers) in different groups. A man performing *salāt* – alone, or a man performing *salāt* with a small group behind him, so 'Umar said: 'In my opinion it would be better to collect these (people) under the leadership of one *qari* (reciter) [i.e.,

---

5. Bukhari: 2012

let them perform *salāt* in congregation]. So, he made up his mind and he congregated them behind Ubai Bin K'ab. Then on another night I went again in his company and the people were performing *salāt* behind their reciter. On that 'Umar remarked: 'What an excellent *bid'a* (i.e., innovation in religion) this is; but the *salāt* which they do not perform, and sleep at its time is superior to the one they are performing now.' He meant the *salāt* in the last part of the night. (In those days) people used to perform *salāt* in the early part of the night."[6]

In another narration Allah's Messenger (ﷺ) said:

قَدْ رَأَيْتُ الَّذِي صَنَعْتُمْ وَلَمْ يَمْنَعْنِي مِنْ الْخُرُوجِ إِلَيْكُمْ إِلَّا أَنِّي خَشِيتُ أَنْ تُفْرَضَ عَلَيْكُمْ وَذَلِكَ فِي رَمَضَانَ

> "I saw what you had done, and the only reason I did not come out to you is that I feared that it would become obligatory upon you." And this occurred in Ramdhan.[7]

An-Nu'man bin Bashir (؂) narrated: "We stood (in prayer) with Allah's Messenger (ﷺ) on the twenty third night of Ramadān up to the first third of the night; then we stood with him on the twenty-fifth night up to the middle of the night; then he led us on the twenty-seventh night (for so long) that we feared missing the *falah* (Predawn meal)."

Al-Hakim said commenting on this *Hadith*: "This carries a clear proof that praying *tarawīh* in the masjids is an established *Sunnah*. 'Ali bin Abi Talib (؂) continued to urge 'Umar (؂) to review it, until he finally did."[8]

Tha'labah bin Abi Malik Al-Qurazi said: "Allah's Messenger (ﷺ) went out (to the Masjid) one night during Ramadān; he saw some people in the corner of the Masjid praying. He asked: "What are they doing?" Some one replied: "O Allah's Messenger, these people do not know much Qur'ān, Ubayy bin Ka'b is reciting and they are behind him following

---

6. Bukhari: 2010
7. Muslim 761, Abu Dawud: 1373
8. Al-Mustadrak: 1/440

his prayer." To which he (ﷺ) replied: "They have done well," and he did not object to their action."[9]

In the narration of Abu Dawud Allah's Messenger (ﷺ) said:

$$أَصَابُوا وَنِعْمَ مَا صَنَعُوا$$

"They have acted correctly, and what a good thing they have done!"[10]

Anas (ﷺ) narrated that Allah's Messenger (ﷺ) was once praying in Ramadān (in the Masjid). He went and stood next to him (in prayer); another man joined them, than another – until there was a small gathering. When Allah's Messenger (ﷺ) sensed that they were all praying behind him, he made his prayer short, concluded it and then entered his house where he resumed praying a much longer prayer than that he prayed with them. In the morning, they asked him: "O Allah's Messenger (ﷺ) did you notice our presence last night?" He (ﷺ) replied:

$$نَعَمْ، ذَاكَ الَّذِى حَمَلَنِى عَلَى الَّذِى صَنَعْتُ$$

"Yes, and that is the reason for what I did."[11]

Abu Hurairah (ﷺ) narrated that Allah's Messenger (ﷺ) said:

$$مَنْ قَامَ رَمَضَانَ إِيمَانًا وَاحْتِسَابًا غُفِرَ لَهُ مَا تَقَدَّمَ مِنْ ذَنْبِهِ$$

"Whoever performed salāt at night in the month of Ramadān with sincere faith and hoping for a reward from Allah, all his past sins will be forgiven."

Ibn Shihab (a narrator) said: "Allah's Messenger (ﷺ) died and the people continued observing that (i.e., Nawafil offered in separate groups), and it remained as it was, during the caliphate of Abu Bakr and in the early days, of 'Umar's caliphate.

These hadiths provide clear evidence for praying tarawīh in congrega-

9. Al-Baihaqi: 2/495
10. Abu Dawud: 1377
11. Ahmad: 3/199, 212, 291

tion, since the Prophet (ﷺ) prayed it on those nights. This conclusion does not conflict with his stopping on the fourth night, because he stated the reason for his action: "I feared that it would become obligatory for you."

There is no doubt that this apprehension dissipated with his (ﷺ) passing after Allah had completed the religion. Thus, the reason for not praying *tarawīh* in congregation was gone, restoring the earlier ruling that it is recommended to pray it in Jama'ah. This is why 'Umar bin Al-Khattab (ﷺ) reviewed it, as is the opinion of the majority of the scholars.

Ibn Shihab narrated that Abdur Rahman bin 'Abdul *Qari* said: "I went out in the company of 'Umar bin Al-Khattab one night in Ramadān to the mosque and found the people performing *salāt* in different groups. A man performing *salāt* alone or a man performing *salāt* with a small group behind him, so 'Umar said: "In my opinion it would be better to collect these (people) under the leadership of one *qari* (reciter) [i.e., let them perform prayer in congregation.] So, he made up his mind and he congregated them behind Ubai bin Ka'b. Then on another night I went again in his company and the people were performing *salāt* behind their reciter. On that, Umar remarked: 'What an excellent *bid'a* (i.e., innovation in religion) this is; but the *salāt* which they do not perform, and sleep at its time is superior to the one they are performing now.' He meant the *salāt* in the last part of the night. (In these days) people used to perform *salāt* in the early part of the night."[12]

Ibn At-Tīn and other jurists have said: "Umar (ﷺ) deduced that he should do this from the Prophet's approval during those nights. When he (ﷺ) later disliked it, it was only because he feared that it would become obligatory for the people. It is probably for this reason that Al-Bukhari, after mentioning 'Umar's action, cited 'Āishah's *hadith*. After the Prophet passed away, such fear was gone and 'Umar realized the importance of gathering the people, because praying behind one *imam* helps the people endure the length of the prayer. This action of 'Umar was adopted by the majority of the scholars (as being the truth)."[13]

---

12. Bukhari: 2010
13. Fathul-Bari: 4/203, 204

In his statement, 'Umar did not intend the shar'i definition of *bid'a,* which is to innovate in the religion something that does not have a precedent. It is clear that he did not innovate anything, but revived several of the Prophet's (ﷺ) *Sunnahs.*

He only meant bid'a according to one of its linguistic meanings, which is a new or novel thing that was not commonly known prior to its initiation. There is no doubt that praying *tarawīh* in congregation behind one *imam* was not a commonly known practice during the Caliphate of Abu Bakr and a portion of Umar's, as preceded. With this understanding, it is a new matter. But since it is in accordance with the Prophet's action, it is a *Sunnah,* and not a *bid'ah.* Describing it as being good is only because of this; and this is the understanding of the great scholars who have explained this statement by 'Umar. For example Abdul Wahhāb As-Subki said:

Ibn 'Abdul-Barr said: "Umar did not legislate except what Allah's Messenger (ﷺ) legislated, and what he loved and accepted. Nothing prevented him from continuing (with the *tarawīh* in congregation) except fear that it would become an obligation for his *Ummah,* because he was kind and merciful toward the believers. 'Umar (ﷺ) learned that from Allah's Messenger (ﷺ) and understood that one may not add to the obligations or take away from them after his (ﷺ) death. He therefore re-established it for the people, revived it, and commanded it; he did this in the 14th year of the Hijrah. That was a (good) thing that Allah reserved for him particularly to do; Allah did not inspire Abu Bakr (ﷺ) to do it, even though he was better than him, and generally faster in performing all that is good. Each of them possessed virtues that the other did not."

Had *tarawīh* not been an ordained *Sunnah,* it would be a rejected innovation, as the case for the *raghaib* prayer on the middle night of Sha'bān and on the first Friday of Rajab. If this was the case, it would be incumbent to forbid it; but that was never done, as is obviously known in the Dīn.[14]

The great scholar Ibn Hajar al-Haythami said:

---

14. Ishraqul-Masābīh fī salātit-Tarawīh: 1/168 as quoted in The Night Prayer by Muhammad Al-Jibali: 45, 46

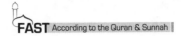

"Driving the Jews and Christians out of the Arabian peninsula and fighting the Turks were not *bid'as* – since these were done by the command of the Prophet (ﷺ) even though they were not done during his lifetime. And in 'Umar's saying regarding the *tarawīh* prayers: 'This is indeed a good *bid'a*,' he meant the linguistic meaning of *bid'a*, which is to do something that was not being done, similar to what Allah says:

$$قُلْ مَا كُنتُ بِدْعًا مِّنَ ٱلرُّسُلِ$$

'I did not bring something unprecedented among the messengers.' (Al-Ahqaf 46:9)

This does not indicate a *bid'a* in the *shar'ī* sense, because such a *bid'a* would be an act of misguidance as was indicated by the Messenger (ﷺ).

Scholars who classify *bid'as* into good and bad only intend the linguistic meaning of *bid'a*; and those who say that every *bid'a* is a misguidance mean *bid'a* in the *shar'ī* sense.

Just look at how the Sahābah (ﷺ), as well as those who followed them in a good way, have objected to giving Adhān for prayers other than the five daily prayers, such as the 'Eīd prayers, even though there is no explicit prohibition in this regard. Also, they disliked people holding onto the two shāmī corners of the Ka'bah, as well as praying after sa'y in analogy to praying after tawāf.

Futhermore, there are things that the Prophet (ﷺ) avoided despite the need and ability to do them during his lifetime. Avoiding such things is then a *Sunnah*, and doing them is a balance worthy innovation. By our saying: Despite the need and ability to do them, we exclude driving out the Jews, compiling the *Mushaf*, and other things that He (ﷺ) did not do because of reasons that prevented doing them. Thus, there was a need to pray *tarawīh* in congregation, but there was also a reason that prevented the Prophet (ﷺ) from continuing to pray it in congregation."[15]

Performing the night prayer in congregation is better than praying individually due to the Prophet's establishing it himself and due to him

---

15. Al-Ibda'fi Madarril-Ibtidā' as quoted in The Night Prayers, pg., 47, 48

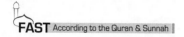

explaning its virtue in his saying.

Abu Dharr (ﷺ) narrated: "We fasted with the Messenger of Allah (ﷺ) the entire month of Ramadān and he did not lead us (in night prayer) for any of it until only seven nights were left. He then led us (in prayer) only six (nights), and he did not lead us until half the night had passed. I said: 'O Messenger of Allah! Why do you not (lead us) in voluntary prayer for the entire night?' He replied:

إِنَّ الرَّجُلَ إِذَا صَلَّى مَعَ الإِمَامِ حَتَّى يَنْصَرِفَ حُسِبَ لَهُ قِيَامُ لَيْلَةٍ

> 'If a person offers prayer with the *Imam* until he leaves, it will be counted as an entire night's prayer for him.'

And when there were four (nights left) he did not stand (in prayer). When only three (nights left) he did not stand (in prayer) When only three (nights) remained, he gathered his family and wives and the people, and led us (in prayer) until we thought that we would miss the *falah*." He (the sub-narrator) said: "I said: 'What is the *Falah*?' He (Abu Dharr) said: 'The *sahur* (pre-dawn meal). Then he did not lead us for the rest of the month.'"[16]

The Legality of Woman Performing the Night Prayer in Congregation

Women can attend the *tarawīh* prayers. It is also permissible to appoint an *imam* specifically for them. It is confirmed that 'Umar (ﷺ) gathered the people for *qiyām*, appointing Ubayy bin Ka'b to lead the men, and Sulaiman bin Abi Hathmah to lead the women, Also, 'Arfajah ath-Thaqafi said: "Ali bin Abi Talib (ﷺ) commanded the people to pray night prayer during the month of Ramadān; he appointed one *imam* for the men and one for the women. I was the women's *imam*."[17]

16. Abu Dawud: 1375
17. Al-Baihaqi, Abdur - Razaaq

The Number of Rak'ahs in the Night Prayer

Abu Salmah bin 'Abdur Rahman narrated that he asked 'Āishah (صلى): "How was the prayer of Allah's Messenger (صلى) in Ramadān?" She replied:

مَا كَانَ يَزِيدُ فِي رَمَضَانَ وَلَا فِي غَيْرِهِ عَلَى إِحْدَى عَشْرَةَ رَكْعَةً يُصَلِّي أَرْبَعَ رَكَعَاتٍ فَلَا تَسْأَلْ عَنْ حُسْنِهِنَّ وَطُولِهِنَّ ثُمَّ يُصَلِّي أَرْبَعًا فَلَا تَسْأَلْ عَنْ حُسْنِهِنَّ وَطُولِهِنَّ

"He did not perform (night) prayer more than eleven *rak'ah* in Ramadān or any other month. He used to perform four *rak'ah* – let alone their beauty and length – and then he would perform four *rak'ah* – let alone their beauty and length – and then he would perform three *rak'ah* (*witr*)." She added: "I asked: O Allah's Messenger ! Do you sleep before praying the *witr*?" He replied: "O Aisha! My eyes sleep but my heart does not sleep."[18]

Jabir bin 'Abdullāh (صلى) narrated: "Allah's Messenger (صلى) led us (one night) during Ramadān, praying eight *rak'ah* and *witr*. On the following night, we gathered in the Masjid hoping that he would come out again (to lead the prayer). We stayed there until the morning. Then we entered the Masjid hoping that he would lead us in the prayer. He replied:

قَدْ رَأَيْتُ الَّذِى صَنَعْتُمْ فَلَمْ يَمْنَعْنِى مِنَ الْخُرُوجِ إِلَيْكُمْ إِلاَّ أَنِّى خَشِيتُ أَنْ تُفْرَضَ عَلَيْكُمْ

'Indeed I feared that it would become an obligation on you.'[19]

As-Sā'ib bin Yazīd (صلى) narrated:

---

18. Bukhari: 2013
19. At-Tabrani: in Al-Mo'jam As-Sagheer: 108, Talkees-ul-Habeer: 119

$$\text{أَمَرَ عُمَرُ بْنُ الْـخَطَّابِ أُبَيَ بْنِ كَعْبِ وَتَـمِيْمًـا الدَّارِيَ أَنْ يَقُوْمُوا}$$
$$\text{لِلنَّاسِ بِإِحْدَى عَشَرَةَ رَكْعَة}$$

'Umar bin Al-Khattab commanded Ubayy bin Ka'b and Tamīm Ad-Dārī to lead the people in *qiyām* with eleven *rak'āh*. The reciter would read one hundred āyāt (in each *rak'āh*), until we had to lean on canes because of the long standing. We would not finish except with the arrival of *Fajr*."[20]

Argument for Twenty Rak'āhs

Hafiz Ibn Hajar said: "As for what was recorded by Ibn Abi Shaybah, from the *hadith* of Ibn 'Abbās (﴿) that Allah's Messenger (ﷺ) used to pray in Ramadān twenty *rak'āh* and *witr*, it has weak isnad; furthermore, it contradicts 'Āishah's *hadith* in two *Sahihs*. And she knows better than other people about the affairs of the Prophet (ﷺ) at night."[21]

Ibn Hajar Al-Haythamī said: "It is extremely weak. The scholars of *hadith* have been severe in criticizing and condemning one of its narrators. He narrates fabricated *hadith*s, such as: 'No nation was destroyed except in March,' and 'The Hour of Doom will not arise except in March.' This *hadith* regarding tarawih is among his munkars. As-Subkī has declared that the condition to accept a weak *hadith* is that its weakness must not be severe. And ath-Thahabī said: 'Anyone whom Shu'bah considers a liar, his *hadith* should not be considered at all.'"[22]

Report from 'Umar (﴿)

Yazīd bin Rūmān reported: "The People stood in *Qiyām* during the time of 'Umar with twently-three *Rak'āh*."

This report is weak because of the disconnection between Yazīd bin Rūmān and 'Umar, and may not be therefore taken as evidence, especially since it conflicts with the authentic report from 'Umar that he com-

---

20. Muwatta': 1/114
21. Fauthul-Bari: 4/205
22. Al-Fatawa al-Kubrā: 1/95 as quoted in Tarawih Prayer by Sheikh Albani, pg. 23

manded the people to pray eleven *rak'āh.*[23]

The Manner of Offering Tarawih Prayer

'Āishah (﷽) narrated about the *salāt* of Allah's Messenger (﷽) during the month of Ramadān. She said:

مَا كَانَ يَزِيدُ فِي رَمَضَانَ وَلَا فِي غَيْرِهِ عَلَى إِحْدَى عَشْرَةَ رَكْعَةً يُصَلِّي أَرْبَعًا فَلَا تَسْئَلْ عَنْ حُسْنِهِنَّ وَطُولِهِنَّ ثُمَّ يُصَلِّي أَرْبَعًا فَلَا تَسْئَلْ عَنْ حُسْنِهِنَّ وَطُولِهِنَّ ثُمَّ يُصَلِّي ثَلَاثًا فَقُلْتُ يَا رَسُولَ اللهِ أَتَنَامُ قَبْلَ أَنْ تُوتِرَ قَالَ يَا عَائِشَةُ إِنَّ عَيْنَيَّ تَنَامَانِ وَلَا يَنَامُ قَلْبِي

"Allah's Messenger (﷽) never exceeded eleven *rak'āh* in Ramadān or in other months; he used to offer four *rak'āh* – do not ask me about their beauty and length – then four *rak'āh* – do not ask me about their beauty and length – and then three *rak'āh.*"

'Āishah (﷽) further said: "I said: O Allah's Messenger! Do you sleep before offering the *witr* prayers?" He replied: "O 'Āishah! My eyes sleep but my heart remains awake!"[24]

Hudahifah (﷽) narrated:

صَلَّيْتُ مَعَ النَّبِيِّ (﷽) ذَاتَ لَيْلَةٍ فَافْتَتَحَ الْبَقَرَةَ فَقُلْتُ يَرْكَعُ عِنْدَ الْـمِائَةِ. ثُمَّ مَضَى فَقُلْتُ يُصَلِّي بِهَا فِي رَكْعَةٍ فَمَضَى فَقُلْتُ يَرْكَعُ بِهَا. ثُمَّ افْتَتَحَ النِّسَاءَ فَقَرَأَهَا ثُمَّ افْتَتَحَ آلَ عِمْرَانَ فَقَرَأَهَا يَقْرَأُ مُتَرَسِّلاً إِذَا مَرَّ بِآيَةٍ فِيهَا تَسْبِيحٌ سَبَّحَ وَإِذَا مَرَّ بِسُؤَالٍ سَأَلَ وَإِذَا مَرَّ بِتَعَوُّذٍ تَعَوَّذَ ثُمَّ رَكَعَ فَجَعَلَ يَقُولُ «سُبْحَانَ رَبِّيَ الْعَظِيمِ». فَكَانَ رُكُوعُهُ نَحْوًا مِنْ قِيَامِهِ ثُمَّ قَالَ «سَمِعَ اللهُ لِـمَنْ حَمِدَهُ». ثُمَّ قَامَ

23. Nasbur-Rāyah: 2/154, Al-Majmū': 4/33 – Tarawih Prayer by Sheikh Albani pg. 61, 62
24. Bukhari: 1147

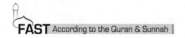
طَوِيلاً قَرِيبًا مِمَّا رَكَعَ ثُمَّ سَجَدَ فَقَالَ «سُبْحَانَ رَبِّيَ الأَعْلَى».

فَكَانَ سُجُودُهُ قَرِيبًا مِنْ قِيَامِهِ.

"I performed *salāt* with the Propeht (ﷺ) one night
and he started reciting Surah Al-Baqarah. I thought
that he would go into *ruku* (bowing posture) at the
end of one hundred verses, but he continued (reciting); and I thought that he would perhaps recite (this
Surah) in the whole *rak'āh*, but he continued the recitation; I thought he would perhaps bow on completing (this *Surah*). He (ﷺ) then started reciting Surah
An-Nisā' which he followd with *Surah Al-Imran*. He
recited at a leisurely pace. When he recited a verse
which mentioned the Glory of Allah, he glorified (by
saying *Subhan Allah* – Glory to Allah the Great) and
when he recited the verse which tells how the Lords
is to begged, Allah's Messenger (ﷺ) would then beg
from him, and when protection, he would seek Allah's protection. Then he bowed and said: '*Subhana
Rabbiyal-Adhim* (Glory be to my Mighty Lord).' His
bowing lasted about the same length of time as his
standing, (and then on returning to the standing posture after *ruku*) he would say: '*Sami Allahu liman
hamidah, Rabbana lakal-hamd* (Allah listens to him
who praises Him. Praise be to You, Our Lord); and
he would then stand about the same length of time as
he had spent in bowing. He would then prostrate and
say: '*Subhana Rabbiyal-A'la* (Glory be to my Lord,
the Most High); and his prostration lasted nearly the
same length of time as his standing (*qiyām*)."[25]

'Abdullāh bin 'Amr bin Al-'Ās (ﷺ) said that the Messenger of Allah
(ﷺ) said:

---

25. Muslim: 772

مَنْ قَامَ بِعَشْرِ آيَاتٍ لَـمْ يُكْتَبْ مِنَ الْغَافِلِينَ وَمَنْ قَامَ بِمِـائَةِ آيَةٍ
كُتِبَ مِنَ الْقَانِتِينَ وَمَنْ قَامَ بِأَلْفِ آيَةٍ كُتِبَ مِنَ الْـمُقَنْطَرِينَ

"Whoever recites ten verses (at night), he will not be
written among the heedless. And whoever recites one
hundred verses (at night), he will be written among
the devout. And whoever recites a thousand verses (at
night), he will be written among the prosperous."[26]

In tarawih, lengthy *qiyām* (standing) is *Sunnah*, but it must be kept in
mind that the Noble Qur'ān must be recited according to the principles
of Ilm-ut-Tajweed (علم التجويد) with a clear and distinct voice and at a slow
pace. Many of the qurra' (reciters) recite so fast that it is hard for one to
understand, let alone concentrate, on what is being recited. Such recitation is a means of retribution rather than reward. A new system is now
in vogue. According to this system, the whole Qur'ān is finished within
a few days and eight to ten parts of it are recited daily in *qiyāmul-lail*.
There are hundreds of thousands of people in the audience. After listening to the Noble Qur'ān for a few days, these people are satisfied that
they have heard the entire Qur'ān in the Night Prayer and are now free to
go back to their business to make the best of the 'Eid season.

'Āishah (🌸) narrated:

لاَ أَعْلَمُ رَسُولَ اللَّهِ قَرَأَ الْقُرْآنَ كُلَّهُ فِي لَيْلَةٍ وَلاَ قَامَ لَيْلَةً حَتَّى
الصَّبَاحِ وَلاَ صَامَ شَهْرًا كَامِلاً قَطُّ غَيْرَ رَمَضَانَ

"I do not know that the Messenger of Allah (🌸) recited the whole Qur'ān in one night, or prayed *qiyām*
until morning, or ever fasted an entire month, except
Ramadān."[27]

Moderation and Regularity in Prayer

Anas bin Malik (🌸) narrated that once the Prophet (🌸) entered (the

26. Abu Dawud: 1398
27. Nasa'i: 2350

mosque) and saw a rope hanging between its two pillars. He said: "What is this rope for?" The people said: "This rope is for Zainab who, when she feels tired, holds it (to keep standing) in the *salat*." The Prophet (ﷺ) said:

لَا حُلُّوهُ لِيُصَلِّ أَحَدُكُمْ نَشَاطَهُ فَإِذَا فَتَرَ فَلْيَقْعُدْ.

"Do not use it. Remove the rope. You should perform *salat* as long as you feel active, and when you get tired, sit down."

'Āishah (ﷺ) narrated that a woman from the tribe of Bani Asad was sitting with me and Allah's Messenger (ﷺ) came to my house and said: "Who is this?" I said: "(She is) so-and-so. She does not sleep at night because she is engaged in *salat*." The Prophet (ﷺ) said, disapprovingly:

مَهْ عَلَيْكُمْ مَا تُطِيقُونَ مِنَ الْأَعْمَالِ فَإِنَّ اللهَ لَا يَمَلُّ حَتَّى تَمَلُّوا.

"Do (good) deeds which are within your capacity as Allah never gets tired of giving rewards till you get tired for doing good deeds."

'Abdullāh bin 'Amr (ﷺ) narrated: Once Allah's Messenger (ﷺ) said to me: "I have been informed that you perform *salat* all night and fast during the day." I said: "(Yes) I do so." He said:

فَإِنَّكَ إِذَا فَعَلْتَ ذَلِكَ هَجَمَتْ عَيْنُكَ وَنَفِهَتْ نَفْسُكَ وَإِنَّ لِنَفْسِكَ حَقًّا وَلِأَهْلِكَ حَقًّا فَصُمْ وَأَفْطِرْ وَقُمْ وَنَمْ.

"If you do so, your eye-sight will become weak and you will become weak. No doubt, your body has a right on you, and your family has a right on you; so fast (some days) and do not fast (some days). Perform *salat* (for some time) and then sleep."[28]

'Āishah (ﷺ) narrated that Allah's Messenger (ﷺ) had a mat and he used

---

28. Bukhari: 1150, 1151, 1153

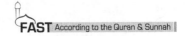

it for making a small apartment during the night and performed *salāt* in it. The people began to pray with him, and he spread it out during the day time. The people crowded around him one night. He (ﷺ) then said:

يَا أَيُّهَا النَّاسُ عَلَيْكُمْ مِنَ الأَعْمَالِ مَا تُطِيقُونَ فَإِنَّ اللهَ لاَ يَمَلُّ حَتَّى تَمَلُّوا وَإِنَّ أَحَبَّ الأَعْمَالِ إِلَى اللهِ مَا دُووِمَ عَلَيْهِ وَإِنْ قَلَّ . وَكَانَ آلُ مُحَمَّدٍ (ﷺ) إِذَا عَمِلُوا عَمَلاً أَثْبَتُوهُ.

"O people, perform such acts as you are capable of, for Allah does not grow tired (of giving reward) until you become tired. The acts most pleasing to Allah are those which are done continuously, even if they are small. And it was the habit of the members of Muhammad's household that whenever they did an act, they did it continuously."

Alqamah narrated: I asked 'Āishah (ﷺ), the Mother of the believers: "O Mother of the believers, how did the Messenger of Allah (ﷺ) act? Did he choose a particular act for a particular day?" She said: "His acts were continuous, and who amongst you is capable of doing what the Allah's Messenger (ﷺ) did?"[29]

'Abdullāh bin Amr bin 'Āl-As (ﷺ) narrated: Allah's Messenger (ﷺ) told me:

أَحَبُّ الصَّلاَةِ إِلَى اللهِ صَلاَةُ دَاوُدَ عَلَيْهِ السَّلاَم وَأَحَبُّ الصِّيَام إِلَى اللهِ صِيَامُ دَاوُدَ وَكَانَ يَنَامُ نِصْفَ اللَّيْلِ وَيَقُومُ ثُلُثَهُ وَيَنَامُ سُدُسَهُ وَيَصُومُ يَوْمًا وَيُفْطِرُ يَوْمًا.

"The most beloved *salāt* to Allah is that of Dawud (David) and the most beloved fast to Allah is that of Dawud. He used to sleep for half of the night and then perform *salāt* for one third of the night and again sleep for its sixth part and used to observe *saūm* on

---

29. Muslim: 782, 783

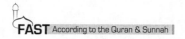

alternate days."[30]

Commanding the Imam to be Considerate of the People

If a person is praying night prayer by himself, he can make it as long as he wishes; if others agree with the *imam*, he may also make it as long as he wishes. The longer it is, the better, but a person should not go to extremes and spend the whole night in *qiyām* except on rare occasions, following the example of the Prophet (ﷺ) who said:

$$ وَخَيْرَ الْهَدْي هَدْيُ مُحَمَّدٍ $$

"The best guidance is the guidance of Muhammad."[31]

If a person is praying as an *Imam*, he should make it only as long as is easy for the people behind him, because the Prophet (ﷺ) said:

$$ إِنِّي لَأَقُومُ فِي الصَّلَاةِ أُرِيدُ أَنْ أُطَوِّلَ فِيهَا فَأَسْمَعُ بُكَاءَ الصَّبِيِّ فَأَتَجَوَّزُ فِي صَلَاتِي كَرَاهِيَةَ أَنْ أَشُقَّ عَلَى أُمِّهِ $$

"When I stand for *salāt*, I intend to prolong it, but on hearing the cries of a child, I cut it short as I dislike to cause trouble to the child's mother."

Anas bin Malik (ﷺ) narrated:

$$ مَا صَلَّيْتُ وَرَاءَ إِمَام قَطُّ أَخَفَّ صَلَاةً وَلَا أَتَمَّ مِنْ النَّبِيِّ (ﷺ) وَإِنْ كَانَ لَيَسْمَعُ بُكَاءَ الصَّبِيِّ فَيُخَفِّفُ مَخَافَةَ أَنْ تُفْتَنَ أُمُّهُ $$

"I never offered behind any *Imam* a *salāt* lighter and more perfect that when behind the Prophet (ﷺ) and he used to cut it short whenever he heard the cries of a child lest he should cause suffering to the child's mother."[32]

---

30. Bukhari: 1131
31. Muslim: 867
32. Bukhari: 707, 708

Abu Mas'ud Al-Ansari (ﷺ) narrated that a man once said to Allah's Messenger (ﷺ): "O Allah's Messenger! I cannot attend the (compulsory congregational) *salāt* because so and so (the *Imam*) prolongs the *salāt* when he leads us in it." The narrator added: "I never saw the Prophet (ﷺ) more furious when giving advice than he was on that day. The Prophet (ﷺ) said:

أَيُّهَا النَّاسُ إِنَّكُمْ مُنَفِّرُونَ فَمَنْ صَلَّى بِالنَّاسِ فَلْيُخَفِّفْ فَإِنَّ فِيهِمْ الْمَرِيضَ وَالضَّعِيفَ وَذَا الْحَاجَةِ

'O people! Some of you make others dislike good deeds (*salāt*, etc.) So whoever leads the people in prayer should shorten it because among them there are the sick, the weak and the one who is in a state that requires urgent relief (such as having some urgent job to do).'"[33]

Jabir bin 'Abdullāh (ﷺ) said: "Mu'adh bin Jabal (ﷺ) used to perform *salāt* with the Prophet (ﷺ) and then go to lead his people in it. Once he led the *'Ishā'* prayer and recited Surat Al-Baqarah. Someone left the *salāt* and Mu'adh (ﷺ) criticized him. The news reached the Prophet (ﷺ) and he said to Mu'adh (ﷺ) 'You are putting the people to trail,' and repeated it thrice (or said something similar) and ordered him to recite two medium-length surahs from *Al-Mufassal*."[34]

All Surahs in the Qur'ān from Surah *Al-Hujurat* to the end of the Qur'ān are called *Al-Mufassal* (partitioned) because that section of the Qur'ān has many partitions between the Surahs (i.e. the Surahs are short). From *Al-Hujurat* to *Al-Buruj* are called *tiwwal* (long). From *Al-Buruj* to *Al-Bayinah* are called *awsat* (middle); and from *Al-Bayinah* to the end of the Qur'ān are called qisar (short). It is *Sunnah* to recite the *tiwwal* in *Fajr* prayer, *awsat* in *'Ishā'* prayer, and the qisar in the *Maghrib* prayer, *Zuhr* prayer is linked with *Fajr* prayer and *'Asr* with *'Ishā'* prayer.[35]

---

33. Bukhari: 90
34. Bukhari: 701
35. Ittihaful-Qiram

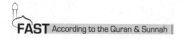

Reciting the Entire Qur'ān in *Tarawīh*

There is a great flexibility in this matter. I do not know of any evidence that suggests that it is better, except that some scholars have mentioned that it is *mustahab* for the *Imam* to recite the entire Qur'ān for the congregation in order that they receive the opportunity to listen to it in its entirety. However, this is not clear evidence. What is most important is that the *Imam* has *khushoo'* in his prayer, that he feels at ease, and that the people benefit from him, even if he were not to complete except half of the Qur'ān. It is not important that he completes it, but rather that the people benefit from him, even if he were not to complete except half of the Qur'ān. It is not important that he completes it, but rather the people benefit and find peace in his prayer, his *khushoo'*, and his recitation. However, if he found it easy to complete, then all praise is for Allah, but if he did not, then what he did recite was sufficient, for his concern should be for the people and that they feel *khushoo'* in their prayer. The benefit of the people is more important than the mere completion of the Qur'ān, but if he were to finish the Qur'ān without causing difficulty for the people, then this is well and good.[36]

The Imam Holding a Mushaf

'Āishah (﷽) was led in the *Salāt* by her slave Dhakwān who used to recite from the *Mushaf* (the written Qur'ān not from memory). *Imam* Bukhari narrated it under the chapter: A slave or a manumitted slave can lead the *salāt*.

One of the Followers holding a Mushaf

I do not know of any evidence to support this. It is apparent though, that one should have *khushoo'* and feel at peace in his prayer and not carry a *Mushaf*. One should put his right hand over one's left hand as is the *Sunnah*. One should place one's right hand on one's left hand, wrist, and forearm and put them on one's chest. This is what is preferred and more correct. Carrying a *Mushaf* prevents one from doing these *Sunnah*

---

36. Concerning *Tarawīh* by Sheikh Ibn Baz, p.16

acts and prevents one from concentrating on the *Imam* and his recitation. Rather, it keeps one's heart and eyes busy in examining its pages and verses. So what I believe is that leaving it is the *Sunnah*. One should listen and concentrate on the recitation; if he knows that the *Imam* has made a mistake, then he should correct him, and if he does not, then someone else should correct him. However, if the *Imam* does happen to make a mistake in recitation and he is not corrected, it does not influence the validity of the prayer. A mistake only harms the prayer if it is made in *Surah al-Fatihah*, for it is a *rukn* (pillar) of the prayer. However, if one were to carry a *Mushaf* and correct the *Imam* when it necessitates, then there may be no harm in that. As for every person carrying a *Mushaf*, this is contrary to the *Sunnah*.[37]

Repetition of One Verse

Abu Dhar (ﷺ) narrated:

قَامَ النَّبِيُّ صلى الله عليه وسلم حَتَّى أَصْبَحَ بِآيَةٍ وَالآيَةُ (إِنْ تُعَذِّبْهُمْ فَإِنَّهُمْ عِبَادُكَ وَإِنْ تَغْفِرْ لَهُمْ فَإِنَّكَ أَنْتَ الْعَزِيزُ الْحَكِيمُ

One night Allah's Messenger (ﷺ) continued reciting one verse till morning: "If you punish them they are Your slaves, and if You forgive them, Verily, You only You, are the All Mighty, the All-Wise."[38]

Supplicating After the Completion of the Qur'ān

Our pious predecessors did not leave reciting the supplications made upon the completion of the Qur'ān during the prayer of Ramaḍān, and we do not know of any difference in this regard. What is best is that the *Imam* should supplicate, but not lengthen the supplication. He should seek to recite those supplications that are beneficial and inclusive in meaning, as 'Āishah (ﷺ) said:

"The Prophet (ﷺ) was fond of those supplications that were inclusive in

---

37. Concerning Tarawih, by Sheikh Ibn Baz, pg. 22, 23
38. Nasa'i: 1011

meaning and refrained from other supplications."

So what is better is that the *Imam* should seek to supplicate with those which are inclusive in meaning without lengthening them. He should recite the supplication: "O Allah guide me from those whom you have guided..." in the *qunoot* as has been reported in a hasan *hadith*. Along with this, he should recite other good and easy supplications, as in the addition of 'Umar (ﷺ) without lengthening them, thus in fact causing burden and inconvenience to the people. This is how the supplication upon the completion the Qur'ān should be; he should be inclusive in meaning. He should start by praising Allah and sending peace and prayers upon the Prophet (ﷺ), and then complete the supplication with what is easy, whether it be in the night prayer or in the *witr*. He should not lengthen it so as to cause distress or inconvenience.

This is what is known from our pious predecessors, and this example was followed by later generations. Our schalors and teachers along with their dedication for the *Sunnah* followed this as well, the latter emulating the former. This is considered to be an obvious fact by the scholars of the *Dawah of Tawheed*, who are known to be keen in the *Sunnah*. The fact of the matter remains that there is no harm or blame in this, if Allah wills, but rather that this is something that is deemed praiseworthy, because by doing this one seeks response to one's supplication after the completion of the Book of Allah. When Anas (ﷺ) would complete the Qur'ān, he would gather his family and supplicate outside of the prayer. This is just as well whether it is within the prayer or outside it because supplication has been legislated at both times, so there can be no objection in this.

And it is well known that upon reciting a verse which describes the punishment or the mercy of Allah, one should supplicate as the Prophet (ﷺ) did in the night prayer. This is similar to the matter at hand in that it is also legislated to supplicate after the completion of the Qur'ān. The point of contention is only whether one should supplicate within the prayer. As for supplicating outside of it, then I do not know of any difference of opinion other than that it is deemed praiseworthy, but the difference lies within the prayer. I do not know anyone from our pious predecessors who has objected to supplicating within the prayer, and I do not know of any who have objected to supplication outside it. So this is what is used as a basis, that it was something known to our predecessors, of which the former as well as the latter acted upon. Whosoever says that this is wrong should come with some evidence, for the burden of proof does not lie upon the one who acts according to what our pious predecessors, did. The evidence is to be established by the one who says that it is wrong and that it is an innovation. This is what our pious predecessors of the *Ummah* chose and tread upon. The latter generations took example from the former, and amongst them were the scholars, the virtuous, and the scholars of *hadith*. The recitation of various supplications in the night prayer is something known to be from the *Sunnah* of the Prophet (ﷺ), and what is recited upon the completion of the Qur'ān is within this class of supplication.[39]

Any Particular Supplication after Completion of the Qur'ān

From what we know, there is no particular supplication which has been mentioned in the Qur'ān or the *Sunnah*. One may supplicate with whatever one pleases: one may choose from any of the beneficial supplications like the seeking of forgiveness for sins, success in attaining *Al-Jannah*, savior from An-Nar, seeking of rufuge from trails, seeking of the blessing in memorizing the Noble Qur'ān, understanding and acting upon it, and any other similar supplications. It has been related of Anas (ﷺ) that he would gather his family and supplicate upon completing the recitation of the Qur'ān. As for the Prophet (ﷺ) what I know, nothing has been mentioned in this regard.

As for the supplication attributed to Ibn Taymiyyah (ﷺ), I do not know of its authenticity. It is known, but I have not come across it in any of his works.[40]

Praying 'Ishā' with the congregation who is praying Tarawih

There is no harm in that one prays with the intention of *'Ishā'* with oth-

---

39. Concerning Tarawih, pg. 34-36
40. Majallah Al-Buhooth Al-Islamiyyah: 20/186, Concering Tawaweeh by Sheikh Ibn Baz

ers who are praying tarawīh. This is the correct of the two opinions held by the scholars. And once the *Imam* pronounces the tasleem, he should stand and complete the remainder of his prayer. It has been reported in Bukhari and Muslim on the authority of Mu'adh bin Jabal (﷽) that he used to pray with the Prophet (﷽), and then return to his people and lead them in theirs, and the Prophet (﷽) did not object to that. This proves the permissibility of praying an obligatory prayer behind one praying a superogatory one. It has been reported in Saheeh Bukhari that the Prophet (﷽) in some types of the prayer of fear prayed two *rak'āh* leading one group, and then prayed another two with the next, making tasleem at the end. So the first two *rak'āh* were considered obligatory for him, while the second was considered superogatory, but obligatory for the congregation.[41]

Reciting the Qur'ān Melodiously

It has been encouraged to recite the Qur'ān melodiously in the authentic *Sunnah* of the Prophet (﷽), but what is meant by this is that one beautify one's voice in recitation without it resembling singing. It has been reported in authentic narrations:

$$مَا أَذِنَ اللهُ لِشَيْءٍ مَا أَذِنَ لِلنَّبِيِّ أَنْ يَتَغَنَّى بِالْقُرْآنِ$$

"Allah does not listen so attentively to anything as He listens to the recitation of the Qur'ān by a Prophet who recites well with a melodious and audible voice."[42]

Abu Musa (﷽) narrated that the Prophet (﷽) said to him:

$$يَا أَبَا مُوسَى لَقَدْ أُوتِيتَ مِزْمَارًا مِنْ مَزَامِيرِ آلِ دَاوُدَ$$

"O Abu Musa! You have been given one of the musical wind instruments of the family of Dawūd (David)."[43]

---

41. Concerning *Tarawīh* by Ibn Baz, p. 49
42. Bukhari: 5024
43. Bukhari: 5048

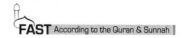

'Abdullāh bin Mas'ūd (⁂) narrated: The Propht (⁂) said to me: "Recite (the Qur'ān) to me." I said: "O Allah's Messenger! Shall I recite (the Qur'ān) to you while it has been revealed to you?" He said: "Yes." So I recited Surah An-Nisā', till I reached the verse:

$$فَكَيْفَ إِذَا جِئْنَا مِنْ كُلِّ أُمَّةٍ بِشَهِيدٍ وَجِئْنَا بِكَ عَلَى هَؤُلَاءِ شَهِيدًا$$

"How (will it be) then, when we bring from each nation a witness and we bring you (O Muhammad ⁂) as a witness against there people?" (V. 4:41)

He said: "Enough for the present." I looked at him and behold! His eyes were overflowing with tears.[44]

'Ubaidullah bin Abi Yazid narrated: Abu Lubabah passed by us, so we followed him back to his home. We saw that he was a person who lived in an austere house, wearing simple clothes. I heared him say: I heard the Messenger of Allah (⁂) say:

$$لَيْسَ مِنَّا مَنْ لَمْ يَتَغَنَّ بِالْقُرْآنِ$$

"He who does not recite the Qur'ān in a pleasant tone is not of us."

He said: "So I said to Ibn Abī Mulaikah: 'O Abu Muhammad what if he does not have a good voice?' His teacher replied: 'He should try as much as he can.'"[45]

The words "is not of us" means that he is not following the way of the Prophet (⁂) with regard to the recitation of the Qur'ān. This hadith also induces us to recite the Qur'ān with a sweet and touching voice because the recitation of the Qur'ān in this manner enhances its effect.

Al-Barā' (⁂) narrated:

$$سَمِعْتُ النَّبِيَّ (⁂) يَقْرَأُ وَالتِّينِ وَالزَّيْتُونِ فِي الْعِشَاءِ وَمَا سَمِعْتُ$$

---

44. Bukhari: 5050
45. Abu Dawud: 1471

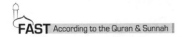

أَحَدًا أَحْسَنَ صَوْتًا مِنْهُ أَوْ قِرَاءَةً

"I heared the Prophet (ﷺ) reciting Wat-tīni Waz-Zai-tuni (Surah 95) in the *'Ishā'* prayer, and I never heard a sweeter voice or better way of recitation than that of the Prophet (ﷺ)."[46]

Weeping in the supplication and not when they hear the words of Allah

This may not necessarily be done by choice, but it may be that a person's soul is moved in supplication and not in recitation. It is necessary, though, that he cures himself of this. It is more important to feel *khushoo'* in the recitation than in supplication. However if he were to feel *khushoo'* both in his recitation and his supplication, then this is all well and good, because having *khushoo'* in the supplication is a means for its acceptance. It is necessary, though, that more importance is paid to the recitation because it is the Speech of Allah, and that it is a Guidance and a Light. The Prophet (ﷺ) and the Sahaabah (ﷺ) would contemplate and comprehend the Qur'ān, and as a result they would weep. An example of this is the Prophet's (ﷺ) saying to 'Abdullāh bin Mas'ood (ﷺ): "Recite to me the Qur'ān." 'Abdullāh replied: "How should I recite to you, when it was you to whom it was revealed?" The Prophet (ﷺ) then said: "I love to hear its recitation from someone other than myself." Thereupon Ibn Mas'ood recited the Qur'ān from the beginning of Surah An-Nisā' until he reached Allah's saying...

فَكَيْفَ إِذَا جِئْنَا مِنْ كُلِّ أُمَّةٍ بِشَهِيدٍ وَجِئْنَا بِكَ عَلَى هَؤُلَاءِ شَهِيدًا

"How (will it be) then, when We bring from each nation a witness, and We bring you (O Muhammad ﷺ) as a witness against these people?" (An-Nisā' 4:41)

The Prophet (ﷺ) said: "That is enough." Ibn Mas'ood (ﷺ) said: "So I turned my gaze towards him," or he said, "So I raised my head towards

---

46. Bukhari: 769

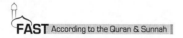

him, and behold! His eyes were overflowing with tears."[47]

What is apparent from this hadeeth is that the Prophet (ﷺ) wept without any sound issuing forth, and that Ibn Mas'ood came to know of his weeping only by the presence of his tears. It has also been reported in the *hadith* of 'Abdullāh bin Shikhir, that he heard wheezing like the wheezing of a cauldron from the Prophet (ﷺ) chest because of his weeping. This evidence shows that his weeping could sometimes be heard, but without it being disturbing.

Compensation of the Night Prayer

'Āishah (ﷺ) narrated:

أَنَّ رَسُولَ اللهِ (ﷺ) كَانَ إِذَا فَاتَتْهُ الصَّلَاةُ مِنَ اللَّيْلِ مِنْ وَجَعٍ أَوْ
غَيْرِهِ صَلَّى مِنَ النَّهَارِ ثِنْتَىْ عَشْرَةَ رَكْعَةً.

"If Allah's Messenger (ﷺ) missed his night prayer because of indisposition or the like, he would perform twelve *rak'āhs* (of voluntary *Salāt*) during the day."

'Umar bin Khattab (ﷺ) narrated that Allah's Messenger (ﷺ) said:

مَنْ نَامَ عَنْ حِزْبِهِ أَوْ عَنْ شَىْءٍ مِنْهُ فَقَرَأَهُ مَا بَيْنَ صَلَاةِ الْفَجْرِ
وَصَلَاةِ الظُّهْرِ كُتِبَ لَهُ كَأَنَّمَا قَرَأَهُ مِنَ اللَّيْلِ

"If any one falls asleep and, because of that, fails to read the share or part (of the Qur'ān he would recite in his night prayers), then if he recites them between the *Fajr* and *Zuhr* prayers, it will be recorded for him as though he had recited it during the night."[48]

---

47. Bukhari: 5050
48. Muslim: 746, 747

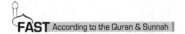

Reciting the Qur'ān or Praying superogatory Prayer: which is better

It is from the guidance of the Prophet (ﷺ) in Ramadān that he would increase in different types of worship. Jibreel would revise the Qur'ān with him, and when Jibreel met him he would be more generous than a fast wind. He (ﷺ) was the most generous of people, but he would be his most generous during Ramadān. He would increase in prayer, spending for the sake of Allah, recitation of the Qur'ān, helping others, *dhikr*, and *i'tikaf*. This is the guidance of the Prophet (ﷺ) in this blessed month. As for the comparison between recitation and prayer, this differs in regards to the different condition and people, and its exact reward is with Allah, for He is All-Encompassing in knowledge.[49]

Ramadān and Qur'ān

The month of Ramadān is the one in which the Qur'ān was sent down. Allah says:

$$\text{شَهْرُ رَمَضَانَ ٱلَّذِىَ أُنزِلَ فِيهِ ٱلْقُرْءَانُ هُدًى لِّلنَّاسِ وَبَيِّنَتٍ}$$
$$\text{مِّنَ ٱلْهُدَىٰ وَٱلْفُرْقَانِ}$$

> "The month of Ramadān in which was revealed the Qur'ān as a guidance for mankind and clear proofs for the guidance and the criterion (between right and wrong)." (Al-Baqarah 2:185)

Our *salaf*, who were undoubtedly the best of generations, their character and way of life stand witness to this fact and is further confirmed by the statement of Allah's Messenger (ﷺ):

$$\text{خَيْرُ أُمَّتِي الْقَرْنُ الَّذِينَ يَلُونِي ثُمَّ الَّذِينَ يَلُونَهُمْ ثُمَّ الَّذِينَ يَلُونَهُمْ}$$

> "The best of the generations are my generation, then those which follow them, then those which follow them."

---

49. Concerning *Tarawīh* by Sheikh Ibn Baz, p. 50

Some of our *salaf* would complete reciting the whole Qur'ān during the night prayer of Ramadān every 3 days, others every seven days, e.g. Qatadah, others in 10 days, e.g. Abu Rajā' Al-Utaridi. The *salaf* would recite the Qur'ān in Ramadān in prayer as well as outside of it. Al-Aswad would finish the Qur'ān every 2 nights in Ramadān, Ibrahim an-Nakh'i would do likewise in the last ten nights specifically, and every 3 nights during the rest of the month. Qatadah would regularly finish the Qur'ān in 7 days, but in three days during Ramadān and in last ten days every night. Az-Zuhair would say when Ramadān began: "It is the month of reciting the Qur'ān and feeding the people." *Imam* Shafi' used to finish the Qur'ān sixty times in Ramadān.

Imam Malik would cease narrating *hadith* and sitting with the people of knowledge, and stick to reciting the Qur'ān from the *Mushaf*. Sufyan ath-Thawri would leave other acts of worship and stick to reciting the Qur'ān. 'Āishah (﷽) would recite from the *Mushaf* at the beginning of the day in Ramadān (i.e. after Dawn), until when the sun had risen, and then she would sleep.

Ibn Rajab further says:

The forbiddance of completing the recitation of the Qur'ān in less than 3 days applies to this being made a regular practice, but as for favoured times such as Ramadān, esp., the nights in which *Laylatul-Qadr* is sought, or favoured places such as Makkah for the visitor, it is recommended to increase reciting the Qur'ān to avail the time and place. This is the view of Ahmad, Ishaq and others, and the practice of others indicates this too."[50]

The *Witr* Prayer

Witr literally means odd number. *Witr* has two different meanings in the *Sunnah*: The last one or three *rak'āhs* of the night prayer, or it means all of the night prayers (because in essence they are odd-numbered). This discussion refers to the former meaning. We learn from the following *hadith* that *witr* is not obligatory but desirable. But it would not be correct

---

50. Lata'iful-Ma'arif: 271

to show any slackness in performing it because every Muslim should do his best to follow the *Sunnah* of the Prophet (ﷺ).

Abu Ayyūb Ansari (ﷺ) narrated that Allah's Messenger (ﷺ) said:

الْوِتْرُ حَقٌّ عَلَى كُلِّ مُسْلِمٍ فَمَنْ أَحَبَّ أَنْ يُوتِرَ بِخَمْسٍ فَلْيَفْعَلْ وَمَنْ أَحَبَّ أَنْ يُوتِرَ بِثَلَاثٍ فَلْيَفْعَلْ وَمَنْ أَحَبَّ أَنْ يُوتِرَ بِوَاحِدَةٍ فَلْيَفْعَلْ

"The *Witr* is a duty of every Muslim, so he who wants to perform five *rak'āhs* (*witr*) should perform five *rak'āhs* and he who wants to perform three *rak'āhs* should perform three *rak'āhs*, and he who wants to perform one *rak'āh* should perform one *rak'āh*."[51]

'Abdullāh bin Umar (ﷺ) narrated that the Prophet (ﷺ) said:

صَلَاةُ اللَّيْلِ مَثْنَى مَثْنَى فَإِذَا أَرَدْتَ أَنْ تَنْصَرِفَ فَارْكَعْ رَكْعَةً تُوتِرُ لَكَ مَا صَلَّيْتَ

"The night prayer is performed as two *rak'āhs* followed by two *rak'āhs* and so on, and if you want to finish it, perform only one *rak'āh* which will be *witr* for all the previous *rak'āhs*."

Qasim said: "Since we attained the age of puberty we have seen some people offering a three *rak'āh* prayer as *witr* and all that is permissible. I hope there will be no harm in it."[52]

'Abdullāh bin Umar (ﷺ) narrated that the Prophet (ﷺ) said:

اجْعَلُوا آخِرَ صَلَاتِكُمْ بِاللَّيْلِ وِتْرًا

"Make *witr* your last *salāt* for the night."[53]

---

51. Abu Dawud: 1422
52. Bukhari: 993
53. Bukhari: 998

Ibn 'Umar (ﷺ) narrated that the Prophet (ﷺ) said:

$$إِذَا طَلَعَ الْفَجْرُ فَقَدْ ذَهَبَ كُلُّ صَلَاةِ اللَّيْلِ وَالْوِتْرُ فَأَوْتِرُوا قَبْلَ طُلُوعِ الْفَجْرِ$$

"When the dawn breaks, then the time of all night prayers, including the *witr*, is over, so observe the *witr* before dawn."[54]

Jabir (ﷺ) narrated that Allah's Messenger (ﷺ) said:

$$أَوْتِرُوا قَبْلَ أَنْ تُصْبِحُوا$$

"Perform *witr* prayer before dawn."[55]

Two *Witrs* in One Night

Talq bin 'Ali (ﷺ) narrated: I heared Allah's Messenger (ﷺ) saying:

$$لَا وِتْرَانِ فِي لَيْلَةٍ$$

"There are no two *witr* (prayers) during one night."[56]

Compensation of the *Witr* Prayer

Abu Sa'īd Al-Khudri (ﷺ) narrated that Allah's Messenger (ﷺ) said:

$$مَنْ نَامَ عَنْ وِتْرِهِ فَلْيُصَلِّ إِذَا أَصْبَحَ أَوْ إِذَا ذَكَرَهُ$$

"Whoever oursleeps and misses the *witr*, or forgets it, should pray in the morning or when he remembers."[57]

One should know that should someone miss a prayer out of sincere oblivion or due to having fallen asleep, he shall not be brought to account

---

54. Tirmidhi: 467
55. Muslim: 754
56. Tirmidhi: 470
57. Tirmidhi: 465,466

in both these cases and he will get an equal amount of reward as if he performed the prayer on time, but it is prohibited to go to sleep at a time when a certain prayer is about to approach. In case such a thing happens inadvertently and beyond one's capability and control, one shall not be blamed for it.[58]

What to Recite in the *Witr* Prayer

Ibn 'Abbās (﷽) narrated:

كَانَ النَّبِيُّ ﷺ يَقْرَأُ فِي الْوِتْرِ بِـ (سَبِّحِ اسْمَ رَبِّكَ الْأَعْلَى) وَ (قُلْ يَا
أَيُّهَا الْكَافِرُونَ) وَ (قُلْ هُوَ اللَّهُ أَحَدٌ) فِي رَكْعَةٍ رَكْعَةٍ

"Allah's Messenger (ﷺ) recited in the *witr* prayer *Surah Al-'Ala* (no. 87), *Surah Al-Kafirun* (no, 113) and *Surah Al-Ikhlas* (no. 114) – in every *rak'āh* (one Surah)."[59]

Invocations for *Qunut* in the *Witr* Prayer

Hassan bin Ali (﷽) stated: The Messenger of Allah (ﷺ) taught me some phrases which I recite in *qunut*:

اللَّهُمَّ اهْدِنِي فِيمَنْ هَدَيْتَ وَعَافِنِي فِيمَنْ عَافَيْتَ وَتَوَلَّنِي فِيمَنْ
تَوَلَّيْتَ وَبَارِكْ لِي فِيمَا أَعْطَيْتَ وَقِنِي شَرَّ مَا قَضَيْتَ إِنَّكَ تَقْضِي
وَلَا يُقْضَى عَلَيْكَ وَإِنَّهُ لَا يَذِلُّ مَنْ وَالَيْتَ وَلَا يَعِزُّ مَنْ عَادَيْتَ
تَبَارَكْتَ رَبَّنَا وَتَعَالَيْتَ

Allaahum-mahddinee fiman hadaita, wa'aafini fiman 'aafaita, watawal-lani fiman tawallaita, wa baarik lee fimaa a'ataita, wa qinee sharra maa qadaita, fa innaka taqdee wa laa yuqdaa 'alaika, innahu laa yat-hillu man waalaita, [walaa ya 'izzu man 'aadaita],

---

58. Ittihaful-Kiram
59. Tirmidhi: 462

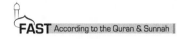

tabaarakta Rabbanaa wa ta' aalaita.

O Allah, guide me with those whom You have guided, and strengthen me with those whom You have given strength. Take me under Your care with those whom You have taken under Your care. Bless me in what You have given me. Protect me from the evil You have ordained. Surely, You command and are not commanded, and none whom You have committed to Your care shall be humiliated [and none whom You have taken as a an enemy shall taste glory]. You are Blessed Our Lord, and Exalted.[60]

Additional Invocations

One may occasionally add to the *salāt* supplication upon the Prophet (ﷺ). Also, durig the second half of Ramadān, one may further curse the disbelievers, say the supplication upon the Prophet (ﷺ), and supplicate for the Muslims. This was practiced by the *Imams* during the time of 'Umar (ﷺ), as 'Abd ur-Rahmān bin 'Abd al-Qārī reported:

"And they cursed the *kuffar* in the (second) half (of Ramadān):

اللَّهُمَّ قَاتِلِ الْكَفَرَةَ الَّذِينَ يَصُدُّونَ عَنْ سَبِيلِكَ، وَيُكَذِّبُونَ رُسُلَكَ، وَلَا يُؤْمِنُوْنَ بِوَعْدِكَ، وَخَالِفْ بَيْنَ كَلِمَتِهِمْ، وَأَلْقِ عَلَيْهِمْ رِجْزَكَ وَعَذَابَكَ، إِلَهَ الْـحَقِّ

'Allahumma qatilil kafarata 'Illathina yasudduna 'an sabilik, wayukath-thibuna rusulak, wala yu'minuna biwa'dik, wakhalif bayna kalimatahim, wa-'alqi 'alayhim rijzaka wa-'athabak, ilaha 'lhaqq

'O Allah, fight the disbelievers who obstruct the people who believe in Your promises. Cause them to be divided, cast terror into their heats, and launch Your

---

60. Abu Dawud: 1425

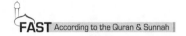
punishment and chastisement upon them. You are the God of Truth.'

Then they offered the *salāt* upon the Prophet (ﷺ), prayer for the Muslims with what they wished for good, and sought forgiveness for the believers. Following this they said:

اللَّهمَّ إِيَّاكَ نَعْبُدُ، ولكَ نُصَلِّي ونَسْجُدُ، وإليكَ نسعى ونَحْفِدُ، ونرجو رَحْمَتَكَ ربَّنَا، ونخافُ عذابَكَ الجِدَّ، إنَّ عذابَكَ لِـمَن عادَيْتَ مُلْحَقٌّ

Allahumma iyyaka na'bu, walaka nusalli wanasjud, wa-ilayka nas'a wanahfid, wanarju rahmataka rabbana, wanakhāfu 'athbakal jadd, inna 'athabaka Liman 'adayta mulhaq.

"O Allah, it is You that we worship, to You we pray and prostrate ourselves, and unto You we run and rush. We hope in Your Mercy Our Lord, and we fear Your severe chastisement; surely, Your severe chastisement is to reach those whom You hate."

Then they said takbir and went to *sujud*."[61]

Qunut before Ruku or after Ruku

Ubai bin Ka'b ﷺ narrated:

أَنَّ رَسُوْلَ الله (ﷺ) كَانَ يُوْتِرُ فَيَقْنُتُ قَبْلَ الرَّكُوْعِ

"The Prophet (ﷺ) used to recite *qunut* before *ruku*."[62]

Muhammad narrated: I asked Ans bin Malik (ﷺ) about *qunut*, and he responded:

قَنَتَ رَسُوْلُ الله (ﷺ) بَعْدَ الرُّكُوعِ

---

61. Ibn Khuzaimah: 3/155, 156 as quoted in *Qiyām* Ramadān by Sheikh Albani, p. 32
62. Ibn Majah: 1182

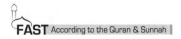

"The Prophet (ﷺ) recited *qunut* after *ruku*."[63]

Long *Qunut*

You find the *Imam*s reciting long supplications, repeating some over and over, tiring their hand and the hands of their followers, allowing the thoughts of the followers to roam in a confused and impatient manner, waiting for the *Imam* to end his stream of unrelated ideas and requests!

This innovation does not have a basis in the practice of the Prophet (ﷺ) or his companions, whose *qunut* was concise and to the point.[64]

Weeping and Loud Crying

Sheikh Ibn Baz (رحمه الله) was asked in regard to the weeping and loud crying. He answered: I have warned many who have inquired against this act. This is not befitting due to the fact that it distracts the *Imam* as well as others. So what is incumbent upon the believer is that he be cautious in that he is not heard weeping, and that he be cautious that he does not show off, for the shaytaan might lead him to this. It is incumbent that he does not disturb the people with his weeping. It is true that some do not weep of their own choice, rather, it being something which overwhelms them without intending it. This is forgiven if it occurs unintentionally. It has been authentically reported that when the Prophet (ﷺ) recited, a sound like the wheezing of a cauldron could be heard beause of his weeping. Also, it has been reported of 'Umar (ﷺ) that his weeping could be heard from the last rows of the congregation. This does not mean, though, that they would intentionally raise their voices while crying; rather, it was something that overwhelmed them because of the khashyah of Allah. Therefore, if one does become overwhelmed with weeping without intending, there is not harm in that.

Wiping the Face after Invocation

There are no authentic reports confirming that the Prophet (ﷺ) ever

---

63. Ibn Majah: 1184
64. The Night Prayers by Muhammad Nasir-ud-Deen Albani & Muhammad Al-Jibali pg. 128, 129

wiped his face with his hands after supplicating, in general, or after *qunut* in particular. Because of this An-Nawai said:

"This is not recommended, in accordance with what al-'Izz bin 'Abdus-Salām said: 'No one does this but an ignorant person.'"[65]

And Al-Bayhaqi said:

"As for wiping the face with the hands after concluding the supplication, I do not know that any of the *salaf* did it."[66]

What to say immediately following the *Witr* Prayer

Ubai bin Ka'b (ﷺ) narrated:

قَالَ كَانَ رَسُولُ اللَّهِ (ﷺ) إِذَا سَلَّمَ فِي الْوِتْرِ قَالَ سُبْحَانَ الْمَلِكِ الْقُدُّوسِ

When Allah's Messenger (ﷺ) made taslim in the *witr* prayer (i.e. finished it), he would say: "Subhannal Malikil Quddoos (Glory is to the King, the Holy)."[67]

---

65. As-Sunan: 1/212 – As quoted in the Nights Prayers p. 128
66. Sifatu-salah by Sheikh Albani: 3/959
67. Abu Dawud: 1430

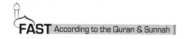

I'tikaf

I'tikāf means to stick to something, whether good or bad, and to block out every thing else. Allah says in the Qur'ān:

إِذْ قَالَ لِأَبِيهِ وَقَوْمِهِۦ مَا هَٰذِهِ ٱلتَّمَاثِيلُ ٱلَّتِىٓ أَنتُمْ لَهَا عَٰكِفُونَ ﴿٥٢﴾

> "When he said to his father and his people: "What are these images, to which you are devoted?" (Al-Anbiyā' 21:52)

That is what they devoted themselves to in worship. What is meant here is seclusion and staying in the mosque with the intention of coming closer to Allah.[1]

Evidence for the Legality of *I'tikāf*

Allah, Most High says:

وَلَا تُبَٰشِرُوهُنَّ وَأَنتُمْ عَٰكِفُونَ فِى ٱلْمَسَٰجِدِ

> "And do not have sexual relations with them (your wives) while you are in *I'tikāf* in the mosques." (Al-Baqarah 2:187)

'Abdullāh bin Umar (ﷺ) narrated:

كَانَ رَسُولُ اللهِ (ﷺ) يَعْتَكِفُ الْعَشْرَ الْأَوَاخِرَ مِنْ رَمَضَانَ

1. Fiqh As-Sunnh: 1/597

"Allah's Messenger (ﷺ) used to practice *I'tikāf* in the last ten days of the month of Ramadān."[2]

'Āishah (﵂) narrated:

$$\text{أَنَّ النَّبِيَّ (ﷺ) كَانَ يَعْتَكِفُ الْعَشْرَ الْأَوَاخِرَ مِنْ رَمَضَانَ حَتَّى تَوَفَّاهُ اللهُ ثُمَّ اعْتَكَفَ أَزْوَاجُهُ مِنْ بَعْدِهِ}$$

"The Prophet (ﷺ) used to practice *I'tikāf* in the last ten days of Ramadān until he died; then his wives practiced *I'tikāf* after him."[3]

The Benefits of *I'tikāf*

There are many hidden benefits in the acts of worship and much wisdom behind them. The basis of all deeds is in the heart, as the Messenger of Allah (ﷺ) said:

$$\text{أَلَا وَإِنَّ فِي الْجَسَدِ مُضْغَةً إِذَا صَلَحَتْ صَلَحَ الْجَسَدُ كُلُّهُ وَإِذَا فَسَدَتْ فَسَدَ الْجَسَدُ كُلُّهُ أَلَا وَهِيَ الْقَلْبُ}$$

"Beware! There is a piece of flesh in the body, if it becomes good (reformed), the whole body becomes good, but if it gets spoilt, the whole body gets spoilt, and that is the heart."[4]

What corrupts the heart most are distraction and preoccupations – such as food, drinks, sex, talking too much, sleeping too much and socializing too much, as well as other distractions – which divert people from turning to Allah and causes the heart to become unfocused and unable to concentrate on worshipping Allah. So Allah has prescribed acts of worship, such as fasting, to protect the heart from the negative effects of these distractions. Fasting deprives a person of food, drink and sex during the day, and this denial of excessive enjoyments is reflected in the heart,

2. Bukhari: 2025
3. Bukhari: 2026
4. Bukhari: 52

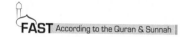

which gains strength for treading the path to Allah and frees it from the chains of these distractions which distract a person from thinking about the Hereafter by occupying him with wordly concerns.

Just as fasting is a shield, which protects the heart from the influences of physical distractions such as excessive indulgence in food, drink and sex, so too does *I'tikāf* offer an immence hidden benefit, which is a protection from the effects of excessive socializing. For people may take socializing to extremes, until it has a similar effect on a person to the effects of over-eating, as the poet said:

فَلَا تَسْتَكْثِرُوْنَ مِنَ الصِّحَابِ   عُدُوُّكَ مِنْ صِدِيْقِكَ مُسْتَفَاد

يَكُونُ مِنَ الطَّعَامِ أَوْ الشَّرَابِ   فَإِنَّ الـدَّاءَ أَكْثَـرَ مَـا تَرَاهُ

"Your enemy was once your friend

so do not have too many companions,

for indeed you see most diseases

are a result from food and drink"

I'tikaf also offers protection from the evil consequences of talking too much, because a person usually does *I'tikāf* on his own, turing to Allah by praying *qiyāmul-layl*, reading Qur'ān, making *dhikr*, reciting *du'ā*, and so on.

It also offers protection from sleeping too much, because when a person makes *I'tikāf* in the mosque he devotes his time to drawing closer to Allah by peforming different kinds of acts of worship and he does not stay in the mosque to sleep.

Undoubtedly, a person's success in freeing himself from socializing, talking and sleeping too much will help him make his heart turn towards Allah and protect him from the opposite.

Al-I'tikāf Nadrah Tarbawiya, Dr. 'Abd al-Lateef ibn Muhammad Baltoo.

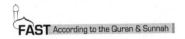

Al-Ithāf fi Bayan Masa'il al-I'tikāf, Abu Umar Haay al-Haay.

The person in *I'tikāf* has committed himself to staying in the mosque for a specific time period. Human nature may not readily accept such restrictions at the specific time period. Human nature may not readily accept restrictions at the beginning of *I'tikāf,* but usually this attitude quickly disappears because of the peace of mind that the soul of the Muslim develops from staying in the House of Allah.

The person in *I'tikāf* understands the importance of his staying in the mosque during his *I'tikāf* from the following things:

The person who stays in the mosque finds that the mosque becomes dear to him, and he understands the value of Allah's houses, may He be Exalted. This love has a great value with Allah, because those who love the houses of Allah will be one of the groups whom Allah will shade on the Day when there will be no shade except His shade.

"Allah will give shade to seven (types of persons) on the Day when there would be no shade but His. One of them is:

وَرَجُلٌ قَلْبُهُ مُعَلَّقٌ فِي الْـمَسَاجِدِ

A person whose heart is attached to the mosque."[5]

When a person stays in the mosque the angels pray for forgiveness for him. Allah's Messenger ﷺ said:

أَنَّ الْـمَلَائِكَةَ تُصَلِّي عَلَى أَحَدِكُمْ مَا دَامَ فِي مُصَلَّاهُ مَا لَـمْ يُحْدِثْ اللَّهُمَّ اغْفِرْ لَهُ اللَّهُمَّ ارْحَمْهُ

"The angels keep on asking for Allah's blessings and forgiveness for anyone of you as long as he remains at his *musalla* (praying place) and does not pass wind. The angels say: 'O Allah! Forgive him and be Merciful to him.'"[6]

---

5. Bukhari: 1423
6. Bukhari: 659

Once Allah's Messenger (ﷺ) delayed the *'Ishā'* prayer until mid-night and after the prayer, he faced us and said: "The people have offered *salāt* and slept, and you remained in *salāt* as long as you waited for it."[7]

Giving up harmful habits

In the light of the fact that the concept of Islamic education is lacking in many Muslim societies and in many homes in those Muslim societies, many habits have become widespread which go against the teachings of this pure religion. These evil habits have become so widespread that they have become almost acceptable and are not seen as having any harmful impact either on the religion or the individual. These habits include smoking, listening to music and watching scenes and events broadcast by satellite channels which go against the *'aqeedah* (belief) of the Muslim and his sense of modesty and chastity, and other habits which affect the religion and the individual.

The time of *I'tikāf* gives the individual the opportunity to see the falsehood of these habits and the futility of the belief which many Muslims have, that they do not have the ability to rid themselves of these habits, because these habits have gained control over them.

During the period of *I'tikāf*, when he is alone with his Creator, the Muslim comes to understand the concept of worship in the most comprehensive sense and that he has to be enslaved to Allah every hour of the day, in both his public and his private life. When he takes the pleasure and love of Allah as the yardstick against which he measures all his actions, he will find that the habits we have referred to above, and many others, do not agree with that love of Allah, and indeed they are the opposite. So he discovers that habits such as these take him out of the circle of sincere *'uboodiyyah* towards Allah. If this is the case, then he is obliged to rid himself of these habits as quickly as possible.

During the period of *I'tikāf*, the Muslim is not allowed to go out except in the case of definite needs which serve to facilitate his staying in the mosque for *I'tikāf*. Apart from that, he should not go out, even if it is for a

---

7. Bukhari: 661

permissible purpose. So, for example, he cannot go out and walk around in the market place, even for a short time, to buy things that have nothing to do with his *I'tikāf*. If he goes out to buy *Siwak*, this will not affect his *I'tikāf* because it is something that is required for his prayer during his *I'tikāf*. But if he went out to buy a gift for his wife or for one of his children, that would invalidate his *I'tikāf* because the Messenger (ﷺ) did not go out except in the case of human need, as mentioned above. So how about if the person in *I'tikāf* goes out to do something *harām* such as smoking cigarettes for example, or to watch a satellite TV show that he usually watches? Undoubtedly this would invalidate his *I'tikāf*.

So if he goes out to drink wine or to smoke, this invalidates his *I'tikāf*. In general, anyone going out for any invalid reason invalidates *I'tikāf*, and more so if the purpose of going out is to commit a sin. Even when he goes out for a legitimate purpose, it is not permissible for him to light a cigratte on the way. *I'tikāf* is an annual opportunity in which a person can get rid of these bad habits by repenting and turning to Allah, and by weaning himself from these sins during the period of *I'tikāf*, not giving in to his desires, and getting used to this.

This continual worship of Allah requires continual patience on the part of the person in *I'tikāf*, which is a kind of training for a person's will and kind of self-discipline for the soul which usually tries to escape this worship to turn towards other matters which it desires.

There is also the kind of patience which is required for dealing with the absence of things that a person may be used to, such as different kinds of food that he eats at home but which are not available in the mosque. So he puts up with having little for the sake of earning the pleasure of Allah, may He be Exalted and Glorified.

And there is the kind of patience which is required for putting up with the place where he is sleeping, for he will not have a bed placed in the mosque for him, or a comfortable mattress on which he could sleep. He sleeps on a very modest mattress or even on the carpet in the mosque.

And there is the kind of patience which is required for putting up with the conditions in the mosque, the crowds of people around him, the lack of peace and quiet such as he enjoys at home when he wants to sleep. And there is the kind of patience which is required for suppressing his desire for his wife, with whom he is not allowed to have sexual relations if he goes home for any purpose; he cannot even kiss or hug her, even though she is *halal* for him. This is the value of patience, strong will power and self-control that is manifested. Through these practices and others, a person can train himself to delay many of the things he desires for the sake of things which are more important, so he puts off these psychological and material needs for the sake of earning the pleasure of Allah, may He be Glorified and Exalted.

(*Al-I'tikāf* Nadrah Tarbawiyyah, Dr Abd Al-Lateef ibn Muhammad Bāltoo. *Al-Ithāf fi Bayan Masā'il al-I'tikaf*, Abdu 'Umar Haay al – Haay)

Fasting While Performing *I'tikāf*

Salaf (pious predecessors) regarded it as recommended to combine fasting and *I'tikāf*. Some scholars say that fasting is a condition of *I'tikāf*, but the most correct view is that fasting is desirable for the one who does *I'tikāf*, but it is not condition of his *I'tikāf* being valid.

Ibn Umar (🙏) narrated that 'Umar (🙏) asked the Prophet (🙏): "I vowed in the Pre-Islamic Period of Ignorance to stay in *I'tikāf* for one night in Al-Masjid al-Haram." The Prophet (🙏) said to him: "Fulfill your vow."

This statement of the Prophet (🙏) shows that fasting is not a condition for *I'tikāf*; otherwise, performing *I'tikāf* at night would not be valid.

'Amra bint 'Abdur Rahmān narrated on the authority of 'Āishah (🙏) that Allah's Messenger (🙏) used to practice *I'tikāf* every year in the month of Ramadān. After offering the morning prayer he would enter the place of *I'tikāf*. 'Āishah (🙏) asked his permission to let her practice *I'tikāf* and he allowed her, and so she pitched a tent in the mosque. When Hafsa heard of that, she also pitched a tent (for herself), and when Zainab heard of that, she too pitched another tent. When, in the morning, Allah's Messenger (🙏) had finished the morning prayer, he saw the tents and asked: "What is this?" He was informed about it. He then said: "What made them do this? Is it Righteousness? Remove the tents, for I do not want to see them." So the tents were removed. The Prophet (ﷺ) did not perform *I'tikāf* that year in the month of Ramadān, but did it in the last ten days of Shawwāl.[8]

It was not proven whether he was fasting or not on these days when he did *I'tikāf*.

Allah's Messenger (ﷺ) During His *I'tikāf*

Abū Sa'īd Al-Khudri (ﷺ) narrated that Allah's Messenger (ﷺ) used to practise *I'tikāf* in the middle ten days of Ramadān; once he stayed in *I'tikāf* until the night of the twenty-first and it was the night in the morning of which he used to come out of his *I'tikāf*. The Prophet (ﷺ) said:

مَنْ كَانَ اعْتَكَفَ مَعِي فَلْيَعْتَكِفْ الْعَشْرَ الْأَوَاخِرَ وَقَدْ أُرِيتُ هَذِهِ اللَّيْلَةَ ثُمَّ أُنْسِيتُهَا وَقَدْ رَأَيْتُنِي أَسْجُدُ فِي مَاءٍ وَطِينٍ مِنْ صَبِيحَتِهَا فَالْتَمِسُوهَا فِي الْعَشْرِ الْأَوَاخِرِ وَالْتَمِسُوهَا فِي كُلِّ وِتْرٍ

"Whoever was in *I'tikāf* with me should stay in *I'tikāf* for the last ten days, for I was informed (of the date) of the Night (of Qadr) but I have been caused to forget it. (In the dream) I saw myself prostrating in mud and water in the morning of that night. So, look for it in the last ten nights and in the odd ones of them."

It rained that night (i.e. the 21st of Ramadān) and the roof of the Mosque dribbled as if it was made of leaf stalks of date-palms. I saw with my own eyes the marks of mud and water on the forehead of the Prophet (ﷺ), i.e., in the morning of the twenty-first (of Ramadān).[9]

Yunūs narrated that Nāfi' informed him from Ibn 'Umar: "The Prophet (ﷺ) used to observe *I'tikāf* in the last ten days of Ramadān." Nāfi' said: "Abdullāh (Ibn Umar) showed me the place where the Messenger of Al-

---

8. Bukhari: 2041
9. Bukhari: 2027

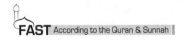

lah (ﷺ) used to observe *I'tikāf* in the Masjid."[10]

Ibn Umar (ﷺ) narrated that when the Prophet (ﷺ) observed *I'tikāf*, his bedding would be spread for him, or his bed would be placed there for him behind the Pillar of Repentance."[11]

The Pillar of Repetance is a particular piller in the Prophet's Mosque. Abu Lubabah (ﷺ), a Companion of the Prophet (ﷺ), made a mistake and when he realized the mistake he tied himself to the pillar on the condition that he would remain tied until Allah forgave him. Three days later the Messenger of Allah (ﷺ) received, through revelation, the good news of Abu Lubabah's repentance being accepted, and thereupon Allah's Messenger (ﷺ) himself came and untied him.

Abū Sa'īd Al-Khudri (ﷺ) narrated that the Messenger of Allah (ﷺ) observed *I'tikāf* in a Turkish tent, over the door of which was piece of reed matting. He pushed the mat aside, then he put his head out and spoke to the people.[12]

The Prophet (ﷺ) used to enter his place before sunset on the twenty-first day if he wanted to spend the last ten days in *I'tikāf*, but he used to enter his tent after *Fajr* prayer as mentioned in the narration of Bukhari and Muslim.

'Āishah (ﷺ) narrated:

$$كَانَ النَّبِيُّ (ﷺ) يُصْغِي إِلَيَّ رَأْسَهُ وَهُوَ مُجَاوِرٌ فِي الْـمَسْجِدِ فَأُرَجِّلُهُ وَأَنَا حَائِضٌ$$

"The Prophet (ﷺ) used to place his head (out) to me while he was in *I'tikāf* in the mosque during my monthly period and I would comb and oil his hair."[13]

In another narration:

---

10. Abu Dawud: 2465
11. Ibn Majah: 1774
12. Ibn Majah: 1775
13. Bukhari: 2028

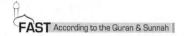

وَكَانَ لَا يَدْخُلُ الْبَيْتَ إِلَّا لِحَاجَةٍ إِذَا كَانَ مُعْتَكِفًا

"While in *I'tikāf* he would not enter the house except for a need."[14]

Alī bin Husain narrated that Safiyya (﷽) the wife of the Prophet told me that she went to Allah's Messenger (ﷺ) to visit him in the mosque while he was in *I'tikāf* during the last ten days of Ramadān. She had a talk with him for a while then she got up in order to return home. The Prophet (ﷺ) accompanied her, when they reached the gate of the mosque, oposite the door of Umm Salamah, two Ansari men were passing by and they greeted Allah's Messenger (ﷺ). He said to them: "Do not run away." And said: "She is (my wife) Safiyyah bint Huyaī." Both of them said: "*Subhan Allah*, (How dare we think of any evil) O Allah's Messenger." And they felt it. The Prophet (ﷺ) said (to them):

إِنَّ الشَّيْطَانَ يَبْلُغُ مِنَ الْإِنْسَانِ مَبْلَغَ الدَّمِ وَإِنِّي خَشِيتُ أَنْ يَقْذِفَ فِي قُلُوبِكُمَا شَيْئًا

"Satan reaches everywhere in the human body as blood reaches in it (everywhere in one's body). I was afraid lest Satan might insert an evil thought in your minds."[15]

The Prophet (ﷺ) thought that it was essential for him to go out with her because it was night, so he went out with her from the palce where he was doing *I'tikāf*, in order to take her home.

'Āishah (﷽) narrated:

كَانَ رَسُولُ اللَّهِ (ﷺ) إِذَا دَخَلَ الْعَشْرُ أَحْيَا اللَّيْلَ وَأَيْقَظَ أَهْلَهُ وَجَدَّ وَشَدَّ الْـمِئْزَرَ.

"When the (last) ten (nights) began, the Messenger of Allah (ﷺ) would stay awake at night, wake his fam-

---

14. Bukhari: 2029
15. Bukhari: 2035

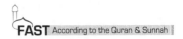

ily, strive hard (in worship) and tighten his izār."[16]

'Āishah (ﷺ) narrated:

$$كَانَ رَسُولُ اللهِ (ﷺ) يَجْتَهِدُ فِى الْعَشْرِ الأَوَاخِرِ مَا لاَ يَجْتَهِدُ فِى غَيْرِهِ.$$

"The Messenger of Allah (ﷺ) used to strive harder in the last ten (nights of Ramadān) then at any other time."[17]

Ubayy bin Ka'b (ﷺ) narrated:

$$أَنَّ النَّبِيَّ (ﷺ) كَانَ يَعْتَكِفُ الْعَشْرَ الأَوَاخِرَ مِنْ رَمَضَانَ فَلَمْ يَعْتَكِفْ عَامًا فَلَمَّا كَانَ الْعَامُ الْـمُقْبِلُ اعْتَكَفَ عِشْرِينَ لَيْلَةً.$$

"The Prophet (ﷺ) used to observe I'tikāf in the last ten days of Ramadān, then he did not observe it for a year, when the next year came, he observed it for twenty nights."[18]

Etiquettes of I'tikāf

The Prophet (ﷺ) used to stay in the mosque all the time and not go out except in the case of human need, i.e. to pass urine or stool.[19]

The Prophet (ﷺ) used to keep clean, as he used to put his head out into 'Āishah's room for her to comb his hair.[20]

Hafiz Ibn Hajar says:

"The *hadith* indicates that it is permissible to keep clean, apply perfume, wash, shave and adorn oneself by analogy with combing. The majority of the scholars agree that there is nothing disliked in I'tikāf except that

---

16. Muslim: 1174
17. Muslim: 1175
18. Abu Dawud: 2463
19. Bukhari: 2029
20. Bukhari: 2028

which is viewed as being disliked in the mosque."[21]

Visiting the Sick and attending the Funerals

'Āishah (※) narrated:

يَمُرُّ بِالْـمَرِيضِ وَهُوَ مُعْتَكِفٌ فَيَمُرُّ كَمَا هُوَ وَلاَ يُعَرِّجُ يَسْأَلُ عَنْهُ

"If the Prophet (※) would pass by a sick person while he was observing *I'tikāf*, he would pass by on his way without stopping to ask about him."

'Āishah (※) said: "I used to enter the house to relieve myself, and there was a sick person there, and I only inquired about him as I was passing through." She said: "And the Messenger of Allah (※) would not enter the house except to relieve himself, when they were observing *I'tikāf*."[22]

'Āishah (※) narrated:

السُّنَّةُ عَلَى الْـمُعْتَكِفِ أَنْ لاَ يَعُودَ مَرِيضًا وَلاَ يَشْهَدَ جَنَازَةً وَلاَ
يَمَسَّ امْرَأَةً وَلاَ يُبَاشِرَهَا وَلاَ يَخْرُجَ لِحَاجَةٍ إِلاَّ لِمَا لاَ بُدَّ مِنْهُ وَلاَ
اعْتِكَافَ إِلاَّ بِصَوْمٍ وَلاَ اعْتِكَافَ إِلاَّ فِي مَسْجِدٍ جَامِعٍ.

"The *Sunnah* is not to vist a sick person while observing *I'tikāf*, not to attend the funeral, not to touch or embrace a woman, not to exit for a need, except out of necessity and their is no I'tikaf without fasting and there is no *I'tikāf* except in a *Jami' Masjid*."[23]

This narration is not authentic, we mentioned it here because Imam Tirmidhi explained these points as we mentioned below. Abu 'Eisa (At-Tirmidh) said: This is acted upon according to the people of knowledge. When a man performs *I'tikāf*, he is not to leave his *I'tikāf* except for some personal need. They agreed upon this: He goes out to relieve him-

---

21. Fathul-Bari: 4/807
22. Ibn Majah: 1776
23. Abu Dawud: 2472, 2473

self from defection and urination. [If a mosque does not have the facilities, like: toilets washing place, privacy, and facility for taking a bath due to sexual impurity, according to the consensus the person making *I'tikāf* is allowed to leave the mosque for these matters. If a mosque has these facilities then he is not allowed to leave the mosque].

The people of knowledge differ about visiting the sick, attending the Friday prayer, and the funeral for the person performing *I'tikāf*. Some of the people of knowledge among the Companions of the Prophet (ﷺ) and others held the view that he may visit the sick, follow the funeral and attend the Friday prayer as long as he made that a condition (before entering the state of *I'tikāf*). This is the view of Sufyān At-Thawri and Ibn Al-Mubārak. Some of them said that he cannot do any of that, and they thought that if a person is in a land where the Firday prayer is held, then he is not to perform *I'tikāf* except in the Friday prayer Masjid, because they consider it disliked for him to leave his place of *I'tikāf* to go for the Friday prayer. They do not think that he should miss the Friday prayer, so they said that he is not to perform *I'tikāf* except in the mosque where Friday prayer is offered, so that he will not have a need to leave his place of *I'tikāf* except to relieve himself and for his personal needs. This is because in their view, leaving it for other than his personal needs will severe his *I'tikāf*. This is the saying of Malik and Ash-Shāfi'i. Ahmad said that he does not visit the sick nor follow the funeral based upon the *hadith* of 'Āishah. Ishaq said that if he makes it a condition then he can follow the funeral and visit the sick.[24]

Conditions of *I'tikāf*

Islam

I'tikāf on the part of the disbeliever or an apostate is not valid.

Puberty

It is not valid on the part of a child who has not yet reached the age of

24. Tirmidhi under *hadith*: 805

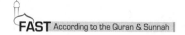

puberty.

Purity

Purity from major forms of impurity (*janabah*), such as sexual impurity, menstruation, and *nifas* (post-partum bleeding). If any of these things happen to a person during his *I'tikāf*, he has to leave the mosque, because it is not permissible for him to stay in the mosque in this state.

The *I'tikāf* at night only

Ibn 'Umar (⬥) narrated that 'Umar (⬥) asked the Prophet (⬥): "I vowed in the Pre-Islamic period of Ignorance to stay in *I'tikāf* for one night in Al-Masjid al-Haram." The Prophet (⬥) said to him: "Fulfill your vow."

If a person vows to do *I'tikāf* in Al-Masjid al-Haram, he has to fulfill his vow and do i'tikāf in al Masjid al-Harm. But if he vows, for example, to do *I'tikāf* in al-Masjid an-Nabawi, then it is permissible for him to do *I'tikāf* in al Masjid an-Nabawi or in al Masjid al-Haram, because al-Masjid al-Haram is better. Likewise if he vowed to do *I'tikāf* in al-Masjid al-Aqsa then he can do it in al-Masjid al-Haram or in Al-Masjid an-Nabawi, because they are better than al-Masjid al-Aqsa.

Staying in the Mosque

I'tikāf should be done in the mosque. Allah says:

$$وَلَا تُبَٰشِرُوهُنَّ وَأَنتُمۡ عَٰكِفُونَ فِي ٱلۡمَسَٰجِدِ$$

> "And do not have sexual relations with them (your wives) while you are in *I'tikāf* (i.e. confining oneself in a mosque for prayers and invocations leaving the wordly activites) in the mosques." (Al-Baqarah: 2/187)

It is preferable for *I'tikāf* to be in a mosque where *Jumu'ah* prayers are held.

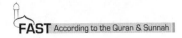

At another place Allah says:

وَعَهِدْنَآ إِلَىٰٓ إِبْرَٰهِـۧمَ وَإِسْمَٰعِيلَ أَن طَهِّرَا بَيْتِىَ لِلطَّآئِفِينَ وَٱلْعَٰكِفِينَ وَٱلرُّكَّعِ ٱلسُّجُودِ

"And we commanded Ibrahim and Isma'il that they should purify My House (the Ka'bah at Makkah) for those who are circumambulating it, or staying (I'tikāf), or bowing or prostrating themselves (there, in prayer)." (Al-Baqarah 2:125)

This is also indicated by the actions of the Prophet (ﷺ) and by his wives and companions after him.

The I'tikāf of a Mustahāda

'Āishah (ﵟ) narrated: One of the wives of Allah's Messenger (ﷺ) practised I'tikāf with him while she had bleeding in between her periods and she would see red (blood) or yellowish traces; and sometimes we put a tray beneath her when she offered the prayer.[25]

---

25. Bukhari: 2037

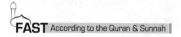

Laylatul-Qadr

Laylatul-Qadr is Better than Thousand Months

Allah says:

إِنَّآ أَنزَلْنَٰهُ فِى لَيْلَةِ ٱلْقَدْرِ ﴿١﴾ وَمَآ أَدْرَىٰكَ مَا لَيْلَةُ ٱلْقَدْرِ ﴿٢﴾ لَيْلَةُ ٱلْقَدْرِ خَيْرٌ مِّنْ أَلْفِ شَهْرٍ ﴿٣﴾ تَنَزَّلُ ٱلْمَلَٰٓئِكَةُ وَٱلرُّوحُ فِيهَا بِإِذْنِ رَبِّهِم مِّن كُلِّ أَمْرٍ ﴿٤﴾ سَلَٰمٌ هِىَ حَتَّىٰ مَطْلَعِ ٱلْفَجْرِ ﴿٥﴾

Verily, We have sent it (this Qur'an) down in the Night of Al-Qadr (Decree). And what will make you know what the Night of Al-Qadr (Decree) is? The Night of Al-Qadr (Decree) is better than a thousand months (i.e. worshipping Allah in that night is better than worshipping Him a thousand months, i.e. 83 years and 4 months). Therein descend the angels and the Ruh [Jibral (Gabriel)] by Allah's Permission with all Decrees. (All that night), there is peace (and goodness from Allah to His believing slaves) until the appearance of dawn.

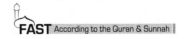

Decree of Every Matter

Allah says:

$$\text{إِنَّآ أَنزَلْنَـٰهُ فِى لَيْلَةٍ مُّبَـٰرَكَةٍ إِنَّا كُنَّا مُنذِرِينَ ۝ فِيهَا يُفْرَقُ كُلُّ أَمْرٍ}$$
$$\text{حَكِيمٍ ۝ أَمْرًا مِّنْ عِندِنَآ إِنَّا كُنَّا مُرْسِلِينَ ۝ رَحْمَةً مِّن رَّبِّكَ إِنَّهُۥ هُوَ}$$
$$\text{ٱلسَّمِيعُ ٱلْعَلِيمُ ۝}$$

"We sent it (this Qur'ān) down on a blessed night [in the month of Ramadān]. Verily, We are ever warning. Therein (that night) is decreed every matter of ordainments. *Amran* (i.e. a command or this Qur'ān or the Decree of every matter) from Us. Verily, We are ever sending (the Messengers), (As) a Mercy from your Lord. Verily! He is the All-Hearer, the All-Knower. (Ad-Dukhan 44:3-6)

Ibn 'Abbas and others have said: "Allah sent the Qur'ān down all at one time from The Preserved Tablet (*al-Lawh Al-Mahfuz*) to the House of Mighty (*Baytul-'Izzah*), which is in the heaven of this world. Then it came down in parts to the Messenger of Allah (ﷺ) based upon the incidents that occurred over a period of twenty – three years." [1]

Abu Hurairah (ﷺ) narrated that when Ramadān would come, the Messenger of Allah (ﷺ) would say:

$$\text{قَدْ جَاءَكُمْ شَهْرُ رَمَضَانَ شَهْرٌ مُبَارَكٌ افْتَرَضَ اللهُ عَلَيْكُمْ صِيَامَهُ}$$
$$\text{يُفْتَحُ فِيهِ أَبْوَابُ الْجَنَّةِ وَيُغْلَقُ فِيهِ أَبْوَابُ الْجَحِيمِ وَتُغَلُّ فِيهِ}$$
$$\text{الشَّيَاطِينُ فِيهِ لَيْلَةٌ خَيْرٌ مِنْ أَلْفِ شَهْرٍ مَنْ حُرِمَ خَيْرَهَا فَقَدْ حُرِمَ}$$

"Verily, the month of Ramadān has come to all of you. It is a blessed month, which Allah has obligated all of you to fast. During it the gates of Paradise are opened, the gates of Hell are closed and the devils are

---

1. Ibn Kathir: 1/440

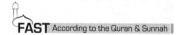

shackled. In it there is a night that is better than one thousand months. Whoever is deprived of its good, then he has truly been deprived."[2]

Abu Hurairah (ﷺ) narrated that Allah's Messenger (ﷺ) said:

إِنَّ الْـمَلَائِكَةَ تِلْكَ اللَّيْلَةَ فِي الْأَرْضِ أَكْثَرُ مِنْ عَدَدِ الْحَصَى

"Indeed, during that night (*Laylatul-Qadr*), they angels on earth are more than the numbers of pebbles."[3]

Abu Sa'īd Al-Khudri (ﷺ) narrated that Allah's Messenger (ﷺ) said:

إِنَّ هَذَا الشَّهْرَ قَدْ حَضَرَكُمْ وَفِيهِ لَيْلَةٌ خَيْرٌ مِنْ أَلْفِ شَهْرٍ مَنْ حُرِمَهَا فَقَدْ حُرِمَ الْخَيْرَ كُلَّهُ وَلاَ يُحْرَمُ خَيْرَهَا إِلاَّ مَحْرُومٌ

"This month (Ramadān) has come to you. There is in it one night that is better than one thousand months. He who is deprived of it is truly deprived of all good. And no one is deprived of its goodness but a deprived person.[4]

Which Night is Laylatul-Qadr?

'Āishah (ﷺ) narrated that Allah's Messenger (ﷺ) said:

تَحَرَّوْا لَيْلَةَ الْقَدْرِ فِي الْوِتْرِ مِنْ الْعَشْرِ الْأَوَاخِرِ مِنْ رَمَضَانَ

"Search for the Night of Qadr in the odd nights of the last ten nights of Ramadān."[5]

Abu Sa'īd Al-Khudri (ﷺ) narrated that Allah's Messenger (ﷺ) used to practise *I'tikāf* (in the mosque) in middle third of Ramadān, and after passing the twenty nights he used to go back to his house on the 21st,

2. Ahamd: 8991
3. Ahmad: 10734
4. Ibn Majah: 1644
5. Bukhari: 2017

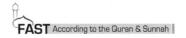

and the people who were in *I'tikāf* with him also used to go back to their houses. Once in Ramadān, in which he practiced *I'tikāf*, he established the night prayers at the night in which it used to return home, and then he addressed the people and ordered them whatever Allah wished him to order and said: "I used to practise *I'tikāf* for these ten days (i.e., the middle 1/3rd) but now I intend to stay in *I'tikāf* for the last ten days (of the month); so whoever was in *I'tikāf* with me should stay at his place of seclusion. Verily, I have been shown (the date of) this night (of Qadr) but I have forgotten it. So, search for it in the odd nights of the last ten days (of this month). I also saw myself (in the dream) prostrating in mud and water." On the night of the 21st (of Ramadān), the sky was overcast with clouds and it rained, and the rain-water started leaking through the roof of the mosque at the *musalla* (praying place) of the Prophet (ﷺ). I saw with my own eyes the Prophet (ﷺ) at the completion of the morning *salāt* leaving with his face covered with mud and water.

Ibn Abbas (ﷺ) narrated that the Prophet (ﷺ) said: "Look for the night of Qadr in the last ten nights of Ramadān; on the night when nine or seven or five nights remain out of the last ten nights of Ramadān [i.e., 21, 23, 25, 27, 29 respectively]."[6]

Ibn Umar (ﷺ) narrated that Allah's Messenger (ﷺ) said:

$$ \text{الْتَمِسُوهَا فِى الْعَشْرِ الأَوَاخِرِ يَعْنِى لَيْلَةَ الْقَدْرِ فَإِنْ ضَعُفَ أَحَدُكُمْ} $$
$$ \text{أَوْ عَجَزَ فَلاَ يُغْلَبَنَّ عَلَى السَّبْعِ الْبَوَاقِى} $$

"Seek it in the last ten (nights)," meaning Lailatul-Qadr, "and if one of you feels weak or tired, that should not cause you to miss the last seven (nights)."[7]

Abu Hurairah (ﷺ) narrated that the Messenger of Allah (ﷺ) said:

$$ \text{أُرِيتُ لَيْلَةَ الْقَدْرِ ثُمَّ أَيْقَظَنِى بَعْضُ أَهْلِى فَنُسِّيتُهَا فَالْتَمِسُوهَا فِى} $$
$$ \text{الْعَشْرِ الْغَوَابِرِ} $$

---

6. Bukhari: 2021
7. Muslim: 1165 (209)

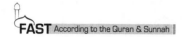

"I was shown Lailatul-Qadr, then one of my family woke me up and I was caused to forget it, so seek it in the last ten (nights)."[8]

Signs of Lalatul-Qadr

Ubayy bin K'ab (&) narrated: "By the signs of which the Messenger of Allah (&) told us:

$$أَنَّهَا تَطْلُعُ يَوْمَئِذٍ لاَ شُعَاعَ لَهَا$$

'On that day the sun rises with no rays.'"[9]

It is only an indicatin that the previous night was the Night of Qadr. If one sees it, he should thank Allah for his good fortune, and if he did not, he should long, and try for it the following year.

Ibn Abbas (&) narrated that Alalh's Messenger (&) said:

$$لَيْلَةٌ طَلْقَةٌ لَا حَارَّةٌ وَلَا بَارِدَةٌ تُصْبِحُ الشَّمْسُ يَوْمُهَا حَمْرَاءُ ضَعِيْفَةٌ$$

"Laylatul-Qadr is an easy and moderate night. It is neither hot nor cold. On the morning following it, the sun rises reddish and weak (in light)."[10]

It is interesting to note that these sings occur after the night ends. Some scholars have indicated that the wisdom behind this is that one whould not rely on definite knowledge in order to limit his worship to just one night of the whole year.

Fake tales about Laylatul-Qadr

Many fables circulate among the common people, claiming unusual incidents happening during *Laylatul-Qadr*. Those fables claim that trees make sujūd, animals act in a strange way, sinners who happen to wake up for a few seconds and ask for wealth become millionaires, etc.

---

8. Muslim: 1166
9. Muslim: 762
10. Ibn Khuzamah: 2192

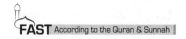
All of this is nonsense! *Laylatul-Qadr* is a blessed night that should be spent in worship and obedience, not in negligence or sinning. Only the one who makes good use of it, in accordance with the *Sunnah* as outlined above, can hope for Allah's acceptance and blessings.

The Superiority of Praying in the Night of Qadr

Abu Hurairah (◈) narrated that the Messenger of Allah (◈) said:

مَنْ قَامَ لَيْلَةَ الْقَدْرِ إِيمَـانًا وَاحْتِسَابًا غُفِرَ لَهُ مَا تَقَدَّمَ مِنْ ذَنْبِهِ

"Whoever stood for the *salāt* in the Night of Qadr with sincere faith and hoping for a reward from Allah, then all his past sins will be forgiven."[11]

Supplication in the Night of Qadr

'Āishah (◈) narrated that she asked: "O Messenger of Allah! If I realize that it is Lailatul-Qadr, what should I supplicate in it?" He (◈) said, "You should supplicate:

اللَّهُمَّ إِنَّكَ عَفُوٌّ تُحِبُّ الْعَفْوَ فَاعْفُ عَنِّي

Allahumma innaka 'afuwwun tuhibbul-'afwa, fa'fu 'anni (O Allah, You are Most Forgiving, and You love forgiveness; so forgive me)."[12]

Hard work in the last ten days of Ramadān

'Āishah (◈) narrated:

كَانَ النَّبِيُّ (◈) إِذَا دَخَلَ الْعَشْرُ شَدَّ مِئْزَرَهُ وَأَحْيَا لَيْلَهُ وَأَيْقَظَ أَهْلَهُ

"With the start of the last ten days of Ramadān, the

---

11. Bukhari: 2014
12. Tirmidhi: 3513

Prophet used to keep awake all night and perform prayer and also used to keep his family awake for the prayer."[13]

In another narration of 'Āishah (ﷺ):

كَانَ رَسُولُ اللهِ يَجْتَهِدُ فِي الْعَشْرِ الأَوَاخِرِ مَا لاَ يَجْتَهِدُ فِي غَيْرِهَا.

"The Messenger of Allah (ﷺ) would struggle (to perform *salāt* more) during the last ten (nights) more than he would struggle in the rest of it."[14]

---

13. Bukhari: 2024
14. Tirmidhi: 796

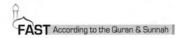

Sadaqatul-Fitr

Obligation of Sadaqatul-Fitr

Ibn Umar (ﷺ) narrated:

فَرَضَ رَسُولُ اللهِ (ﷺ) زَكَاةَ الْفِطْرِ صَاعًا مِنْ تَمْرٍ أَوْ صَاعًا مِنْ شَعِيرٍ عَلَى الْعَبْدِ وَالْحُرِّ وَالذَّكَرِ وَالْأُنْثَى وَالصَّغِيرِ وَالْكَبِيرِ مِنَ الْـمُسْلِمِينَ وَأَمَرَ بِهَا أَنْ تُؤَدَّى قَبْلَ خُرُوجِ النَّاسِ إِلَى الصَّلَاةِ .

"Allah's Messenger (ﷺ) made obligatory the payment of one Sā' (2.6 KG) of dates or one Sā' of barely as zakatul-fitr on every Muslim slave or free, male or female, young or old; and he ordered that it be paid before the people went out to offer 'Eid prayer."[1]

Ibn 'Umar (ﷺ) said: "The Prophet (ﷺ) made obligatory on every male or female, free man or slave, the payment of one Sā' of dates or barely as *sadaqatul-fitr*." The people then substituted one-half Sā' of wheat for that. Ibn 'Umar used to give dates. Nafi' added: Once there was scarcity of dates in Madinah and Ibn 'Umar gave barely (instead). And Ibn 'Umar used to give *sadaqatul-fitr* for every young and old person. He even used to give it on behalf of my children.

Ibn 'Umar (ﷺ) used to give *sadaqatul-fitr* to those who had been officially appointed for its collection. People used to give *sadaqatul-fitr* to those who had been officially appointed for its collection. People used to

---

1. Bukhari: 1503

give *sadaqat*ul-fitr even a day or two before Eid.[2]

'Abdullāh bin Umar (ﷺ) used to give *sadaqatul-fitr* on behalf of his servants who were in the Wadi Qura and Khaibar.[3]

Sadaqatul-Fitr on Fetus

No *zakah* is obligated on the fetus, according to the majority of the jurists. Ibn Hazm disagrees, saying that if the fetus completes one hundred and twenty days before the dawn of the last day of Ramadān, then *zakah* al-fitr must be paid on its behalf. The hundred and twenty days is taken from the saying that indicates that it is at this time that the soul is blown into the fetus. Allah's Messenger (ﷺ) said:

إِنَّ أَحَدَكُمْ يُجْمَعُ خَلْقُهُ فِي بَطْنِ أُمِّهِ فِي أَرْبَعِينَ يَوْمًا ثُمَّ يَكُونُ عَلَقَةً
مِثْلَ ذَلِكَ ثُمَّ يَكُونُ مُضْغَةً مِثْلَ ذَلِكَ ثُمَّ يُرْسَلُ إِلَيْهِ الْمَلَكُ فَيَنْفُخُ
فِيهِ الرُّوحَ وَيُؤْمَرُ بِأَرْبَعِ كَلِمَاتٍ رِزْقِهِ وَأَجَلِهِ وَعَمَلِهِ وَشَقِيٌّ أَمْ
سَعِيدٌ

"The creation of anyone of you is gathered for forty days in his mother's womb as a nutfah, then he becomes a clot for a similar period of time, then he becomes a little lump of flesh for a similar length of time. Then the angle is sent to him and he breaths the soul into it, and four things are decreed; his provision, his life-span, his deeds and whether he will be wretched or blessed."[4]

Ibn Hazm argues that the fetus is included by the word of the Prophet (ﷺ) "young" and reports that Uthman bin Affan (ﷺ) used to pay *sadaqatul-fitr* on behalf of the young, old and unborn babies. Abu Qilabah says, "They (the Companions) used to like paying *sadaqatul-fitr* on behalf of the young, the old, and the fetus in the womb." Ibn Hazm clarifies that

2. Bukhari: 1511
3. Muwatta: 1/283
4. Ahmed: 1/382

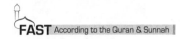

Abu Qilabah met many Companions and narrates from them.

Sulaiman bin Yasar answered "Yes" to a question about *sadaqatul-fitr* on behalf of the fetus and adds: "No companion is known to have differed with Uthman on this issue."[5]

The truth is that there is no evidence on the obligation of *sadaqat*ul-fitr on unborn babies in what Ibn Hazm quotes, and it is gross arbitration to include the fetus in the meaning of the "young". Uthman's action is not indicative of the obligation, although it may mean encouragement of this action. So to be on the safe side we can say that it is permissible. Ash-Shawkani relates from Ibn al-Mundhir as reporting ijma that "it is not obligatory on unborn babies," and Ahmad considers this payment desirable and not obligatory.[6]

Conditions for the Obligation of *Sadaqatul-Fitr*

The majority of the scholars believe that there are only two conditions that are obligatory: Islam and owing the amount of *zakahtul-fitr* above what is needed as provision for the day of 'Eid for the person and his family. *Imam* Ash-Shawkani says that this is correct because the texts are general and inclusive of the rich and poor. The term of the ability of *zakah* is not subject to human opinion in this case, since the purpose of this *zakah* is the clearing of vain speech, etc., includes both the poor and the rich. On the other hand, the condition for owning food for the day of 'Eid is indispensable, because without this condition, the person deserves to receive *sadaqatul-fitr* and to be satisfied on that day.[7]

The Wisdom Behind Sadaqatul-Fitr

Ibn Abbas (ﷺ) narrated:

فَرَضَ رَسُولُ اللهِ (ﷺ) زَكَاةَ الْفِطْرِ طُهْرَةً لِلصَّائِمِ مِنَ اللَّغْوِ
وَالرَّفَثِ وَطُعْمَةً لِلْمَسَاكِينِ مَنْ أَدَّاهَا قَبْلَ الصَّلَاةِ فَهِىَ زَكَاةٌ

---

5. Muhalla: 6/132
6. Nail al-Awtar: 4/181
7. Nail al-Awtar: 4/181

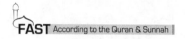

مَقْبُولَةٌ وَمَنْ أَدَّاهَا بَعْدَ الصَّلاَةِ فَهِىَ صَدَقَةٌ مِنَ الصَّدَقَاتِ.

"The Messenger of Allah (ﷺ) obligated zakatul-fitr for the one who fasts as a means of purifying him from vain speech and immoral deeds, and as a means of feeding the poor. Whoever gives it before the (Eid) prayer will have it counted as an accepted sadaqah, and whoever gives it after the prayer will have it counted as a charity among charities."[8]

When it Must be Given

As described in above mentioned narration: "Whoever gives it before the (Eid) prayer will have it counted as accepted sadaqah."

Ibn Umar (ﷺ) used to give *sadaqatul-fitr* to those who had been officially appointed for its collection. People used to give *sadaqatul-fitr* (even) a day or two before the Eid.[9]

Paying *Zakatul-Fitr* During the First or Second Ten Days of Ramadān

Zakatul-fitr is connected to al-fitr (breaking of the fast) because al-fitr is the reason for it. So, if the breaking of the fast of Ramadān is the reason for this expiation, then it is dependent upon it and it should not precede it. This is why the best time to pay it is on the day of Eid, prior to the prayer. However, it is permissible to pay it one or two days before Eid, as this makes things easier for the giver and the recipient. Before that, according to the most authoritative opinion of the scholars, it is not permissible, and according to this there are two times for it; the permissible time, which is one or two days before the Eid and the preferred time, which is on the day of 'Eid prior to the prayer.

As for delaying it until after the prayer, that is unlawful and it will not be counted as *zakatul-fitr*. Unless the person was ignorant of the day of Eid, such as if he was out in the desert and he did not know until it was

8. Abu Dawud: 1609
9. Bukhari: 1511

too late, and something like that. In that case, there is no sin upon him in paying it after the Eid prayer and it will be counted as zakatul-fitr.[10]

It says in 'Awnul-Māʿbōd Sharh Abi Dawud: "Obviously, the one who gives zakatul-fitr after the prayer is like one who did not give it, because both have in common the fact that they did not give this obligatory charity. Most of the scholars think that giving it before the Eid prayer is only *mustahab* (desirable), and they confirmed that it is acceptable to give it at any time until the end of the day of fitr, but this opinion is refuted by the *hadith*. With regard to delaying it until after the day of Eid, Ibn Raslōn said: "This is *harām* by consensus, because it is *zakah*, so the one who delays it must be committing a sin, as is the case when one delays a prayer."[11]

So it is *harām* to delay giving it for no good reason, because this defeats the purpose, which is to save the poor from having to ask on the day of joy. If a person delays giving it without any excuse, he has committed a sin but he still has to make it up.

Zakatul-fitr has to be handed over to someone who is entitled to it or someone who has been appointed to collect it, at the right time before the Eid prayer. If a man wants to give it to a particular person but cannot find him or a trustee who can accept it on his behalf and he is afraid that time is running out, he has to give it to another entitled person and not delay giving it. If a person wants to give zakatul-fitr to a specific needy person and is afraid that he may not see him at the appropriate time, he should tell him to appoint someone to accept it on his behalf.[12]

Amount of *Zakatul-Fitr*

The amount to be given is one Sāʿ of food according to the measure of Sāʿ used by the Prophet (ﷺ). Ibn Umar (ؓ) narrated: "Allah's Messenger (ﷺ) made the payment of *sadaqatul-fitr* obligatory (and it was), either one Sāʿ of barely or one Sāʿ of dates."[13]

10. Fatawa Arkanul-Islam: 2/605, 606
11. 'Awnul-Maʿbōd: 5/3, 4
12. Zakatul-Fitr by Muhammad Salih Al-Munajjid
13. Bukhari: 1512

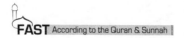

One Sā' equals to 2.6 kilograms

Increasing the amount of Zakatul-Fitr with the Intention of Giving Voluntary Charity

It is permissible for a person to increase the zakatul-fitr payment and make the intention that what was in excess of the obligatory amount be considered as voluntary charity. Included in this is the practice of some people nowadays who have zakatul-fitr for ten persons to distribute for example, so they buy a bag of rice which holds more than the zakatul-fitr for ten persons, and he gives all of it as payment for himself and for his family. This is permissible if the person is certain that the bag holds what is incumbent upon him or more, because measuring the amount of zakatul-fitr is not obligatory, except to know if it is sufficient, so if we know that the amount is sufficient in this bag and we pay it to the poor person, then there is no sin in this.[14]

Types of Things that May be Given

Abu Sa'īd Al-Khudri (ﷺ) narrated:

كُنَّا نُخْرِجُ زَكَاةَ الْفِطْرِ صَاعًا مِنْ طَعَامٍ أَوْ صَاعًا مِنْ شَعِيرٍ أَوْ
صَاعًا مِنْ تَمْرٍ أَوْ صَاعًا مِنْ أَقِطٍ أَوْ صَاعًا مِنْ زَبِيبٍ

"We used to give one Sā' of meal, or one Sā' of barely or one Sā' of dates, or one Sā' of iqt (dried yoghurt or cottage cheese), or one Sā' of raisins (dried grapes) (per head) as zakatul-fitr."[15]

'Abdullāh bin 'Umar (ﷺ) narrated: "The Prophet (ﷺ) ordered (the Muslims) to give one Sā' of dates or one Sā' of barely as zakatul-fitr. The people regarded two mudd of wheat as equal to that."[16]

Abu Sa'īd Al-Khudri (ﷺ) narrated: "In the life time of the Prophet (ﷺ) we used to give one Sā' of meal or one Sā' of dates, or one Sā' of barely,

14. Fatawa Arkanul-Islam: 2/606, 607
15. Bukhari: 1506
16. Bukhari: 1507

or one Sā' of raisins (dried grapes) (per head) as *sadaqatul-fitr*. When Mu'āwiyah become the caliph and the wheat was (available in abundance) he said: 'I think that one mudd (of wheat) equals two mudd (of any of the above mentioned things).'"[17]

'Ammār bin Sa'īd, the mu'adhdhin of the Messenger of Allah (ﷺ), narrated from his father that the Messenger of Allah (ﷺ) enjoined *sadaqatul-fitr* one Sā' of dates, one Sā' of barely, or one Sā' of sult (a kind of barely without skin on it, resembling wheat).[18]

Giving Something Other Than Above Mentioned Things

Some scholars say that if the five types of food are available, which are: wheat, dates, barely, raisins and cottage cheese, then zakatul-fitr will not be fulfilled by giving something other than these. This view completely contradicts the view of those who say that it is permissible to pay zakatrul-fitr with any of these things and others, even with money. So there are two conflicting opinions.

The correct view is that paying it with any human food will be counted, because Abu Sa'īd Al-Khudri said as confirmed in Sahih Bukhari: "We used to pay it during the time of the Prophet (ﷺ) with a Sā' of food, and our food consisted of dates, barely, raisins and cottage cheese."

He did not mention wheat, and I do not know of any clear, authentic *hadith* in which wheat is mentioned as being given as zakatul-fitr but there is no doubt that wheat is valid.

Then there is a *hadith* of Ibn Abbas (﷜) in which he said: The Messenger of Allah (ﷺ) enjoined the payment of zakatul-fitr as a purification for the fasting person from vain talk, obscenity and in order to feed the destitute.

Therefore, the correct view is that any human food is valid for the payment of zakatul-fitr, even if it is not one of the five types which have been reported by the scholars of Islamic Jurisprudence because four of these types as indicated earlier, were the food of the people during the

---

17. Bukhari: 1508
18. Ibn Majah: 1830

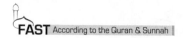

time of the Prophet (ﷺ).[19]

Opinions of the Scholars of Islamic Jurisprudence

An-Nawawi (ﷺ) said: "Our companions (fellow scholars of the shafi'i school of thought) said: It is a condition of giving something as zakatul-fitr that it should be one of the foodstuffs on which *zakah* is paid at the rate of one-tenth (i.e., *zakah* of grains and fruits). Nothing else is acceptable except aqit (dried yoghurt), cheese and milk."

Ash-Shafi'i (ﷺ) said: "If the staple food of a people is corn, pearl millet (dukhn) thin husked barely (sult), rice or any grain on which *zakah* is obligatory, then they may give it as zakatrul-fitr."[20]

Ibnul Qayyim (ﷺ) said: "If it was said: You must give a Sā' of dates everywhere, whether it is the staple food or not, this is a disputed matter which is subject to ijtihād. There are some people who say that it is obligatory, and others who say that in each country it is obligatory to give a Sā' of whatever is the staple food there. This is more correct and is closer to the principles of shariah, for how can you make it obligatory for people whose staple food is fish, for example, or rice or pearl millet, to give dates?"[21]

Conclusion

Any human food is valid for the payment of zakatul-fitr.

Giving Money for Zakatul-Fitr

Zakatul-fitr is an act of worship according to the consensus of the Muslims, and the fundamental principle regarding acts of worship is that they are tawqeef (i.e., limited to whatever there is a text for). Therefore, it is not permissible for anyone to seek to worship Allah with any act of worship except with what is taken from the wise person who was the source of Islamic legislation (i.e., Prophet Muhammad ﷺ). He is the one for

---

19. Fatawa Arkanul-Islam: 2/607, 608
20. Al-Majmō'
21. I'lamul-Muwaqq'aīn:

whom His Lord, blessed is He the Most High, said:

$$وَمَا يَنطِقُ عَنِ ٱلْهَوَىٰ ۝ إِنْ هُوَ إِلَّا وَحْيٌ يُوحَىٰ ۝$$

"And he (Muhammad ﷺ) does not speak from (his own) desire. It is only a revelation that is revealed (to him)." (An-Najm 53: 3,4)

He (ﷺ) said concerning that:

$$مَنْ أَحْدَثَ فِي أَمْرِنَا هَذَا مَا لَيْسَ فِيهِ فَهُوَ رَدٌّ$$

"Whoever introduces into this matter of ours that which is not of it is rejected."[22]

He (ﷺ) legislated zakatul-fitr by that which is confirmed from him in the authentic *hadith*s as a Sā' of food or a Sā' of dried dates or a Sā' of barely or a Sā' of raisins or a Sā' of cottage cheese.

Hence, this is the *Sunnah* of Muhammad (ﷺ) regarding zakatul-fitr. It is known that during the time of the legislating dinars and dirhams (i.e., gold and silver coins) existed – especially in Madinah among the Muslims. There were the two leading forms of currency at that time and yet he, the Prophet (ﷺ), did not mention them in regards to zakatul-fitr. If either of them were acceptable for zakatul-fitr, he would have clarified that, as it is not permissible to delay explanation past the time of need. If this explanation had occurred, the Companions would have acted upon it (i.e., by giving money). The fundmental principle regarding acts of worship is tawqeef. We do not know of anyone of the Prophet's Companions giving money for zakatul-fitr, and they were the most knowledgeable people of his *Sunnah* and the most devout people in following it. If anything like this had occurred among them, it would have been reported just as other things were reported from their statements and deeds that were related to the matters of Islamic legislation. Indeed Allah, Glory is unto Him the Most High, said:

---

22. Bukhari: 2697

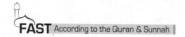

لَّقَدۡ كَانَ لَكُمۡ فِى رَسُولِ ٱللَّهِ أُسۡوَةٌ حَسَنَةٌ

"Verily there is an excellent example for you all in the Messenger of Allah (Muhammad ﷺ)." (Al-Ahzab 33:21)

And He, the Mighty and Majestic, said:

وَٱلسَّـٰبِقُونَ ٱلۡأَوَّلُونَ مِنَ ٱلۡمُهَـٰجِرِينَ وَٱلۡأَنصَارِ وَٱلَّذِينَ ٱتَّبَعُوهُم بِإِحۡسَـٰنٍ رَّضِىَ ٱللَّهُ عَنۡهُمۡ وَرَضُوا۟ عَنۡهُ وَأَعَدَّ لَهُمۡ جَنَّـٰتٍ تَجۡرِى تَحۡتَهَا ٱلۡأَنۡهَـٰرُ خَـٰلِدِينَ فِيهَآ أَبَدٗا ذَٰلِكَ ٱلۡفَوۡزُ ٱلۡعَظِيمُ ﴿١٠٠﴾

"And the first and foremost (to believe) from the Muhajirūn (immigrants to Al-Madinah) and the Ansar (the citizens of Al-Madinah who helped the Muhajirūn) and those who followed them in goodness, Allah is pleased with them and they are pleased with Him. And He has prepared for them Gardens with rivers flowing beneath them. They will abide therein forever. That is the supreme success. (At-Tawbah 9:100)

From what we mentioned, it becomes clear to the person who follows the truth that giving money for zakatul-fitr is not permissible and it does not suffice for whoever gives it because he is opposing what has been mentioned of the legislative evidences.[23]

Shaykh Salih Al-Munajjid says: "There are obvious benefits to giving it in the form of staple foods, such as at times when businessmen are hoarding certain goods, prices have gone up, or at time of war and inflation. If someone were to say: "But money is more useful for the poor, because then they can buy what they want, and they might need something other than food, so the poor person might sell the food and loose the money. The response to this is that there are other sources for meeting the needs of the poor with regard to shelter, clothing and so on, which are provided

---

23. Majm'u Fatwa, Ibn Baz: 14/208-211

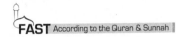

for from the *zakah* paid on people's wealth, general charity and other kinds of donations. Let us put things into the proper Islamic perspective and adhere to what was set out by the Prophet (ﷺ) who told us that giving a Sāʿ of food to feed the poor is obligatory. If we give food to a poor person, he will eat it and will benefit from it sooner or later, because it is the kind of food he uses away.

On this basis, it is not permissible for the purposes of zakatul-fitr to give money for a person to pay off his debts or to cover the cost of surgery for a sick person or to pay for tuition for a needy student and so on. There are other sources for this kind of help as stated above.[24]

To Whom it May be Given

Those entitled to receive obligatory *zakah* are entitled to receive zakatul-fitr, though it should not be understood that they are all the types of recipients mentioned in the Quranic verse, for it is not paid to those whose hearts are inclined towards Islam, nor to those who are employed to collect it.

We should also remember it is not permissible for the one who gives zakatul-fitr to buy it back from the one to whom he has given it.

Payment and Distribution

1. It is preferable for the person, who is giving it, to distribute it out himself. (Ash-Shafʿi said): "I prefer to distribute zakatul-fitr myself rather than give it to one who is collecting it."

2. An-Nawawi (رحمه الله) said: Ash-Shafi'i said in Al-Mukhtasar: "Zakatul-Fitr is to be distributed among those to whom zakat is distributed. I prefer that it should be given to relatives on whom it is not obligatory to spend at all. He said: If he prefers to give it to the one who is collecting it, this should be fine, insha'Allah – but it is better for him to distribute it himself. If he gives to the Muslim leader or the collector or the one who is collecting the people's zaktul-fitr, and he is given permission to give it, this is fine, but

---

24. Zakatul-Fitr by Salih Al-Munajjid

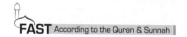

distributing it himself is better than all of this."[25]

3.   It is permissible to appoint a trustworthy person to hand it over to those who are entitled to it, but if he is not trustworthy, then it is not allowed. 'Abdullāh bin Al-Muammal said: "I heard Ibn Abi Mulaykah when a man was saying to him, so and so told me to leave my zakatul-fitr in the mosque, Ibn Abi Mulaykah said: 'He does not know what he is talking about. You go and distribute it (yourself), otherwise Ibn Hisham (The governor who was collecting it in the mosque) will give it to his guards and whoever he wants (i.e., he would give it to people who were not entitled to it).'"[26]

Imam Ahmed (ﷺ) stated that it is permissible to share out one Sā' among a group of people, or to give many Sā's to one person.

Malik said: "There is nothing wrong with a man giving *sadaqat*ul-fitr on behalf of himself and his family to one needy person."[27]

If one is giving less than a Sā' to a poor person this must be pointed out, because he might use it to pay his own zakatul-fitr.

It is permissible for a poor person, if he receives zakatul-fitr from someone and he has more than he needs, to give it on his own behalf or on behalf of one of those who are dependent on him if he is sure that the food is acceptable (i.e., it is the right type of food and the quantity is sufficient).[28]

Where to Give Sadaqatul-Fitr

The *Sunnah* is to distribute zakatul-fitr among the poor people of the land. Allah's Messenger (ﷺ) said about every type of *zakah*:

$$\text{تُؤْخَذُ مِنْ أَغْنِيَائِهِمْ وَتُرَدُّ عَلَى فُقَرَائِهِمْ .}$$

"It is to be taken from the wealthy among them and

25. Al-Majmo
26. Al-Umm
27. Al-Mudawanah
28. Zakatul-Fitr by Muhammad Salih Al-Munajjid

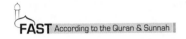

given to the poor among them."[29]

Shaykh Ibn Baz (رحمه الله) says: "If someone, who must pay zakatul-fitr, travels two days or more before the 'Eid', he should give it in the Islamic land that he is travelling to. If he is travelling to lands that are not Islamic, he should find some poor Muslims and give it to them. If his travel was after the permitted time to give it, then he should give it to the poor of his land because its intent is to show beneficence and kindness to them (the poor) and prevent them from begging from the people during the days of 'Eid.[30]

It is permissible for a person to pay zakatul-fitr for his family if they are not in the city or country with him. For example, if he was in Makkah and they were in Riyadh, it is permissible to pay zakatul-fitr for them in Makkah, but it is better for a person to pay zakatul-fitr in the place in which the time for its payment overtakes him, so if it overtakes him when he is in Makkah he should pay it in Makkah and if he is in Riyadh then he should pay it in Riyadh. If some of his family members are in Makkah and some of them in Riyadh, then those in Riyadh should pay it in Riyadh and those in Makkah should pay it in Makkah, because zakatul-fitr is due from each person.[31]

---

29. Bukhari: 1395
30. Majmo Fatawa: 14/214,215
31. Fatawa Arkanul-Islam: 2/610

Ramadan and Unity

The most important goal of the Sharee'ah is uniting the people together, unifying their ranks and keeping away from them all that would split their comprehensive unity from the individual opinions. So the Sharee'ah does not give any weight to the individual opinion in matters concerning collective acts of worship such as fasting, Eīd, Jumuah, and prayer in congregation even if the opinion is correct, from one angle. Do you not see that the Companions of Allah's Messenger (ﷺ) used to pray behind one another. So from them were those who held the view that touching a woman or blood flowing from body invalidates the ablution, along with those who did not hold this view. From them were those who would complete the prayer whilst travelling, whilst others shortened it. Yet these, and other such differences, did not prevent them from collectively praying behind a single Imām and deeming it to be acceptable. This is because they knew that splitting up in the Religion is more evil than having differences in some opinions. Indeed, the matter with one of them reached the extent that he would not even deem acceptable any opinion which differed with the Caliph in the major gatherings; such as the gathering at Mina during Hajj, to the extent that he would totally abandon acting upon his opinion in that gathering – fleeing from that which could result from this evil, because of acting to his own opinion. Uthman ؓ prayed four *rak'ahs* at Mina, 'Abdullāh bin Mas'ud criticized him saying: "I prayed two *rak'ahs* with the Prophet (ﷺ) and two *rak'ahs* with Abu Bakr, and two *rak'ahs* with Umar, and two *rak'ahs* with Uthman in the beginning of his rule, then he completed it (i.e. by praying four *rak'ahs*). After that the ways became divided with you all. So I hope two

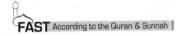

rak'ahs from these four *rak'ahs*." So it was said to him: "You criticized 'Uthman, yet you prayed four?" So he said: "Differing is evil."

The same situation is for Ramadān. Allah's Messenger (ﷺ) said:

$$الصَّوْمُ يَوْمَ تَصُوْمُوْنَ وَالْفِطْرُ يَوْمَ تُفْطِرُوْنَ وَأَلْأَضْحَى يَوْمَ تُضَحُّوْنَ.$$

"That fast is the day the people fast, the breaking of the fast is the day the people break their fast, and the sacrifice is the day the people sacrifice."

Imām Tirmidhi said: "Some of the people of knowledge explained this *hadith* by saying that this *hadith* only means that the fast and the breaking of the fast is done with the community and the majority of the people."[1]

Imām Sanani said: "In this *hadith* is a proof that being in agreement with the people in establishing the 'Eīd, and that the individual person who believes that it is the day of 'Eīd – because of the sighting of the moon – then it is obligatory upon him to be in agreement with the people, and that the ruling of the people concerning the prayer, breaking the fast and sacrificing is binding upon the individual."[2]

Ibn Al-Qayyim (رحمه الله) said: "It is said that within it is a refutation of those who say that whosoever knows the positions of the moon due to astronomical calculation, then it is permissible for him to fast and end the fast, even if others do not know. It is also said that the individual who sees the moon, but the judge has not accepted his testimony, then there is no fasting for him, just as there is no fasting for the people."[3]

---

1. Tirmidhi: 397
2. Sublus Salam: 2/72
3. Tahdheebus Sunan 3/214; Silsilatul Ahadeeth As-Sahehah: 1/442-445

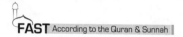

Medical Aspects of Fasting

Food is needed by the body to provide energy for immediate use by burning up carbohydrates, which is sugar. Excess carbohydrates, which cannot be used, are stored as fat tissue in muscles, and as glycogen in the liver for future use. Insulin, which is a hormone from the pancreas, lowers blood sugar and diverts it to other forms of energy storage, that is, glycogen. To be effective, insulin has to be bound to binding sites called receptor. Obese people lack receptor; therefore they cannot utilize their insulin, which leads to insulin resistance and glucose intolerance.

When one fasts (or decreases carbohydrate intake drastically), it lowers his blood glucose and insulin level. This causes a break down of glycogen from the liver to provide glucose for energy need and breakdown of fat from adipose tissue to provide for energy needs.

On the basis of human physiology described above, semi-starvation (ketogenic) diets have been devised for effective weight control. These diets provide calculated amount of protein in divided doses with plenty of water, multivitamins, etc. These effectively lower weight, blood sugar, but because of their side effects, should be used only under supervision of physicians.

Complete fasting reduces or eliminates hunger and causes rapid weight loss. In 1975, Allan cott in his paper: "Fasting as a way of life" noted that fasting brings a wholesome physiological rest for the digestive tract and central nervous system and normalizes metabolism. It must be pointed out, however, that there are also many adverse effects of total fasting. That includes hypokalemia and cardiac arrhythmia associated with low

calorie starvation diets used in unsupervised manner.

Studies on Islamic Fasting

There have been many studies on Ramadān Fasting. In 1996, an international conference was held in Casablanca, Morocco, under the king Hasan Foundation for health in Ramadān and about 50 papers were presented including those from Dr. Soliman (Jordon), Azizi (Iran), Noo*mani* (USA) and Athar (USA). The conclusions of these presentations were that Ramadān Fasting had beneficial effects on health, especially on blood glucose, blood pressure lipid profile and weight. No serious adverse effects were noted (ref 7-10)

Why Islamic fasting is different than other types of Fasting (ref.7)

1- As compared to other diet plans, fasting during Ramadān contains no malnutrition or inadequate calorie intake since there is no restriction on the type or amount of food intake during *iftar* or *sahar*. This was confirmed by M. M. Hussaini (ref.6) during Ramadān in 1974 when he conducted dietary analysis of Muslim students at the University of North Dakota and the State University at Fargo. He concluded that calorie intake of Muslim students during fasting was at two thirds of NCRRDA.

2- Fasting, in Ramadān is voluntarily undertaken. It is not a prescribed imposition from a physician. In the hypothalamus part of the brain there is a center called "lipostat" which controls the body mass. When sever and rapid weight loss is achieved by a starvation diet, the center does not recognize this as normal and, therefore re-programs itself to cause weight gain rapidly once the person goes off the starvation diet. So the only effective way of losing weight is slow, self-controlled, and gradual weight loss by modifying our behavior, and the attitude about eating while eliminating excess food. Ramadān is a month of self-regulation and self-training in terms of food intake thereby causing hopefully a permanent change in lipostat reading.

3- In Islamic fasting, we are not subjected to a diet of selective food only (i.e protein only, fruits only etc). An early breakfast, before dawn in taken and then at sunset fast is broken with something sweet i.e. dates, fruits, juices to warrant any hypoglycemia followed by a regular dinner later.

4-   Additional prayers are prescribed after the dinner, which helps metabolize the food. Using a calorie counter, I counted the amount of calories burnt during extra Prayer called Taraweeh. It amounted to 200 calories. Islamic prayer called *salāt* uses all the muscles and joints and can be placed in the category of a mild exercise in terms of caloric output.

5-   Ramadān fasting is actually an exercise in self discipline. For those who are chain smokers, nibble food constantly, or drink coffee every hour. It is a good way to break the habit, hoping that the effect will continue after the month is over.

6-   Psychological effect of Ramadān fasting are also well observed by the description of people who fast. They describe a feeling of inner peace and tranquility. The prophet (ﷺ) advised them: "If one slanders you or oppresses you, tell him I am fasting." Thus personal hostility during the month is minimal.

Dr. Shahid Athar author of "Health Concerns for Believers" wrote: It is my personal experience that within the first few days of Ramadān, I begin to feel better even before losing a single pound. I work more and pray more; physical stamina and mental alertness improve. As I have my own lab in the office, I usually check my chemistry, that is, blood glucose, cholesterol, triglyceride before the commencement of Ramadān and at its end. I note marked improvement at the end. As I am not over weight, thank GOD, weight loss is minimal. The few pounds I lose, I regain soon after. Fasting in Ramadān will be a great blessing for the overweight whether with or without mild diabetes (type 11). In benefits those also who are given to smoking or nibbling, can rid themselves of these addictions in this month. (Fasting for Medical Patients: suggested Guide-line).

Reference:

1- Bristrian, B.R., "Semi-starvation Diet Recent Development," Diabetic Care, November 1978

2- Blackbum, G.L., et el, " Metabolic changes on PSMF diet" diabetes, June 1976.

3- Cott, A., " Fasting is a way of life." New York: Bantam books 1977.

4- Hirsch, Jules, "Hypothalmic Control of Apetite" Hospital practices, February 1984.

5- Khurane, R.C, " Modified Ketogenic Diet For Obesity," Cancer Monthly Digest, July 1973.

6- Hussaini, N.M., Journal of Islamic Medical Association, October 1982.

7- Athar, S., "Therapeutic Benefits of Ramadān Fasting." Islamic Horizon May 1984.

8- Soliman, N., "Effects of Fasting during Ramadān," Journal of Islamic Medical Association, November 1987.

9- F. Azizi et el, "Evaluation of certain Hormones and blood constituents during Islamic Fasting Month." Journal of Islamic Medical Association, Nov, 1987.

10- Athar, S., "Fasting for Medical Patients – Suggested Guide – line" Islamic Horizon, May 1985

"Shahid Athar, "Medical Aspects of Islamic Fasting."

Spiritual and Physical benefits of Fasting

The spiritual lessons learnt through fasting in Ramadān are countless. Ramadān teaches us sincere, true love for Allah, as we perform this act only for Him. Allah says in this *hadith* qudsi: "All human deeds are for themselves, except fasting: it is for Me and I will reward them for it."[1]

---

1. Muslim: 1151(160)

Fasting is a lesson in patience and self-control; it disciplines the body by giving the mind control over physical desires and temptations, building strong willpower and effective devotion. Fasting frees the soul from the slavery of earthly cravings, from whatever it takes as essential in life to restore its command over the body, regaining dignity, freedom and total peace with its Creator, with itself and with the entire universe.

Dr. Hammudah Abd al-Ati, in his book *Islam in Focus*, points out further spiritual features of fasting as it is performed by Muslims: During the daytimes of Ramadān, no one except Allah can see us if we sneak to the kitchen and grab a bite of our favourite dessert, but we never do it; even young children who start practicing the fast at an early age never do it. This is a test and training lesson for our conscious mind and our willpower, our self-respect and moral dignity. Ramadān fasting improves our economic skills, teaching us adaptability, patience and forbearance. During Ramadān we learn to alter our eating schedule to only two meals per day, in which we consume less food and consequently spend less time, effort and money on the purchase and preparation of food – or at least, this is what we are supposed to do!

Fasting is also a lesson in self-denial, evoking in us feelings of compassion for the poor and others less fortunate than we. It strengthens family ties and instills a sense of social belonging. In Ramadān, people are urged to preserve family ties by gathering the whole family for *iftar* (breaking the fast); this extends to distant family members, friends and even neighbours, as it is highly encouraged to invite others to break the fast with you, and if this is not feasible, to sent *iftar* meals to neighbours and the poor. In this way, fasting is a reminder of Allah's coutless blessings, prompting us to be always humble, gratefull and content. Zayd ibn Khalid Juhani related that Prophet Muhammad (ﷺ) said: "He who provides for the breaking of the fast (*iftar*) of another will acquire the same reward as the fasting person without diminishing in any way the latter's reward." (Tirmidhi)

Fasting in Islam is never practiced in isolation from society and life. Muslim should keep their normal daily routine – including work, exercise, exams and appointments. However, extra time should be taken for the purification of the soul through reading the Qur'ān and *dhikr* of Allah, and more effort should me made to increase and strengthen social ties, developing a real spirit of unity and brotherhood. In Ramadān, we are urged to search out the needy and to give extra charity. Ibn 'Abbas related that the Prophet (ﷺ) was the most generous of people, and he was even more generous during Ramadān when Gabriel visited him every night and recited the Qur'ān with him. During this period the bounty of the Prophet became faster than the rain-bearing wind. (Bukhari)

The Islamic method of fasting is a true lesson in morality and ethics; it spreads the spirit of forgiveness. The peace you make with your creator and your soul extends as it were to the whole universe, increasing your feelings of tolerance, and giving you a sense of harmony and peaceful coexistence. Prophet Muhammad's (ﷺ) teachings of Ramadān ethics also stressed the importrance of guarding our senses: restraining the eyes from looking at any sinful act or event, the ears from listening to and the tongue from uttering any gossip or bad language. At the same time we must guard all our body parts: restraining our hands from wrongdoing, our limbs from taking us towards any sinful act or event and above all, he (ﷺ) urged us to control our tempers. Abu Hurairah (ﷺ) related that Prophet Muhammad (ﷺ) said: "If a person does not give up falsehood and false conduct, Allah has no need that he should abstain from food and drink." He also said: "Some people who fast gain nothing beyond hunger and thirst."

Prophet Muhammad (ﷺ) also taught us in different hadiths: "Satan flows through a human being like blood in his veins, so restrain his paths with hunger." By emptying the stomach, we relax the whole body, which of course helps to clear the mind and invigorates the soul. Abstaining from eating when one is hungry is not easy, but practicing it frees the mind and aids in developing concentration and wisdom, by providing time to focus on spiritual matters – the food of the soul: prayers, supplication, *dhikr* of Allah, and reading and reciting the Qur'an.

Besides the various spiritual benefits of fasting, recent research has shown its valuable effects on physical health. According to Al-Dhahabi in his Medicine of the Prophet, it was thought that the stomach was "the seat of disease". The Prophet (ﷺ) told his people: "Fasting is Paradise," (According to the scholars, it is not saying of Allah's Messenger ﷺ. It is saying of a fmous Arab physician) and this can be interpreted as indicating both the immediate and long-term benefits of abstaining from food, drink and sexual activity. Allah says in the Qur'ān:

$$وَأَن تَصُومُواْ خَيْرٌ لَّكُمْ إِن كُنتُمْ تَعْلَمُونَ ۝$$

"...And if you fast, it is better for you, if only you knew."

Fasting gives the digestive system a rest and makes the body feel lighter. The energy usually consumed in digestion and food metabolism will be directed towards body detoxification, tissue repair and system healing.

Leon Chaitow recommended fasting in his book Natural Alternatives to Antibiotics as an effective way to 'supercharge' the immune system. He states that fasting boosts the activity of the essential parts of the body's natural defence mechanism. During fasting the ability of the lymphocytes and other blood cells to encounter any bacterial attack is greatly improved, and since the level of free radicals in the body is reduced by reducing food intake, the activity of the antioxidants is retained for better cell protection. From this we can see the wisdom in the Prophet's (ﷺ) advice: "Do not force your patients to eat or drink as Allah feeds them and gives them what they need of water."

In addition, fasting gives a chance for the stomach and intestines to regenerate their mucous cell lining, as digestive secretions are reduced during the day. Fasting also boosts the detoxification powers of the hepatic (liver) cells, cleans the kidneys and colon and purifies the blood. Futhermore, it helps overcome obesity, aids in ridding the body of any excess water, and clears the blood from extra fats, which in turn frees the tissues from stored fatsoluble toxins such as pesticides or drug metabolities.

Allah, the Most Gracious and Merciful, adapted the human body to withstand this difficult yet very beneficial fasting process. Dr. Hamed Muhammad, in his book Journey of Faith through the Human body, explains the natural changes occurring in the body to accommodate the daily fast-

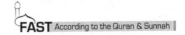

ing in Ramadān. These changes include a reduction in the activity of the thyroxin hormone, thus the energy needed by the fasting Muslim to perform his or her daily functions is reduced, making him or her less susceptible to fatigue. In addition the blood sugar level has been found to remain constant during the fasting hours and insulin secretion is kept under control, which is crucial to keeping the brain supplied with glucose for mental concentration and optimum brain performance.

Sami Mosuli, in his book Islam, the Physician of Modern Diseases, demonstrated the role of autosuggestion and inspiration, gained through faith, devotion and divine love, in changing body physiology, thus reducing in the fasting Muslim the feeling of thirst and hunger. This autosuggestion can be even more powerful than the neurotransmitter messages sent by the hypothalamus in the brain to the stomach for it to feel the hunger and start asking for food. Instead, the body refers to its stored glycogen and fat deposits for energy supply.[2]

---

2. Healing Body & Soul, pg. 420-424

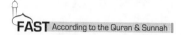

Wisdom and other Benefits of Ramadân

There is much wisdom and numerous benefits in fasting which is related to the taqwa that Allah mentions in the *ayah* (verse):

لَعَلَّكُمْ تَتَّقُونَ

"....that you may become *al-muttaqoon* (the pious)."
(Al-Baqarah 2:183)

The interpretation of this *ayah* is that if a person refrains from *halal* things, hoping to gain the pleasure of Allah and out of fear of His punishment, it will be easier for him to refrain from doing *harām* things.

When a person's stomach is empty and he is hungry, many of his other faculties are kept from feeling hunger or desires; but when his stomach is satisfied, his tongue, eyes, hands and private parts start to feel hunger. Fasting leads to the defeat of Shaytaan; it controls desires and protects one's faculties.

When the fasting person feels the pangs of hunger, he experiences how the poor feel, thus he feels compassion towards them and gives them something to ward off their hunger. Hearing about them is not the same as sharing their suffering, just as a rider does not understand the hardship of walking until he gets down and walks.

Fasting trains the person to avoid desires and to keep away from sin; it helps a person to overcome his own nature and to wean himself away

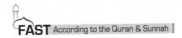
from bad habits. It also trains a person to get used to being organized and punctual, which will solve the problem that many people have of being disorganized, if only they realized.

Fasting is also a demonstration of the unity of the Muslims, as the *ummah* (Islamic nation) fasts and breaks its fast all at the same time.

Fasting also provides a great opportunity for those who are calling other to Allah. In this month many people come to the mosque for the first time, and also those who have not been to the mosque for a long time, and their hearts are open, so we must make the most of this opportunity by preaching in a gentle manner, teaching appropriate lessons and speaking beneficial words, whilst also cooperating in righteousness and good deeds. The teacher should not be so preoccupied with others though that he forgets his own soul and becomes like a candle the lights the way for others while it is itself consumed.